Palgrave Close Readings in Film and Television

Series Editors

John Gibbs
Head of Department
Department of Film, Theatre & Television
University of Reading, UK

Douglas Pye
Senior Visiting Fellow
Department of Film, Theatre & Television
University of Reading, UK

Palgrave Close Readings in Film and Television is an innovative new series of research monographs dedicated to extending the methods and subjects of detailed criticism. Monographs in the series written from a variety of standpoints and dealing with diverse topics are unified by attentiveness to the material decisions made by filmmakers and a commitment to develop analysis and reflection from this foundation. The series is based in the belief that, while a scrupulous attention to the texture of film and television programmes requires the focus of concept and theory, the discoveries that such attention produces become vital in questioning and re-formulating theory and concept. Each monograph will be committed to the appreciation of new areas and topics in the field, but also to strengthening and developing the conceptual basis and the methodologies of critical analysis itself.

More information about this series at
http://www.springer.com/series/14712

James MacDowell

Irony in Film

palgrave
macmillan

James MacDowell
University of Warwick
Coventry, United Kingdom

Palgrave Close Readings in Film and Television
ISBN 978-1-349-67333-9   ISBN 978-1-137-32993-6   (eBook)
DOI 10.1057/978-1-137-32993-6

Library of Congress Control Number: 2016956616

Cover illustration: © Rope, 1948, Alfred Hitchcock, © Warner Bros / The Kobal Collection

Printed on acid-free paper

This Palgrave Macmillan imprint is published by Springer Nature
The registered company is Macmillan Publishers Ltd.
The registered company address is: The Campus, 4 Crinan Street, London, N1 9XW, United Kingdom

In memory of Victor Perkins, 1936–2016.

ACKNOWLEDGEMENTS

First, I thank John Gibbs and Doug Pye for inviting me to contribute to this exciting and essential series. I am also grateful for their kindness and insightfulness throughout all stages of the writing of *Irony in Film*, as well as for setting such inspiring critical and pedagogic examples—both in their criticism and as colleagues at the University of Reading, where this project was conceived. With an eye to the other end of this book's evolution, I thank the team at Palgrave Macmillan, especially Lina Aboujieb, for shepherding me through the publication process with skill and care.

Great thanks are due to all the staff of the University of Warwick's Department of Film & Television Studies for fostering such a stimulating and supportive professional environment, including José Arroyo, Charlotte Brunsdon, Stella Bruzzi, Jon Burrows, Catherine Constable, Adam Gallimore, Stephen Gundle, Tracey McVey, Rachel Moseley, Richard Perkins, Karl Schoonover, Lauren Thompson, Helen Wheatley, and Lynsey Wilmore. I would also like to single out for thanks my fellow teachers on the module 'Hollywood Cinema'—Jo Oldham, Patrick Pilkington, Charlotte Stevens, James Taylor, and Owen Weetch—as well as this module's students, for many conversations that have helped develop my thinking about popular American filmmaking during the book's gestation. Amongst other present and former Warwick colleagues, the thoughts, intellectual inspiration, and friendship of Paul Cuff, Ed Gallafent, Victor Perkins, Michael Pigott, Nic Pillai, Martin Pumphrey, and Rick Wallace in particular have been important to the growth and fruition of ideas presented in this book. Finally, it would have been impossible to have completed this study in good time without the study leave granted to me by the University of Warwick, and I thank my head of department, Alastair Phillips, for helping me secure this and for supporting me expertly and warmly in numerous other ways.

I have presented versions of arguments relevant to *Irony in Film* at a number of conferences, and I thank my fellow panellists on these occasions for their own great work, as well as for helping me improve and refine my ideas: Dieter Declercq, Lucy Fife Donaldson, Manuel Garin, Nessa Johnston, Pete Kunze, Richard McCulloch, Phil Oppenheim, and Tim Vermeulen. Among the many other friends, colleagues, and students who have encouraged, guided, supported, or motivated me in various ways during the writing of this book, I would especially like to thank Ian Banks, Becky Bartlett, Eve Bennett, Tom Brown, Daniel Chan, Pete Falconer, Ian Garwood, Annie Holden, Tom Hughes, Laura Ingeri, Neon Kelly, Geoff King, Simone Knox, Ricky Leach, Lisa Purse, Jonmichael Rossi, Chris Sanders, James Whitfield, and Mark Willetts. I also raise a glass to the staff at Coffee in the Wood, The Royal Standard, The Charles Holden, The Castle, and The Doric Arch, where a surprising proportion of this book was written.

My gratitude to the mighty M.I!M.S collective—John Kokot-Blamey, Andy Holden, Roger Illingworth, and Johnny Parry—with whom I have been talking and arguing about irony of various kinds for around fifteen years; Andy warrants special thanks for our discussions in preparation for his exhibition 'Maximum Irony! Maximum Sincerity: Towards a Unified Theory of M.I!M.S (1999–2003)', which sowed the seeds for this book. Great thanks, too, go to my friend James Zborowski for reading the entirety of this study and always being on hand to offer consistently trenchant advice throughout the writing process; for this, and for long having been my chief counsel on all things film and film studies, he will always have my deepest appreciation and admiration. Enormous thanks are also due to my parents, Robert and Sylvia MacDowell, for their careful reading, illuminating comments, and invaluable help of all kinds, especially during the book's closing stretch.

Finally, I am immensely indebted to Fiona Parry for her unfailing emotional support, as well as for the countless incisive questions, perceptive suggestions, and exciting conversations—not to mention copious reading—which have made such crucial contributions to this work. My sincere thanks too, Fiona, simply for putting up with me while I needed perpetually to keep writing 'that book about irony in film', day after day; I dedicate it to you, with my love.

James MacDowell
London, UK

CONTENTS

LIST OF FIGURES

CHAPTER 1

Introduction

This is a book about irony in film. Surprisingly, it is also the first book about this topic.[1] Irony has been regarded as a vital subject by a great many disciplines—from literary theory, philosophy, and psychology to linguistics, theology, and anthropology; yet it has remained startlingly underexplored by film scholars. This is not to say that film critics and theorists do not allude to irony regularly in connection with other topics, and a smattering of (frequently valuable) books and articles do address the subject in relation to particular movies, directors, cycles, and so forth.[2] There has, though, been very little work dedicated to investigating what it might mean either to create irony in the medium of film or to interpret it. That is what this book attempts.

Across its three main chapters, *Irony in Film* focuses on three fundamental questions. Chapter 2 asks what capacities a filmed, audiovisual medium might have for creating irony; it does so in part by posing this question of other mediums, too, and by exploring how film's apparent relationship to these mediums may inform its ironic potential. Chapter 3 turns its attention to specific properties, devices, and conventions of filmmaking, asking how they can and have been used to ironic effect. Chapter 4 asks how we might best interpret irony in film and confronts theoretical issues that irony seems to raise concerning intention, rhetoric, and the possibility of misinterpretation.

© The Author(s) 2016   1
J. MacDowell, *Irony in Film*, DOI 10.1057/978-1-137-32993-6_1

Before tackling any of these rather imposing questions, though, it is first necessary to address what I mean by describing this as a book about irony in film in the first place. Every word in this book's title in fact begs several further questions; as such, I will expand on the aims and scope of this study by making clear what I mean by each one of them in turn.[3]

IRONY

There are, to say the least, disagreements about how best to define 'irony' (Dane 1991). Indeed, definitions of the term have historically been so contentious that studies of the subject quite frequently feature variations on the joke that it is 'somewhat ironic that, for all the effort...[scholars] have devoted to understanding and using irony, no one can define irony' (Littman/Mey 1991: 131).[4] And yet, of course, the further irony is that this joke itself seems to rely on general agreement about at least one definition of irony. It is therefore not without a little trepidation—though not also without some hopefulness—that I attempt the task faced by any scholarly engagement with irony: explaining how one intends to use this treacherous term.

Certain fundamental fault-lines have emerged within the fraught theoretical literature on irony. The most profound of these, though, may be between those who address irony primarily as a particular kind of communication or expression and those who define it considerably more broadly. The latter approach is usually traced back to thinkers such as Schlegel, Hegel, and Kierkegaard and to the concept of Romantic irony.[5] Understood as 'both a philosophical conception of the universe and an artistic program' (Mellor 1980: 4), the conceptual horizons of Romantic irony stretch far beyond communication or aesthetic devices, and theorists building upon this tradition have produced some of the most ambitious accounts of irony and its significance.[6] Moreover, the general tendency to approach irony as representing something infinitely more inclusive and general than a means of expressing oneself—as, say, scepticism or detachment, ambiguity or paradox—is also prevalent in many studies of irony in philosophy, anthropology, history, theology, critical theory, and psychoanalysis.[7] Although I have no doubt that definitions offered by such conceptual frameworks could plausibly serve as the basis for a study of irony in film,[8] the concerns of this book lie elsewhere.

One way of defining the parameters of this study might be to invoke one of the foremost theorists of literary irony, Wayne Booth, and say that

I am attempting here 'only a rhetoric of irony [in film]—not a psychology or sociology or metaphysics or ethics of irony' (1974: 176). From the Socratic dialogues to contemporary scholarship in linguistics and cognitive science,[9] ironic communication has long been approached in terms of rhetoric, which is to say: 'the art of persuasion, or a study of the means of persuasion'—often, in the case of irony, 'persuasion "to attitude"' (Burke 1969: 46, 50). In arts scholarship, too, a great deal of work on irony can be defined as broadly rhetorical. This means, in part, that much of this critical and theoretical work is dedicated to analysing and interpreting irony as a particular kind of *expression*—the methods artworks have found to create it, and how it can be understood (Booth 1974: ix–xii).[10] It is perhaps this final assumption—that much ironic expression is intended to be and can be understood—which most clearly sets rhetorical approaches apart from some others. Thus, in contrast to Jonathan Culler, who claims (following Kierkegaard) that 'the true ironist does not wish to be understood' (1975: 154), I begin from the premise that all the films analysed in this book wish us to understand their ironies to greater or lesser extents, consciously or intuitively, and I shall be attempting to reach such understandings.[11] This in itself could be said to characterise this study as offering a rhetoric of irony in film.

Even among those who approach irony in the arts rhetorically, though, a firm definition can sometimes still appear elusive. The literary critic I.A. Richards, for example, conceived of irony in poetry as 'the bringing in of the opposite'—a poem's balancing of apparently contradictory but in fact complementary themes, attitudes, or impulses (1925: 250). Similarly broad definitions abound in arts criticism, being especially common in other literary scholarship associated with the so-called New Criticism, where irony gradually came almost to represent something like 'literariness itself' (Dane 1991: 2).[12] Writing in 1951 of the uses critics had by then made of the concept, Cleanth Brooks suggested that 'we have doubtless stretched the term too much, but it has been almost the only term available by which to point to a general and important aspect of poetry' (1951: 732). Clearly, comparably general aspects of filmmaking also deserve pointing towards: thematic tensions, syntheses of opposing impulses, ambivalence, ambiguity, and so on. However, I suggest we risk lessening the utility of irony as a term if we habitually apply it to such multifarious phenomena. This book, at least, concerns itself primarily with other—rather narrower, but widely accepted—definitions of irony.

Beyond Romantic and New Critical definitions, three of the most common forms of irony are usually taken to be *situational*, *dramatic*, and *verbal* (or *communicative*) irony. *Situational irony* is observable in the real world, and it is this we speak of when claiming 'It is ironic *that…*'. It is this form of irony that is invoked by those recurring jokes about millennia worth of attempts to define irony coming up empty-handed. In situational irony, then, circumstances effectively conspire to subvert or invert expectations in a paradoxically fitting fashion (Lucariello 1994). *Dramatic irony*, meanwhile, is an expressive strategy found in aesthetic objects, and especially in storytelling. Dramatic irony is generally understood as the creation of significant and revealing degrees of 'discrepant awareness' (Evans 1960) between audiences and fictional characters; the canonical instance of this is Oedipus searching for the person who has caused a plague to be visited upon Thebes, when the audience knows Oedipus himself to be responsible. Finally, there is what is commonly called *verbal* irony, but which this book will be referring to as *communicative irony*.[13] Again a form of either communication or artistic expression, when we use communicative irony we ourselves act as if we were in some sense like Oedipus—that is, as if we possessed a limited or naïve perspective—when in fact we are adopting that perspective in order to ironise it. The simplest linguistic manifestation of this kind of irony is sarcasm; an example used repeatedly in scholarship, for instance, is the gesture of turning to one's friend while trudging through the pouring rain and announcing, 'Lovely weather!' Yet communicative irony is by no means restricted merely to meaning the opposite of what you say.[14] Numerous theories attempt to define this kind of irony in different ways,[15] but one account I have found particularly useful is the 'pretence theory', which takes communicative irony to be 'the pretended adoption of a defective outlook' (Currie 2006: 121); as such, I will also frequently refer to this form of expression as *ironic pretence*.

These, then, are the main understandings of irony with which this book engages.[16] I will not, it should be noted, be concerned to make claims about the inherent or potential aesthetic or cultural value of ironic expression in film.[17] Nor, for the most part, do I intend to periodise filmic irony by arguing that certain strategies might have become more common during certain putative historical moments—'classical', 'modern', 'postmodern', and so forth. Such subjects would certainly repay further study, and I have in fact touched upon them elsewhere.[18] Here, though, I am primarily interested in three main issues: film's potential for creating the kinds of irony I have outlined (Chapter 2), some specific resources it might have for doing so (Chapter 3), and certain critical and theoretical questions raised by interpreting irony in this medium (Chapter 4). I eagerly look forward to future studies that pursue alternative understandings of and approaches to irony in relation to film. However, it seems to me that the first necessary task is to offer film scholarship some ways of conceptualising our medium's relationship to these fundamental forms of irony, which have received quite thorough exploration in other fields.

IN

This book is called *Irony in Film*—rather than, for example, 'irony *and* film'. This simple choice of preposition in fact already reflects a series of theoretical assumptions, commits my study to a particular focus, and suggests a methodological approach.

It is in keeping with my broadly rhetorical approach to the subject that I believe we are justified in speaking of the irony *in* films, and artworks more generally. This, again, immediately sets me apart from certain scholars, including some who have written about irony in relation to filmmaking. Lars Elleström, for instance—intentionally echoing theorists such as Stanley Fish (1989)—argues that any ironies we might attribute to films are never 'actual qualities of the filmic texts' (2002: 150); instead, irony should always be understood as 'an interpretive strategy employed by the spectator' (ibid.: 149). I delve into this issue in some depth in Chapter 4, but it may be worth pointing here to one merely practical reason for resisting this theoretical premise. On the very same page as Elleström derides certain critics for believing that 'ironies are "found" in films and are hence supposed to "be" there' (ibid.: 147), he nonetheless proceeds to use this very formulation while advancing his own argument that the 'irony found in movies is not always specifically "filmic"' (ibid.: 147). I suggest that such contradictions arise because, if we do not allow ourselves to describe irony as something that can be 'found' in films, we render ourselves virtually unable to make critical or theoretical claims about it. This offers, at least, one provisional pragmatic argument for continuing to speak of irony as something that can exist in film: without admitting this possibility, it would seem that scholars of filmic irony are simply left with no reasonable way of mounting arguments about the object of their attention.

A necessary corollary of conceptualising irony in this way is that I must offer some explanation for how irony can come to be present *in* films. In one sense, that is what this whole study attempts. Yet, more basically,

I am in need of a definition of what it might mean for a film to *contain* irony—a theoretical question taken up most rigorously in Chapter 4. For now, however, I offer the following as an operative assumption. I assume, with those such as Douglas Muecke, that—if considering irony as a form of expression—'a work can be ironical only by intention; being ironical means deliberately being ironical' (1969: 57). Clearly, as Linda Hutcheon notes, it can seem controversial to 'raise issues of intentionality in a post-Derridean, post-Barthesian, and post-Foucaultian age'; and yet, as she also goes on to acknowledge, when studying irony, 'it seems to me to be unavoidable' (1994: 11). I too join many others in considering the concept of intention indispensable for the discussion of ironic expression.[19] There are several reasons for claiming this, not least of which is that intention appears to be a non-negotiable feature of what makes irony a particular form of expression in the first place. In advance of this argument being pursued in greater depth, though, suffice it to say that the claims offered throughout this book depend upon the supposition that to speak of irony *in* a film is to attribute ironic intentions to that film or its makers.

Another outcome of concentrating on irony in film is that my focus is drawn away from something Elleström alluded to earlier: ironic reception strategies. It is plainly possible to discuss all aspects of aesthetics in relation to, for instance, cultural capital (Bourdieu 1984) or taste cultures (Gans 1974); but irony may be especially conducive to such methodologies.[20] There is certainly a valuable book to be written about irony *and* film which focuses on 'one of irony's most common manifestations: as a strategy of interpretation' (Hutcheon 1994: 112) and the contexts in which such interpretations might take place. Some research into ironic reception as a way of watching films already exists: for instance, work on 'cult' cinema, camp culture, and films appreciated for being 'so bad they're good' (indeed, I have myself previously written on the last of these subjects).[21] My particular focus here on irony *in* film, however, means that this methodology cannot be my own.

This book instead dedicates itself to the detailed analysis and theoretical investigation of films themselves. The methodology of close analysis is another necessary consequence of committing myself to the premise that irony is something intentionally present in films. Chapter 3 offers perhaps the most sustained engagement with the material particulars of individual movies, consisting almost entirely of close analyses of moments where sound, editing, mise-en-scène, cinematography, and performance help create irony in a host of disparate movies. Chapters 2 and 4 analyse far fewer films in far greater detail, with these analyses also assisting me in addressing certain theoretical questions. Thus, when I ask in my first chapter what kinds of irony a filmed medium might be capable of creating, I attempt to answer this question partly via extended analyses of three films: *Dr. Strangelove* (Stanley Kubrick 1964), *Rope* (Alfred Hitchcock 1948), and *There's Always Tomorrow* (Douglas Sirk 1956). Chapter 4, meanwhile, focuses primarily on a single film—*Apocalypse Now* (Francis Ford Coppola 1979)—in order to contend with some questions that irony raises for the practice of interpretation, especially concerning intention, as well as the proposition that 'irony always offers the possibility of misunderstanding' (Culler 1975: 154). I suggest that detailed close analysis remains equally essential when addressing such theoretical questions, since I am generally in agreement with Andrew Britton that 'no film theory is worth anything which does not stay close to the concrete, and which does not strive continually to check its own assumptions and procedures in relation to producible texts' (2009: 373).

FILM

It could seem strange that a book calling itself *Irony in Film* should draw its examples almost entirely from the one—admittedly broad—filmmaking tradition considered by this study: namely, American narrative cinema. This decision, though, was made for a number of reasons. First, this happens to be my research specialism. Moreover, choosing to focus a book on one's area of greatest expertise seems particularly advisable when grappling with irony. It is a generally acknowledged fact about linguistic irony that ironic communication has a greater chance of being understood 'the greater the mutual familiarity of speaker and hearer with the presuppositions involved in the act of irony' (Warning 1982: 258). The same is surely true across all means of expression, which ensures that we seem bound to write the most incisive studies of irony in relation to those contexts with which we are most familiar. It is, then, perhaps first and foremost the contextual nature of ironic expression and interpretation—that is, 'the shared context necessary to understand irony' (Hutcheon 1994: 87)—that has guided my choice of corpus. Second, within the existing film scholarship on irony, American cinema is also by far the most frequently referenced. It therefore seems logical for the first book on this topic to be able to draw together and draw upon that literature with reference to the filmmaking tradition that overwhelmingly gave rise to it.[22] Finally, in selecting this focus I am following the example of many works that attempt to grasp comparably generalised aspects of film art.[23] When first trying to understand a subject with potential relevance for any and all filmmaking traditions, it has often seemed beneficial initially to concentrate primarily on what we might broadly call popular American cinema. Not only has this cinema's mode of filmmaking to a significant extent also constituted 'the world's mainstream film style' (Bordwell/Staiger/Thompson 1985: 4), but many other filmmaking traditions can fruitfully be understood, 'in part, as reactions against the traditional patterns of narrative and narration that popular commercial film has so heavily relied upon' (Wilson 1986: 12). Thus, if we can begin to understand the medium's capacities for ironic expression in films like these, we may place ourselves in a better position to address the topic in filmmaking traditions that oppose or diverge from this cinema's tendencies.[24] I therefore believe that American narrative cinema can represent a productive starting point—by no means a terminus—for the investigation of a subject as far-reaching in its relevance as filmic irony.[25]

One reason that, regardless of its corpus, the concerns of this book have such potentially broad implications is that the medium of film in general has often been accused of finding it difficult to create irony.[26] It is perhaps not hard to see why this suspicion might arise. In many discussions of the subject, irony is repeatedly tied to definitions of meaning that are rooted firmly in written or spoken language. We frequently encounter variations on the argument that communicative irony, at least, is created by establishing differences between a 'literal' meaning and the 'implied' meaning an ironist intends to communicate.[27] Clearly, such concepts as 'literal', 'implied', and even 'meaning' become far less secure when applied not to spoken or written language, but to a medium such as film, whose expressive properties are not—or not only—linguistic but rather constitute a 'mongrel' (Durgnat 1976) admixture of linguistic, pictorial, dramatic, narrative, and aural forms of address.

I suggest, though, that there is at least one available route past this apparent problem. Taking stock recently of a broad swathe of work dedicated to defining ironic communication in general, Marta Dynel notes that 'besides...agreeing on the literal vs. implied meaning distinction, most authors are unanimous that irony inherently expresses the speaker's *attitude*, and thus serves as a vehicle for an *evaluative judgment*' (2014: 540; original emphases). We do indeed find variations on this proposition in a wide range of theoretical writings on irony.[28] In fact, surveying the literature on the subject, it quite quickly becomes evident that terminology of this sort appears virtually unavoidable—whether we agree with H. P. Grice that irony is 'intimately connected with the expression of [an] attitude, or evaluation' (1978: 124) or with Dell Hymes' argument that 'when the notion of irony is pursued, it can be found to be a matter of perspective' (1987: 300). Perspective, evaluation, attitude—while not interchangeable, terminology of this kind helps emphasise one apparent corollary of ironic communication: what we might call an *implied stance*.

Much scholarship addressing irony in relation to different artistic fields similarly suggests that—rather than irony necessarily being confined to contrasts between literal and implied *meanings*—it is instead '*perspectival* difference [which] is the necessary canvas upon which ironies are aesthetically constructed' (Kaufer 1983: 462; emphasis mine). For instance, referring primarily to literature, Brooks regards irony as 'a device for definition of attitudes by qualification' (1947: 257). Addressing theatre, William Storm proposes that 'irony arises in juxtaposition..., with a point of view that is generally implied rather than stated' (2011: 3). Recognising the usefulness of such concepts for discussing music, too, Robert Hatten argues that 'irony [is] a bracketing or framing of musical discourse, such that it...might constitute a "perspective"' (1996: 94). Finally, approaching the pictorial arts via the aforementioned 'pretence theory', Gregory Currie defines irony in this medium in terms of a picture 'pretending to adopt a point of view, thereby expressing a view about the defects of that point of view' (2011: 152).

Approaches like these begin to suggest some possible ways of conceptualising irony in film and gesture towards terminology appropriate to this task. For example, given the language frequently used to describe the phenomenon, a term that would seem indispensable to a critical dialogue about ironic filmmaking is *point of view*. In particular, one concept common to much of the voluminous theoretical work on point of view in both literature and film seems especially apposite to discussions of irony: the 'relations of proximity to and distance from...characters' (Wilson 1986: 5). Such 'proximity' and 'distance' may be affected by many factors, including our spatial and temporal access to the narrative, our degree of knowledge relative to characters' knowledge, and the ethical evaluations we feel encouraged to make of characters.[29] The potential relevance of these aspects of point of view for a discussion of irony suggests itself immediately. The 'discrepant awareness' associated with dramatic irony, for instance, is only possible if a film highlights for us salient facts about the story of which certain characters remain ignorant; equally, we might think of what Northrop Frye calls the 'ironic mode' in fiction, which is said to feature a protagonist who is 'inferior in power or intelligence to ourselves' (1957: 33). Perhaps unsurprisingly, then, point of view is a concept referred to not infrequently in the few extant scholarly engagements with filmic irony[30] and one to which this book will often return.

Another term that seems appropriate to the cluster of terminology associated with irony is *tone*. Douglas Pye, who has done most to theorise this underexplored concept in relation to film, suggests that, whereas point of view refers primarily to the perspectives a film provides of its characters and narrative world, tone also encompasses 'the relationships of a film to its material, its traditions and its spectator' (2007: 8). In particular, tone is useful for articulating the way films can assume an ironically distanced attitude towards generic, stylistic, or representational conventions. Pye suggests that registering that a film may be adopting such an attitude towards its own stylistic conventions, say,

> has something in common with registering in conversation that someone is employing conventional phrases with a certain ironic distance...[or] that their use of a phrase carries implied "quotation marks"....The difference in the use of film conventions is that we do not hear a voice. We have to make a judgement about the film's relationship to its methods, based on our assessment of how particular decisions function in their context. (ibid.: 44)

In the absence of the tonal inflections of a human voice, in such cases we must seek to discern a film's tone by determining the degree of distance at which it appears to be holding not merely its characters or fictional events but its own representational conventions and modes of address (Pye 2000: 12). I shall be arguing that this aspect of filmmaking is especially relevant for understanding communicative irony in this medium. As we might expect, tone is another concept that recurs relatively frequently in existing work on ironic filmmaking[31] and is another to which we will return throughout the book.

Of course, a single volume cannot address all the manifold varieties of irony a medium can create, nor attempt to answer all the theoretical issues the subject raises. Nonetheless, I hope that much of what follows might prove useful beyond the scope of my corpus and beyond my particular conceptual field. I suggest that, regardless of where we find ironic expression, and whatever definitions of it we use, we will be required to confront the sorts of questions this book tries to tackle: what capacities does this medium have for creating irony? How can the medium's characteristic devices be put to ironic effect? And how should we go about interpreting irony in this medium? The aim of this book is to offer some theoretical groundwork and analytical tools that might help us better answer such questions.

NOTES

1. There do, though, exist two PhD theses on the topic: Doane (1979) and Roth-Lindberg (1995); Thomas' (2009) thesis also discusses filmic irony in relation to American indie 'smart' cinema (Sconce 2002) specifically.
2. For instance: Elsaesser (1974), Kozloff (1989: 102–126), Robertson (1990), Babington/Evans (1990), Collins (1993), Davis (1999), Sconce (2002), Allen (2007), Perez (2009), Perkins (2011), Gibbs (2012), Leigh (2012), King (2013: 23–76), Brütsch (2015), or Roche (2015). There are also studies that address film briefly but usefully in the context of broader discussions of irony; see, for instance, Hutcheon (1994), Elleström (2002), or Currie (2010). I will be drawing upon the insights of many of these scholars throughout the book.
3. A hat-tip to Richard Dyer's *Pastiche* is due for inspiring this introductory structure (2007: 1–6).
4. See de Man (1996: 165), Enright (1986: 7), or Barbe (1995: 71).
5. Schlegel, for instance, defined irony in poetry not as a discrete device used to create particular effects but more holistically as 'permanent parabasis' (1958: 85). Kierkegaard, for his part (via Hegel), famously regarded irony as 'infinite absolute negativity' (1966: 26)—a philosophical worldview or attitude of radical scepticism towards existence and the self. For a useful overview of various traditions related to Romantic irony, see Garber (1988).
6. Claims, for example, that it is 'inseparable from the evolution of the modern consciousness' (Behler 1990: 111), that it is 'built into the formal representation-relation that is the basis of human culture' (Gans 1974: 74), or that it possesses the power to 'destroy the immediacy and sincerity of life' (Colebrook 2004: 3).

7. For instance: Rorty (1989), Fernández/Huber (2001), White (1973), Holland (2000), Newmark (2012), and Stringfellow (1994), respectively.

8. I certainly agree with Elleström, for example, that 'irony as a worldview or a philosophy of life may be found in movies' (2002: 148). Indeed, some existing film and television scholarship could broadly be described as proposing or debating the attribution of such a worldview to specific directors or texts; see, for example, Comolli (1985) on Hawks; Brill (1988) and Allen (2007) on Hitchcock; Leigh (2012) on Rohmer; Toles (2001) and Rothman (2011) on the Coen Brothers; or Melbye (2016) on *The Twilight Zone* (CBS 1959–1964).

9. See Vlastos (1991), for instance, on Plato's Socrates. For a valuable overview of various linguistic and cognitive accounts of irony, meanwhile, see Gibbs/Colston (2007).

10. As Kenneth Burke notes, in the realm of literature, the study of rhetoric frequently involves 'the analysis of…attitu des, as expressed in literary tactics' (ibid.: 126). It is for this reason, for example, that Burke considers William Empson's analyses of literary ironies in *Seven Types of Ambiguity* (1930) to deserve 'an important place in the New Rhetoric' (ibid.: 126)—even if Empson might not consider himself a scholar of rhetoric *per se*.

11. Whether or not this means they have been created by 'true ironists' I leave to the reader to decide. It may be that most of the examples of irony I engage with could be described as 'stable', as opposed to 'unstable', in Booth's (1974) terms; yet, as he notes, even irreducibly ambiguous ironies, which may not admit singular understandings, nonetheless 'rule out some readings—namely, the *un*ambiguous!' (ibid.: 127).

12. For an overview, see Dane (1991: 149–158).

13. This is due to the immediately obvious inappropriateness of the term *verbal irony* for film; in referring to this form of irony as *communicative irony*, I follow Currie (2011).

14. For criticism of this merely 'antiphrastic' definition, see Hutcheon (1994: 56–64) and Currie (2006).

15. For instance, see too the Gricean (Grice 1978) and 'echoic' accounts (e.g. Sperber/Wilson 2007).

16. Although, for reasons that should be apparent, dramatic and communicative ironies receive greater attention than the largely real-world phenomenon of situational irony.
17. In their own distinct ways, Davis (1999), Toles (2001), Sconce (2002), Thomas (2009), and Leigh (2012), for instance, each offer considerations of ethical issues associated with irony in film.
18. See MacDowell (2010, 2012a/b, 2014, 2015).
19. For instance, Booth (1974), Hermerén (1975), Dutton (1987), and Carroll (2002).
20. Two scholars who have profitably approached irony in film in such terms are Sconce (2002) and King (2013: 23–76).
21. MacDowell/Zborowski (2013); see also Dyer (1987), Sconce (1995), Taylor (1999), McCulloch (2011), and Bartlett (2015).
22. Though this is not to say, of course, that we should not hope for and expect future studies to broaden these horizons considerably.
23. Say, Perkins' *Film as Film* (1972), Wilson's *Narration in Light* (1986), Kozloff's *Invisible Storytellers* (1989), Branigan's *Narrative Comprehension and Film* (1992), or Plantinga's *Moving Viewers* (2009).
24. Since this book is also focused for the most part squarely on fiction films, there is certainly, for instance, much work still to be carried out on irony in documentary filmmaking; though see Perez (2009) for one useful discussion of this.
25. Having said this, even the 'classical' Hollywood films I analyse exhibit extremely disparate approaches to irony—due partly to the disparate nature of their genres. Furthermore, my examples in fact take us some way beyond this already-roomy tradition, encompassing areas such as the 'Hollywood Renaissance', 1980s blockbuster cinema, American independent filmmaking, and even—on occasion—non-narrative experimental film.
26. For instance, Ong (1976: 18), Elleström (2002: 147), Kroeber (2006: 59), or Currie (2010: 169).
27. Marta Dynel observes that one premise most theorists of irony agree upon is that 'the literal import of an ironic utterance differs from the implicit meaning the speaker intends to communicate' (Dynel 2014: 540).
28. Helga Kotthoff, for instance, considers 'the special achievement of irony to be its ability to signal a contrast in evaluation. An attitude is attributed...from which the ironist wishes to contrastively dis-

tance him/herself' (2003: 1392). Sperber and Wilson's influential 'echoic' account of linguistic irony similarly stresses the importance of attitude—specifically, 'the speaker's attitude to the opinion echoed' (2007: 40). Even philosophical definitions of irony are often indebted to such terminology: Claire Colebrook, for example, uses comparable language to define irony as a philosophical disposition, describing it as both a 'sensibility or attitude' (2004: 7) and 'the adoption of a point of view' (ibid.: 133).

29. See, for instance, Booth (1961) in relation to literature and Wilson (1986), Pye (2000), and Zborowski (2015) in relation to film. Smith (1995) also usefully investigates these aspects of our relationship to characters (though he distances himself from the concept of point of view); in her turn, Thomas (2009) has made use of Smith's models to discuss ironic distance from characters in American indie 'smart' films (Sconce 2002).

30. See, for instance, Wilson (1986: 103–125), Allen (2007), and Leigh (2012).

31. In addition to Pye (2007), see Smith (2000), Sconce (2002), Allen (2007), Thomas (2009), Perkins (2011) Gibbs (2012), MacDowell (2012b), and King (2013: 23–76).

BIBLIOGRAPHY

Allen, Richard. (2007). *Hitchcock's Romantic Irony*. New York: Columbia University Press.

Babington, Bruce & Peter Evans. (1990). 'Another Look at Sirkian Irony', *Movie* 34/35, 47–58.

Barbe, Katharina. (1995). *Irony in Context*. Philadelphia: John Benjamins Publishing.

Bartlett, Rebecca. (2015). 'How Failure Works: Understanding and Analysing the Characteristics of Badfilm, 1950–1970'. PhD Thesis, University of Glasgow.

Behler, Ernst. (1990). *Irony and the Discourse of Modernity*. Seattle: University of Washington Press.

Booth, Wayne C. (1961). *The Rhetoric of Fiction*. Chicago: University of Chicago Press.

Booth, Wayne C. (1974). *A Rhetoric of Irony*. Chicago: University of Chicago Press.

Bordwell, David, Janet Staiger, and Kristin Thompson. (1985). *The Classical Hollywood Cinema: Film Style and Mode of Production to 1960*. New York: Columbia University Press.

Bourdieu, Pierre. (1984). *Distinction: A Social Critique of the Judgement of Taste.* Cambridge: Harvard University Press.

Branigan, Edward. (1992). *Narrative Comprehension and Film.* New York: Routledge.

Brill, Lesley. (1988). *The Hitchcock Romance: Love and Irony in Hitchcock's Films.* Princeton: Princeton University Press.

Britton, Andrew. (2009). *Britton on Film: The Complete Film Criticism of Andrew Britton,* Barry Keith Grant (ed). Detroit: Wayne State University Press.

Brooks, Cleanth. (1947). *The Well-Wrought Urn: Studies in the Structure of Poetry.* New York: Harcourt Brace.

Brooks, Cleanth. (1951). 'Irony as a Principle of Structure', in Zabel, Morton D. (ed) *Literary Opinion in America.* New York: Harper & Row, 729–741.

Brütsch, Matthias. (2015). 'Irony, Retroactivity, and Ambiguity: Three Kinds of "Unreliable Narration" in Film', in Nünning, Vera (ed) *Unreliable Narration and Trustworthiness: Intermedial and Interdisciplinary Approaches.* Berling: De Gruyter, 221–244.

Burke, Kenneth. (1969). *A Rhetoric of Motives.* Los Angeles: University of California Press.

Carroll, Noël. (2002). 'Andy Kaufman and the Philosophy of Interpretation', in Krausz, Michael (ed) *Is There a Single Right Interpretation?* University Park: Pennsylvania State University Press, 319–344.

Colebrook, Claire. (2004). *Irony.* New York: Routledge.

Collins, Jim. (1993). 'Genericity in the 90s: Eclectic Irony and the New Sincerity', in Collins, Jim, Hilary Radner & Ava Preacher (eds) *Film Theory Goes to the Movies.* New York: Routledge, 242–264.

Comolli, Jean-Louis. (1985). 'The Ironical Howard Hawks', in Hillier, Jim (ed) *Cahiers du Cinéma: 1960–1968: New Wave, New Cinema, Reevaluating Hollywood.* Cambridge: Harvard University Press, 181–186.

Culler, Jonathan. (1975). *Structuralist Poetics: Structuralism, Linguistics and the Study of Literature.* New York: Routledge.

Currie, Gregory. (2006). 'Why Irony is Pretence', in Nichols, Shaun (ed) *The Architecture of the Imagination: New Essays on Pretence, Possibility, and Fiction.* Oxford: Oxford University Press, 111–133.

Currie, Gregory. (2010). *Narratives and Narrators: A Philosophy of Stories.* Oxford: Oxford University Press.

Currie, Gregory. (2011). 'The Irony in Pictures', *The British Journal of Aesthetics,* 51: 2, 149–167.

Dane, Joseph A. (1991). *The Critical Mythology of Irony.* Athens: University of Georgia Press.

Davis, Kimberly Chabot. (1999). 'White Filmmakers and Minority Subjects: Cinema Vérité and the Politics of Irony in *Hoop Dreams* and *Paris Is Burning*', *South Atlantic Review,* 64: 1, 26–47.

De Man, Paul. (1996). *Aesthetic Ideology*. Minneapolis: University of Minnesota Press.

Doane, Mary Ann. (1979). 'The Dialogic Text: Filmic Irony and the Spectator'. PhD Thesis, University of Iowa.

Durgnat, Raymond. (1976). 'The Mongrel Muse', in *Durgnat on Film*. London: Faber & Faber, 17–28.

Dutton, Dennis. (1987). 'Why Intentionalism Won't Go Away', in Cascardi, A. J. (ed) *Literature and the Question of Philosophy*. Baltimore: Johns Hopkins University Press, 194–209.

Dyer, Richard. (1987). 'Judy Garland and Gay Men,' in *Heavenly Bodies: Film Stars and Society*. London: Macmillan, 137–191.

Dyer, Richard. (2007). *Pastiche*. New York: Routledge.

Dynel, Marta. (2014). 'Linguistic Approaches to (Non)humorous Irony', *Humor* 27: 4, 537–550.

Elleström, L. (2002). *Divine Madness: On Interpreting Literature, Music, and the Visual Arts Ironically*. London: Bucknell University Press.

Elsaesser, Thomas. (1974). 'The Cinema of Irony', *Monogram* 5: 1–2.

Empson, William. (1930). *Seven Types of Ambiguity*. London: Chatto and Windus.

Enright, Dennis Joseph. (1986). *The Alluring Problem: An Essay on Irony*. Oxford: Oxford University Press.

Evans, Bertrand. (1960). *Shakespeare's Comedies*. Oxford: Clarendon Press.

Fernández, James W. & Mary Taylor Huber. (2001). *Irony in Action: Anthropology, Practice, and the Moral Imagination*. Chicago: University of Chicago Press.

Fish, Stanley. (1989). 'Short People Got No Reason to Live: Reading Irony', in *Doing What Comes Naturally: Change, Rhetoric, and the Practice of Theory in Literary and Legal Studies*. Durham: Duke University Press, 180–196.

Frye, Northrop. (1957). *Anatomy of Criticism: Four Essays*. Princeton: Princeton University Press.

Gans, Herbert. (1974). *Popular Culture and High Culture: An Analysis and Evaluation of Taste*. New York: Basic Books.

Garber, Frederick, (ed). (1988). *Romantic Irony*. Philadelphia: John Benjamins.

Gibbs, John. (2012). 'Balancing Act: Exploring the Tone of *The Life Aquatic with Steve Zissou*', *New Review of Film and Television Studies* 10: 1, 132–151.

Gibbs, Raymond W & Herbert L. Colston, (eds). (2007). *Irony in Language and Thought: A Cognitive Science Reader*. New York: Lawrence Erlbaum Associates.

Grice, H. P. (1978). 'Some Further Notes on Logic and Conversation', in Cole, P. (ed), *Pragmatics, vol. 9*. New York: Academic Press, 113–127.

Hatten, Robert. (1996). 'Review of *The Practice of Performance*, by John Rink', *Indiana Theory Review*, 17: 1, 87–117.

Hermerén, Göran. (1975). 'Intention and Interpretation in Literary Criticism', *New Literary History*, 7: 1, 57–82.

Holland, Glenn S. (2000). *Divine Irony*. London: Associated University Press.

Hymes, Dell. (1987). 'A Theory of Verbal Irony and a Chinookan Pattern of Verbal Exchange', in Verschueren, Jeff & Marcella Bertuccelli-Papi (eds), *The Pragmatic Perspective: Selected Papers from the 1985 International Pragmatics Conference*. Amsterdam: Bejamins, 293–338.

Hutcheon, Linda. (1994). *Irony's Edge: The Theory and Politics of Irony*. New York: Routledge.

Kaufer, David. (1983). 'Irony, Interpretive Form and the Theory of Meaning', *Poetics Today* 4, 451–464.

Kierkegaard, Søren. (1966). *The Concept of Irony, with Constant Reference to Socrates* (Translated by Lee M. Capel). London: Collins.

King, Geoff. (2013). '*Indie 2.0: Change and Continuity in Contemporary American Indie Film*', New York: I. B. Tauris.

Kotthoff, Helga. (2003). 'Responding to Irony in Different Contexts: on Cognition in Conversation', *Journal of Pragmatics*, 35: 9, 1387–1411.

Kozloff, Sarah. (1989). *Invisible Storytellers: Voice-over Narration in American Fiction Film*. Los Angeles: University of California Press.

Kroeber, Karl. (2006). *Make Believe in Film and Fiction: Visual vs. Verbal Storytelling*. London: Palgrave Macmillan.

Leigh, Jacob. (2012). *The Cinema of Eric Rohmer: Irony, Imagination, and the Social World*. London: Continuum.

Littman, David C. & Jacob L. Mey. (1991). 'The Nature of Irony: Toward a Computational Model of Irony', *Journal of Pragmatics*, 15: 2, 131–151.

Lucariello, Joan. (1994). 'Situational Irony: A Concept of Events Gone Awry', *Journal of Experimental Psychology: General*, 123, 129–145.

MacDowell, James. (2010). 'Notes on Quirky', *Movie: A Journal of Film Criticism* 1: 1–16. Available at: http://www2.warwick.ac.uk/fac/arts/film/movie/contents/notes_on_quirky.pdf (Accessed 6 February 2016).

MacDowell, James. (2012a). 'Quirky: Buzzword or Sensibility?', in King, Geoff, Claire Molloy & Yannis Tzioumakis (eds), *American Independent Cinema: Indie, Indiewood and Beyond*. New York: Routledge, 53–64.

MacDowell, James. (2012b). 'Wes Anderson, Tone and the Quirky Sensibility', *New Review of Film and Television Studies*, 10: 1, 6–27.

MacDowell, James. (2014). 'The Andersonian, the Quirky, and "Innocence"', in Kunze, Peter (ed), *The Films of Wes Anderson: Critical Essays on an Indiewood Icon*. London: Palgrave Macmillan, 153–169.

MacDowell, James. (2015). '*Buffalo '66*: The Radical Conventionality of an Indie Happy Ending', in Claire Perkins and Constantine Verevis (eds), *US Independent Filmmaking After 1989: Possible Films*. Edinburgh: Edinburgh University Press, 35–44.

MacDowell, James & James Zborowski. (2013). 'The Aesthetics of "So Bad it's Good": Value, Intention, and *The Room*', *Intensities*, Autumn/Winter 2013, pp. 1–30.

McCulloch, Richard. (2011). '"Most People Bring Their Own Spoons": *The Room*'s Participatory Audiences as Comedy Mediators.' *Participations: Journal of Audience & Reception Studies* 8: 189–218.

Melbye, David. (2016). *Irony in The Twilight Zone: How the Series Critiqued Postwar American Culture.* London: Rowman & Littlefield.

Mellor, Anne. (1980). *English Romantic Irony.* Cambridge: Harvard University Press.

Muecke, Douglas Colin. (1969). *The Compass of Irony.* London: Methuen.

Newmark, Kevin. (2012). *Irony on Occasion: From Schlegel and Kierkegaard to Derrida and de Man.* New York: Fordham University Press.

Ong, Walter J. (1976). 'From Mimesis to Irony: the Distancing of Voice', *The Bulletin of the Midwest Modern Language Association*, 9: 1/2, 1–24.

Perez, Gilberto. (2009). 'Errol Morris's Irony', in Rothman, William (ed), *Three Documentary Filmmakers.* Albany: State University of New York, 13–18.

Perkins, Claire. (2011). *American Smart Cinema.* Edinburgh: Edinburgh University Press.

Perkins, V. F. (1972). *Film as Film: Understanding and Judging Movies.* London: Penguin Books.

Plantinga, Carl. (2009). *Moving Viewers: American Film and the Spectator's Experience.* Los Angeles: University of California Press.

Pye, Douglas. (2000). 'Movies and Point of View', *Movie*, 36, 2–34.

Pye, Douglas. (2007). 'Movies and Tone', in Gibbs, John & Douglas Pye (eds), *Close-Up 02: Movies and Tone/Reading Rohmer/Voices in Film.* London: Wallflower Press, 1–80.

Richards, I.A. (1925). *Principles of Literary Criticism.* New York: Harcourt Brace and World.

Robertson, Pamela. (1990). 'Structural Irony in *Mildred Pierce*, or How Mildred Lost Her Tongue', *Cinema Journal* 30: 1, 42–54.

Roche, David. (2015). 'Irony in *The Sweet Hereafter* by Russell Banks (1991) and Atom Egoyan (1997)', *Adaptation* 8: 2, 237–253.

Rorty, Richard. (1989). *Contingency, Irony, and Solidarity.* Cambridge: Cambridge University Press.

Roth-Lindberg, Örjan. (1995). 'Skuggan av ett Leende: Omfilmisk Ironi och den Ironiska Berättelsen', PhD Thesis, University of Stockholm: Bokförlaget T. Fischer & Co.

Rothman, Stephen. (2011). '"Isn't It Ironic": The Films of the Coen Brothers', *Comedy Studies* 2:1, 55–62.

Schlegel, Friedrich. (1958). *Kritische Friedrich-egel-Ausgabe* (edited by Ernst Behler), Munich: Schoningh.

Sconce, Jeffrey. (1995). 'Trashing the Academy: Taste, Excess, and an Emerging Politics of Cinematic Style', *Screen* 36: 4, 371–393.

Sconce, Jeffrey. (2002). 'Irony, Nihilism and the New American "Smart" Film', *Screen* 43: 4, 349–369.

Smith, Murray. (1995). *Engaging Characters*. Oxford: Clarendon Press.

Smith, Susan. (2000). *Hitchcock: Suspense, Humour and Tone*. London: BFI.

Sperber, Dan & Deirdre Wilson. (2007). 'On Verbal Irony', in Gibbs, Raymond W. & Herbert L. Colston (eds), *Irony in Language and Thought: A Cognitive Science Reader*. New York: Lawrence Erlbaum Associates, 35–55.

Storm, William. (2011). *Irony and the Modern Theatre*. Cambridge: Cambridge University Press.

Stringfellow, Frank. (1994). *The Meaning of Irony: A Psychoanalytic Investigation*. Albany: State University of New York Press.

Taylor, Greg. (1999). *Artists in the Audience: Cults, Camp, and American Film Criticism*. Princeton: Princeton University Press.

Thomas, Deborah J. (2009). *Ambivalent Fictions: Youth, Irony and Affect in American Smart Film*. PhD Thesis, The University of Queensland.

Toles, George. (2001). *A House Made of Light: Essays on the Art of Film*. Detroit: Wayne State University Press.

Vlastos, Gregory. (1991). *Socrates: Ironist and Moral Philosopher*. Cambridge: Cambridge University Press.

Warning, Rainer. (1982). 'Irony and the "Order of Discourse" in Flaubert', *New Literary History*, 13: 2, 253–286.

White, Hayden. (1973). *Metahistory: The Historical Imagination in Nineteenth-Century Europe*. Baltimore: Johns Hopkins University Press.

Wilson, George M. (1986). *Narration in Light: Studies in Cinematic Point of View*. Baltimore: John Hopkins University Press.

Zborowski, James. (2015). *Classical Hollywood Cinema: Point of View and Communication*. Manchester: Manchester University Press.

CHAPTER 2

Irony in Film: Theorising Irony for a Mongrel Medium

It has frequently been suggested that films might find it difficult to be ironic. Karl Kroeber, for instance, argues of filmmaking that 'the weapon of irony' is simply 'unavailable to the visual storyteller' (2006: 59); Walter Ong claims that 'the height of irony in the movies can probably never reach that possible in print' (1976: 18); Gregory Currie too believes that films have only a 'limited palette' for ironic expression (2010: 169); and, despite ultimately suggesting that films *can* be ironic, Lars Elleström nonetheless concedes that it is 'understandable that one might feel slightly uncomfortable with the notion of "filmic irony"' (2002: 147). This chapter addresses some of the reasons behind arguments like these.

Given their medium-specific nature, it would seem that interrogating such claims requires, in part, considering the nature of ironic expression in film relative to other media. Elleström suggests that 'irony found in movies is not always specifically "filmic" in the sense that it is not always generated by the particulars of the film medium' (2002: 147). However, while not all ironies in film will be *exclusively* filmic, I suggest that this does not mean we should consider them any less specifically so. And, in contrast to those whose belief in film's limited ironic palette stems from its resemblance or dissimilarity to one medium or another, I suspect that film's particular ironic capacities are bound to lie precisely in this medium's ability to draw simultaneously upon the properties of many other art forms.

© The Author(s) 2016
J. MacDowell, *Irony in Film*, DOI 10.1057/978-1-137-32993-6_2

As has frequently been acknowledged, the 'specific' nature of the film medium in fact appears to be its hybridity—its capacity to synthesise aesthetic features and possibilities associated with numerous different media. In the space of a few pages, James Monaco's influential textbook *How to Read a Film* asserts variously that '"moving pictures" are at first glance most closely parallel to the pictorial arts' (2009: 39), that 'on the surface, theatrical film seems most closely comparable to the stage drama' (ibid.: 48), and that 'the narrative potential of film is so marked that it has developed its strongest bond not with painting, not even with drama, but with the novel' (ibid.: 44). Film is thus, as Raymond Durgnat (1976) famously dubbed it, a 'mongrel' medium. In such an 'impure' (Perkins 1972: 151) art, 'the particulars of the film medium' must be understood to be not merely those properties belonging *only* to film, but also those that film seems to share with other media.[1]

Each of the mediums whose expressive possibilities film seems able to draw upon, furthermore, instinctively appear especially suited to creating different *kinds* of irony. While no medium is likely to be restricted to generating a single type of irony alone, we might say that pictures appear particularly capable of depicting *situational* ironies, drama seems well placed to create *dramatic* irony, and prose fiction is especially apt to be *communicatively* ironic. These, at least, are the kinds of irony that I will be primarily concerned with in my discussion of each medium. I propose that comparing film's ironic capacities to those of pictures, drama, and prose fiction may allow us to recognise that film exhibits—at the very least—the capacity to create these various kinds of irony by its own means.

Of course, comparing the expressive properties of film with those of other mediums always demands caution. In some sense, then, the task faced by this chapter is itself necessarily mongrel: we must consider which of film's ironic capacities appear comparable to those of other media, while never losing sight of their particular character in this mongrel medium. With this in mind, my exploration begins with certain possibilities of filmmaking that seem particularly indebted to its nature as, in part, a pictorial medium.

The Irony in Moving Pictures: Pictorial, Situational, and Filmic

As Elleström notes, 'There are thousands of books and articles dealing with irony in literature. In the case of...[visual] art, it is not so. The word irony is hardly to be found in dictionaries of [this] discipline' (1996: 198).

One reason for this may be the widespread belief that 'irony in pictures is surely rare' (Kennedy 2008: 458). This assumption also appears partly responsible for the accompanying lack of detailed investigations of irony in filmmaking. The link between these media is certainly one reason cited by Gregory Currie for his views about film's limited ironic capacities (2010: 168). Currie has offered one of the only extended theoretical defences of this position, and I will engage with his arguments on this matter later in the chapter. However, it is first necessary to consider the source of his doubts, which stem less from his assumptions about filmmaking in particular than from his belief that, in general, 'pictorial irony is…a notably difficult effect to bring off' (2011: 167).

In a thought-provoking article called 'The Irony in Pictures', Currie argues that many descriptions of pictures as 'ironic' commit 'the error of confusing an ironic picture with a picture of an ironic situation' (2011: 149). To help illustrate this, he cites a Depression-era photograph by Margaret Bourke-White, commonly called *Kentucky Flood* (1937) (Fig. 2.1). The picture shows a group of dispossessed African Americans queuing to receive flood relief beneath a baldly propagandist poster depicting a happy, smiling,

Fig. 2.1   *Kentucky Flood*: Flood victims beneath the 'American Way' poster

white nuclear American family (and their dog) driving through a pictur-
esque natural landscape.[2] The poster carries the headline 'World's Highest
Standard of Living,' as well as the proclamation that 'There's no way like
the American way'; meanwhile, the queue of displaced and poverty-stricken
black men, women, and children lined beneath it punctures powerfully the
billboard's optimistic insinuation that the available 'standards of living'
made possible by its lauded 'American way' might be equal for everyone.

This photograph has been widely referred to as ironic; Currie, however,
disagrees. Although granting that it depicts a painfully ironic situation,
Currie asks whether the photograph can be described as *'being* ironic'
(ibid.: 151; original emphasis) or whether it constitutes merely 'a representation of situational irony' (ibid.: 162). This question arises because of
the intentional narrowness of Currie's definition of what pictures must do
in order to be ironic. This is a definition worth probing, since it also lies at
the heart of his arguments about film's ironic capacities.

Currie is committed to a specific theoretical approach to irony known as
the 'pretence theory'. This theory holds that ironic expression inherently
involves pretending to express a particular point of view, which one does
not endorse, in order implicitly to convey a contrasting point of view—as
in the case of sarcasm, for example (see also Currie 2006). I will be drawing upon this useful theory later in the chapter to help explain film's ability to create *communicative* irony specifically. However, Currie's analysis
of Bourke-White's photograph suggests that the pretence theory should
perhaps not be our sole framework for approaching all ironic expression,
regardless of medium.

For Currie, in order to be called ironic, an artwork must be practising
communicative irony; and in order to practise communicative irony, it
must be pretending. He thus claims of *Kentucky Flood* that, to be an ironic
photograph, 'it would have to be…pretending to adopt a point of view,
thereby expressing a view about the defects of that point of view' (2011:
152). Contrasting this firmly against the act of depicting an ironic situation, Currie asserts that 'only the first of these is a case of a picture *being*
ironic' (ibid.: 151; original emphasis). This will only remain true, however,
if we grant an underlying premise, which to me appears questionable: 'the
irony of pictures, where it occurs, is the same thing as the irony of verbal
remarks' (ibid.: 167). Why, we might ask, should we necessarily expect pictures—or indeed films—always to express themselves ironically in the same
manner as verbal remarks? I suggest that a more productive assumption
is that we will give ourselves a better chance of elucidating the nature of

irony, in any medium, not by demanding that a medium satisfy our theory of ironic expression, but rather by moulding our theorising better to fit the ways a medium seems able to express itself ironically.

It seems likely that there will be ways of 'being ironic' in certain mediums that may not be available to verbal remarks, and I believe that our theories of irony in such mediums should endeavour to articulate what those might be. In the case of photography—and pictures more generally—I suggest that our theorising should not prematurely exclude the possibility that central to the medium's particular ironic capacities is likely to be, precisely, its ability to depict ironic situations. That ability, furthermore, is clearly one of several things this medium shares with film. Thus, although fiction films (and perhaps photographs too)[3] may indeed be capable of achieving precisely the kind of ironic pretence Currie demands, I suggest that we should not necessarily assume this is the only way in which they can '*be*' ironic.

I stress *fiction* film here not because of anything Currie claims about the Bourke-White photograph, nor about the irony in pictures generally. Interestingly, since he is concerned with pictorial representation of all kinds (rather than merely photographic images), Currie's conclusions about the ironic capacities of Bourke-White's picture do not rest upon the fact that it (presumably) depicts a situation that happened in the real world.[4] Indeed, he explicitly addresses what it would mean for his thesis were the photograph to have been staged and concludes that this would not affect his argument (ibid.: 161–162). By contrast, I would argue that a medium's ability not only to capture but also *construct* ironic situations is in fact of great significance, and this will be addressed in my subsequent discussion of dramatic irony. Given Currie's premises, though, we will benefit from limiting our present investigation to issues concerning pictorial representation itself, namely: to the matter of what any picture or film must do in order to create a 'picture of an ironic situation'.

To proceed, we will be in need of an example that can serve for our discussion something like the function Bourke-White's photo serves for Currie's. *Dr. Strangelove* (Stanley Kubrick, 1964) contains several shots that use a compositional strategy strikingly similar to that of *Kentucky Flood*, and for analogous purposes. At numerous points throughout this film, we are shown on screen the phrase 'Peace is Our Profession', which was the official motto of Strategic Air Command—the military organisation that coordinated the United States' nuclear strike capabilities during the Cold War. This phrase is displayed often on various signs and murals, which are positioned around the air force base in which much of the movie is set. These signs, moreover, are regularly juxtaposed in the frame against dramatic materials that clash ironically with the phrase's proclamation, creating similar contrasts between words and image as are established in Bourke-White's picture.[5] I am interested in asking what an examination of this compositional strategy in both *Kentucky Flood* and Kubrick's film may be able to tell us about each medium's capacities for ironic expression.

To help address this question, it is worth taking account of one final, important point made by Currie. Currie argues that a picture can be said to be ironic 'if and only if [it] has properties expressive of an ironic intent' (2011: 154). This seems to me correct, and crucial. If, as suggested in the introduction (and as will be argued further in Chapter 4), ironic expression always depends upon an intention to be ironic, then we should certainly expect ironic pictures (and films) to have been made with ironic intent. The only question, then, is what might count as ironic intent. Because of his theoretical project, Currie is concerned with only one kind of intention: an intention to '[pretend] to a point of view' (2006: 119). If we do not share his theoretical commitments, however, we can agree absolutely on the importance of point of view to pictorial irony and also that a picture must be able to imply 'ironic intent' in order to be called ironic; yet we can equally presume that an intention to *pretend* to hold a point of view is not the only kind of ironic intention for which we should be seeking evidence. I suggest, rather, that our conception of what constitutes 'ironic intent' should be able to encompass *any* ironic intentions that seem to be implied by a photograph or film's approach to point of view. For, as we shall see, point of view will indeed always be fundamental to the ways in which a picture or a film can express ironic intentions—even when it apparently 'simply records an ironic situation' (Currie 2011: 152).

Pictures and Film: Ironic Points of View, Tones, and Intentions

We might reasonably say that Bourke-White photographed an ironic situation. However, to ensure that she captured and emphasised this situation's all-important irony, certain elementary decisions about point of view plainly had to be made. I suggest that these decisions can be characterised as attesting to ironic intent.

A photograph, as Roland Barthes notes, 'can choose its subject, its point of view and its angle' (1977: 43). We can thus begin to approach the question of how *Kentucky Flood*'s point of view attests to ironic intentions by drawing some basic conclusions from how this photograph frames its subject. David Davies writes of photography:

> While the perspective and angle from which a scene is viewed in ordinary perception rarely admits of an explanation in terms of purposes and intentions, the manner in which a subject is presented in a photograph is almost always to be referred to a choice on the part of the photographer, who is showing us the scene from this perspective for a reason. (2010: 178)

Given this fact, the perspective and angle from which *Kentucky Flood* views its scene bespeaks choices, and those choices will imply certain purposes and intentions. The picture's perspective most immediately informs us that a choice has been made to include within the frame, prominently and in focus, both the billboard and the queue. Since this perspective creates a conspicuous and precise compositional contrast between the claims of the poster and the nature of the event in progress beneath it, that choice implies an intention that appears to demand an explanation in which irony plays at least some role. The question is what exactly that explanation should be and whether or not it involves ascribing 'ironic intent' to the picture or its maker.

I suggest that Bourke-White's framing the scene in this manner—that is, so as to create and emphasise the relevant juxtaposition—constitutes, in part, an implicit invitation to the viewer to join her in recognising the situation's irony. The picture, in other words, implies an intention to frame something as bitterly ironic and to communicate that bitter irony to an audience. As an aesthetic intention, I see no reason not to define this as ironic in nature. Intending to offer something as ironic has nothing to do with pretence, yet pretending is also surely not the sole way in which we are able to express ironic intentions. Imagine, for instance, that a friend taps you on the shoulder and directs your attention towards some event occurring within your immediate vicinity that they deem to be ironically amusing—saying nothing, at most offering a knowing glance or look of surprise. I suggest that, while not intending to pretend anything, your friend is nevertheless expressing another kind of ironic intention: he or she intends us to register the presence of irony in the world or—put another way—is encouraging us momentarily to look at the world ironically. It seems to me that comparable kinds of ironic intentions can frequently be implied by artworks,[6] and pictorial artworks no less so than any other. Douglas Muecke notes that, when an artist presents us with an ironic situation, rather than 'the ironist...say[ing] something in order to have it rejected as false..., [instead] the ironist presents something as ironic—a situation, a sequence of events, a character, a belief, etc.' (1970: 56). I agree that the latter action might reasonably earn someone the label 'ironist' as readily as the former and that this is because, as an aesthetic gesture, it can be said to be equally 'expressive of an ironic intent' (Currie, 2011: 154).

I thus propose that, because *Kentucky Flood* is framed as it is, its very point of view expresses an ironic intention. Beyond the mere fact of the picture's central contrast, though, other aspects of its point of view also seem to suggest additional, more complex ironic intentions. To consider just one of these: the framing on the right, left, and top parts of the image is so close to the edges of the billboard that the poster makes up virtually the entirety of the background, while the bottom of the frame seems to come almost as close as possible to the feet of the people in the queue. One result of this is that the scene is denied much of a sense of location. Together with the flattening of the image by a long focal length, this painstaking neatness in the composition lends an almost surreal tone to the picture's irony. It makes it momentarily appear either as if the people in the line are standing in front of an unreal landscape populated by grinning giants—or else, as John Tagg puts it in his fine interpretation of Bourke-White's picture, 'as if the line has been pasted over the bottom of the billboard' (2009: 113). We might say that decisions about point of view are here beginning to affect another property relevant to irony: tone. This is a matter not only of a work's point of view towards its subject but also its implied *attitudes* towards both that subject and its own stylistic conventions.[7] On the one hand, the forcefulness of *Kentucky Flood*'s rhetorical contrasts (e.g. prosperity/destitution, white/black, painting/photography) suggests an angry polemic; at the same time, the extremely precise control of the image's compositional irony implies a meticulous aesthetic sensibility. Tonally speaking, then, although the picture's irony certainly feels pointed and satirical, the particular way it is created contributes to 'the image's oddly detached effect' (Tagg 2009: 111).

In these ways and more, despite 'simply record[ing] an ironic situation' (Currie 2011: 152), the picture's particular ironic effects depend absolutely upon decisions concerning its point of view, since it is those decisions that attest to various ironic intentions. This symbiotic relationship between point of view and ironic intention could be said to be similar, though perhaps rather more complicated, in the case of film.

We should first take stock of what photography and film have in common in this regard. It is true to say of (depictive uses of) both these media what V.F. Perkins writes of film: 'a single image is made to act both as a recording, to show us what happens, and as an expressive device to heighten the effect and significance of what we see' (1972: 78). Because every photograph and every film image will perform the dual functions of record and expressive device, to show something is always to create specific sorts of significance and effects through the act of showing. In showing a situational irony, a major part of the significance will usually be to present it *as* ironic, and a major effect of doing so will be to imply an *intention* to convey that irony. Both of these will necessarily be dependent, furthermore, upon the adoption of a particular point of view.

As in Bourke-White's photograph, then, whenever *Dr. Strangelove* shows Strategic Air Command's motto, it will thus unavoidably simultaneously be implying a variety of intentions by the showing, and achieving both by virtue of the film's point of view. We shall soon see that point of view is a rather more multifarious phenomenon in feature-length fiction films than in photographs. However, let us nonetheless remain with the comparison as long as possible by first considering an aspect of point of view that is as important to the pictorial medium of film as to the pictorial medium of photography: composition.

Picturing Situational Irony in Dr. Strangelove

As in a photograph, so in an individual shot of a film, recording a situational irony will rely upon composition—at the very least if a situation's irony is to be conveyed within a single shot. In such cases, one basic compositional requirement will clearly be the same for film as for photography: create the necessary juxtaposition by virtue of framing. To explore this further, we might consider one of the most ostentatiously ironic shots in the whole of *Dr. Strangelove*.

About two-thirds of the way into the film, the Burpelson Air Force base—from which General Ripper (Sterling Hayden) has launched his crazed scheme to incite World War III—is under siege by the US Armed Forces. Their aim is to force Ripper to recall the numerous planes he has dispatched to bomb Soviet targets. The Strategic Air Command motto is made visible in several shots during this siege, but one in particular stands out for its rhetorical frankness. A handheld, shaky camera picks out a group of soldiers in wide shot through a wire fence. Five soldiers are

Fig. 2.2   *Dr. Strangelove*: Soldiers shelter beneath 'Peace IS OUR PROFESSION'

returning fire on Ripper's men in the base; they are huddled around a jeep for cover, while the dead body of one of their compatriots lies sprawled on the tarmac between them and us. Just behind them, looming very promi-nently in the frame, stands a huge sign on which we can read the legend '843rd BOMB WING, STRATEGIC AIR COMMAND', the logo of that command, and—rendered in by far the largest letters—its motto: 'Peace IS OUR PROFESSION' (Fig. 2.2).

Viewed as a stand-alone image, we might say that the irony of this shot is similarly dependent upon angle and perspective as Bourke-White's photograph. Most obviously, as in *Kentucky Flood*, its irony relies upon keeping in frame juxtaposed elements: the sign, plus the huddled sol-diers, their weaponry, and their fallen comrade. Also as in a photograph, for the film to adopt this particular point of view implies an ironic intent: since the shot's angle has undoubtedly been chosen in order to make the ironic incongruity conspicuous, we are entitled to attribute this choice to the ironic sensibility of those responsible for the composition.

Another clear similarity between how this shot and the Bourke-White photo convey ironic intent is through the way both use written language. It must be stressed here that making use of written words is entirely inessential to the ability of either photography or film to depict situational ironies. The practice does, though, have the benefit of assisting in something that *is* essential to depicting ironic situations, in either medium: juxtaposing one set of perspectives against another. When offered in the form of statements or assertions, verbal language has the appeal of being able instantly to suggest perspectives and attitudes. In a pictorial medium, these can in turn be placed in ironic contrast with visual elements seeming to embody oppositions to those perspectives and attitudes. The ironic potential, then, of the words on the billboard in *Kentucky Flood* and the motto of Strategic Air Command is the same: they represent claims from certain perspectives, which strongly imply certain attitudes—the complacent, laudatory patriotism of the pronouncement about the 'American way', for instance, or the pretentious and pious sloganeering of the claim 'Peace IS OUR PROFESSION'. To the extent that both *Kentucky Flood* and Kubrick's image adopt points of view relative to these attitudes such that they become undermined, both works imply additional attitudes of their own. And, to the extent that we can characterise those attitudes as being (among other things) ironic, we are entitled to consider this another way in which both works imply ironic intentions.

Such are the similarities between the ways Bourke-White's photograph and *Dr. Strangelove*'s shot imply ironic intentions. We can begin to approach how they differ—and how *any* still picture and any fiction film must differ in this regard—by drawing attention to a phrase I found myself needing to use earlier: 'Viewed as a stand-alone image.'

The most pressing difference between all individual pictures and all isolated film images is, of course, that the latter in fact are never isolated. First, the cinematic image is almost always *moving*—both the elements within it and (often) the frame itself. Second, individual film images are almost always just one among many more, meaning that *patterned relationships* are necessarily established between any single image and innumerable others. Third, any individual image and those to which it is related are almost always (at least outside silent film, and even to some extent there) placed into further relationships with a proliferation of *sounds*,[8] bringing an additional aural dimension to the image's expressive powers. Even this noticeably incomplete list of obvious ways in which individual images in films differ from individual pictures begins to suggest what markedly more multifaceted phenomena ironic points of view and tones are bound to be in fiction filmmaking.

Point of view in fiction films has been defined as 'the ways in which a form of narration can systematically structure an audience's overall epistemic access to narrative' (Wilson 1986: 3); furthermore, in a film, '*everything* can convey point of view: camera angle, focal length, music, mise-en-scène, performance,' and so on (Hutcheon 2006: 55; emphasis mine). Tone, meanwhile, has been characterised as the ways in which a movie 'implicitly invites us to understand its attitude to its material and the stylistic register it employs' (Pye 2007: 7) and similarly encompasses both 'dominant or systemic aspects' and 'more local and variable' effects (ibid.: 2007). Our epistemic access and a film's attitudes, its point of view and its tone, are thus cumulative phenomena built up over a text's entirety while also being created moment by moment. Because they are such immanent and all-pervasive features of a film's address, they will unavoidably be affected by decisions taken in all of the areas of filmmaking itemised earlier: movement, patterns of imagery, and sound. Given this, attending even only to how these properties help contribute to the point of view and tone of a single shot from *Dr. Strangelove* should begin to suggest how the modest act of depicting an ironic situation in film can imply a whole host of ironic intentions.

Irony in Movement, Patterns of Imagery, and Sound

'The arresting of time,' suggests Janet Malcolm, 'is photography's unique capacity' (1980: 36). While this capacity is perhaps not quite wholly alien to film (we might think of the 'freeze-frame'), movement does nonetheless offer 'one of the greatest differences, doubtless the greatest, between still photography and the movies' (Metz 1974: 7). Given this, it is certainly worth considering the contrasting temporal tendencies of a medium that was once, after all, regularly referred to as 'animated photography' (Arnheim 1957: 2). I will raise here in relation to Kubrick's film just two aspects of style made possible by the medium's temporal nature: the camera's capacity for mobility and the relationships films construct between different images.

Regarding the former: among the most immediately striking facts about the aforementioned shot from *Dr. Strangelove* is that it is filmed with a camera whose shakes, bumps, and wobbles suggest it is held by human hands, which in turn lends the image the harried immediacy of documentary or newsreel footage. The significance of this for the irony of the shot lies partly in the rhetoric of reportage it summons. In particular, there is the way the camera peers curiously but cautiously through the fence in the foreground and the fact that it whips rightwards *into* its framing of the soldiers and the sign—sitting for some time on this composition before continuing on its path. Both these stylistic decisions create the sense that the camera (or its operator) has been briefly struck by 'finding' the shockingly ironic juxtaposition in the midst of the ongoing violence. This chimes with the film's overall satiric strategy of representing itself as highlighting, and only somewhat exaggerating, real absurdities associated with the contemporaneous political philosophy of 'mutually assured destruction'.[9] Also significant, though, is the somewhat contrasting tonal quality of faint parody the style implies towards the aesthetics of documentaries and newsreels themselves—summoned here by this style being applied to a scenario that, in context, remains comically heightened and hyperbolically crazed, however terrifyingly plausible in theory.[10]

More important still, though, is that this shot represents only one image arranged amidst a multitude of others. Especially relevant is the fact that the composition assumes a place within a pattern of other shots across the film that similarly use Strategic Air Command's motto to create various ironic effects. In addition to being seen elsewhere during this siege, the phrase was first glimpsed at the beginning of the film on a plaque behind General Ripper when he telephoned his executive officer, Group Captain Mandrake (Peter Sellers), to tell him (falsely) that the United States is in a 'shooting war'. When, seconds later, it also becomes visible on a poster behind Mandrake as he receives this call (Fig. 2.3), we might intuit that a motif is being developed; and, indeed, we come to be presented with the words at numerous other points, too. The motto is visible in many later scenes set in Ripper's office—perhaps most notably in shots that permit the plaque to linger at the edge of the frame as Ripper is either preparing or operating the imposingly huge machine gun he uses to fire upon U.S. troops who are advancing towards his headquarters. Signs featuring the legend are also rendered prominent in several earlier tableau-like shots that form a sequence showing groups of soldiers on Ripper's base listening attentively to the public address system as the general proudly delivers a speech about combat readiness (Fig. 2.4). As well as simply increasing the rhetorical emphasis granted the motto, the decision to make this slogan into a motif also allows these words to be put to various distinct

Fig. 2.3   *Dr. Strangelove*: Mandrake flanked by slogan

Fig. 2.4   *Dr. Strangelove*: Ripper's troops listen to his address on PA system

tonal purposes. For instance, shots that associate the motto with Ripper seem dedicated to ironising his psychotic interpretation of what it means to have peace as his profession. Meanwhile, those that connect the slogan to the soldiers under Ripper's charge—especially shots that place us close by those soldiers—might be said to extend a kind of rueful, sardonic sympathy to these nameless grunts, who have unknowingly found themselves caught up in the horrifying ironies of Cold War politics.

Dr. Strangelove's aural dimension is also crucial to the irony of the shot of the sign during the siege—particularly the gunfire that echoes alongside the image: a sporadic but steady series of rifle cracks. These noises of mechanised warfare are nearly as essential as the composition itself to the shot's ironic effects. In their visceral sonic embodiment of all that we are least likely to associate with 'peace' (in any of its connotations), these hammering bangs make a pivotal contribution to the ironic contrasts established with the platitudinous promise espoused by the sign. Furthermore, we might begin to deepen our understanding of sound's substantial potential for implying ironic intentions by imagining a close-up of the 'Peace IS OUR PROFESSION' sign that featured *no* soldiers or guns but was nonetheless accompanied by the gunfire. In such a shot, no visible evidence of the situation in progress would even be necessary to capture its irony so long as these sounds were bringing to the image their powerful contrary associations.

Of course, a similarly indispensable aural contribution to irony can often be made by a film's dialogue and music. At least in films with synchronised sound, in this medium it is not only the written but also the spoken word that has the potential to alert us to a work's ironic intentions. What is President Muffley's (Peter Sellers) famous line, 'You can't fight in here: this is the War Room!', for example, if not a clear signal as to the nature of this film's particular ironic address? And, while no dialogue accompanies the shot of the sign during the siege, we might note suggestive connections between one of the key words of the sign's motto and ironic lines heard elsewhere in the film: for instance, the Soviet Ambassador's (Peter Bull) reference to the Soviet Union's commitment to 'the peace race,' along with the 'space race' and, of course, the 'arms race'. Regarding music, meanwhile, again, none is heard during the siege itself; however, the film's score is certainly used to help create irony elsewhere. We might think, for example, of the several occasions when a martial arrangement of the American Civil War song 'When Johnny Comes Marching Home' is made to accompany scenes set in the bomber that will ultimately drop the inaugural payload. This use of music represents another example of a strategy that is also being pursued by any shot containing the words 'Peace is our Profession': ironically undermining the optimistic attitudes implied by a piece of militaristic propaganda.

I have merely gestured here towards a few of the many ways in which even just camera movement, relationships between images, and sound are relevant to the ironic point of view and tone of one shot in *Dr. Strangelove*. I suggest that, although we *could* say this shot 'simply records an ironic situation' (Currie 2011: 152), the decision to record this ironic situation in just this fashion, and to place it within the film in just this way, in fact attests to numerous interrelated ironic intentions. As such, if we are prepared to define ironic intention more broadly than merely pretending to adopt a point of view, then I believe we must consider the depiction of situational irony to represent a key means by which works in this medium can '*be* ironic' (Currie 2011: 151).

This, moreover, is before attending to the greatly important matter of the placement of any individual shot of *Dr. Strangelove* within a carefully constructed *story*. While the act of surrounding the words 'Peace IS OUR PROFESSION' with warlike activities might be considered an intrinsically ironic gesture, the specific nature of this irony is actually, of course, determined in large part by its place within a film whose whole narrative is dedicated to satirising Cold War politics. To note this much is to acknowledge the fundamental fact that the fiction film's ironic capacities are by no means restricted to its ability to depict situational irony—nor merely to patterns of images, sounds, and the relationships between them—but also to storytelling. This, however, is to begin a discussion about a different aspect of irony altogether.

Filming Ironic Dramas: Drama, Dramatic Irony, and Film

Fiction films have numerous means at their disposal for using storytelling to help create irony, but one moment from *Dr. Strangelove* mentioned earlier hints at an especially common practice. The scenes set onboard the bomber offer an opportunity for *dramatic* irony: the plane's personnel do not know, whereas we do, that they have been ordered to attack their targets under false pretences by a deluded homicidal paranoiac, and that under no circumstances will they ever 'come marching home again'. This section of the chapter explores dramatic irony in film and addresses how a film's ability to create this kind of irony might be related to the medium's dramatic qualities. This task is necessary, in part, because certain aspects of fiction filmmaking are at least as indebted to the dramatic as to the pictorial arts.

Aristotle famously held that there are two fundamental ways in which a story can be conveyed: an artist 'may imitate by narration…or he [*sic*] may present all his characters as living and moving before us' (1961: 53). Conveying a story in the former manner constitutes for Aristotle a narrative, wherein a story is *narrated* to an audience; the latter, meanwhile, constitutes a drama, wherein a story is *presented* in front of them. These categories have frequently been used by theorists to demonstrate that an art form such as prose fiction typically constitutes a narrative—in which a story is *told*—while an art form such as a play typically constitutes a drama—in which a story is *enacted*.[11] What, though, of film?

It would seem, as Douglas Pye observes, that 'movies disturb this ancient duality' between narrative and drama (2013: 133). While fiction films are now usually discussed as narratives, Gilberto Perez notes that 'it used to be assumed that film is a dramatic medium' (1998: 60). In one sense, this is theoretically appealing. A live-action movie, after all, is not the result of narrating a story by means of words, whereas it *is*, in part, usually the result of 'enacting' (portions of) a story. As Bordwell puts it: 'staging an event…is no less part of fictional moviemaking than is camera placement or editing' (1985: 11). Indeed, such staging frequently produces the most meaningful aspects of a film, wherein 'much of the creative effort takes place *in front of* the camera. It is the face and the performance of the actor, the sets and lighting that between them carry most of a film's meaning' (Durgnat 1976: 32; original emphasis). Creating fictions on film thus appears in some respects a fundamentally similar enterprise to creating fictions on stage: a story suggested by a script is conveyed (in part) through enacting dramatic situations; actors embody characters; decisions must be made about blocking, set design, lighting, costume, and so on. Due to these partial but nonetheless undeniable similarities, I am in agreement with those such as Perez (1998), Pye (2000: 3), Rodriguez (2010), and Zborowski (2015: 48–49), who ultimately conclude that 'film is both a dramatic and a narrative medium' (Perez 1998: 85).

Later in this chapter I will be discussing how the apparently narrative components of the film medium affect what ironic capacities it may share with prose fiction. Here, though, I shall explore what both its narrative *and* dramatic aspects mean for the ironic capacities it might or might not share with drama. My particular focus will be film's capacities for creating dramatic irony relative to those of drama. It is true, as Manfred Pfister suggests, that 'it would be wrong to equate dramatic irony with irony in drama' as a whole (1991: 55),[12] and indeed we will also be touching in this section upon other kinds of irony available to dramatic media. Yet dramatic irony nonetheless represents an essential subject—partly because it is central to the ways that irony has been theorised in drama, but also because much of what gets called irony in films is related in some fashion to dramatic irony.

The term *dramatic irony* dates back only to the early nineteenth century, coming to refer to an experience made possible when a story's audience are granted information or perspectives pointedly denied to one or more of the story's characters.[13] Certainly not restricted to theatre alone, dramatic irony is defined in Germaine Collette Dempster's study of Chaucerian irony as 'a strong contrast, unperceived by a character in a story, between the surface meaning of his [*sic*] words or deeds and something else happening in the same story' (1932: 7). This contrast is perceivable due to there being 'discrepant awareness' (Evans 1960) between characters' knowledge and the audience's knowledge. Referring, furthermore, not merely to the fact but rather particular *effects* of discrepant awareness, dramatic irony has been called both 'the sense of contradiction felt by spectators of a drama who see a character acting in ignorance of his [*sic*] condition' (Sedgewick 1948: 43) and an effect of 'dissonance between what the audience may see and the limitations of the character's own self-awareness' (Storm 2011: 5–6).

The capacity to create dramatic irony seems critical to ironic expression in both drama and film, and both media appear to share certain means for doing so. Yet there are also undeniable differences between film's and drama's abilities in this regard, many of which are due to film's peculiar status as both a dramatic *and* a narrative medium. In what follows I shall attend to both those similarities and differences. As in the previous section, we require a concrete example to assist our theorising. The film I have chosen for this task is *Rope* (Alfred Hitchcock, 1948). This is not merely because it is adapted from a theatrical work (Patrick Hamilton's 1929 play of the same name), nor simply because both play and film create such ingenious dramatic ironies. Nor, indeed, will I be concerning myself with questions of adaptation. Hitchcock's *Rope* differs from Hamilton's play in many telling respects, but I am concerned here not to compare this film and that play, but rather to compare the expressive possibilities of film and drama. For *Rope* is a film with a fascinating relationship to drama. Thanks to its theatrical origins, its continuous 'real-time' staging, its action's (almost) total confinement to a single contiguous set, and its famed reliance upon unusually long takes, few fiction films owe so much to the medium's dramatic properties. And yet, precisely *because* of all its debts to drama, few films allow us to register more precisely what nonetheless distinguishes the two media. I shall focus first, though, on several things that *Rope*'s ironies owe to film's dramatic capacities.

Drama and Irony in Film: Perspective, Staging, and Performance in Rope

The action of *Rope*'s story gets under way when we see two young men strangling a third young man to death before loading his body into a large, antique chest. The victim's name is David Kentley (Dick Hogan). He has been murdered by two of his school 'friends', Brandon (John Dall) and Phillip (Farley Granger), for what they consider to be intellectual and 'artistic' reasons: they (especially Brandon) believe conventional codes of morality do not apply to the intellectually 'superior' in society and that murder is 'a crime for most men' but 'a privilege for the few'. David stands for them as an arbitrary representative of 'most men,' and, for Brandon at least, his murder constitutes what he refers to as 'a work of art'. The murderers have contrived to celebrate their killing by hosting a dinner party in this very room, while their victim's body remains ever nearby, concealed in the chest. The invited guests, meanwhile, consist primarily of David's friends and family: his father, Mr Kentley (Cedric Hardwicke); his aunt, Mrs Atwater (Constance Collier); his fiancée, Janet (Joan Walker); and a fellow school friend (and Janet's former beau), Kenneth (Douglas Dick). Also present is Brandon and Phillip's housekeeper, Mrs Wilson (Edith Evanson), as well as their (and David's) former teacher, Rupert Cadell (James Stewart). We will come to discover that Rupert is responsible for introducing his ex-pupils to the philosophical theories that (unbeknownst to him) led them to commit what they regard as this 'immaculate murder'. Upping the audacity of their scheme even further, Brandon will soon decide to serve the evening's buffet from the chest that contains David's corpse—a gesture that he believes '[makes] our work of art a masterpiece'.

Many of *Rope*'s ironies are rooted in film's dramatic capacities. This is to say, in part, that it engineers many moments of irony that could also be created in similar ways by a work of theatre. William Storm has suggested a number of possible means for creating irony in theatre:

> With respect to character, irony can be conscious—as in the observations of a deliberate ironist—or unconscious, as in situations where an irony catches a stage figure unawares. In addition, theatrical irony can be authorial—in the sense of a mastered or overarching irony that marks the dramatic representation overall. (2011: 4)

I will have more to say shortly about the first type of irony mentioned here, but we will be best served by first attending to the remaining types, which relate more closely to dramatic irony specifically.

Regardless of medium, the fact that we are allowed to know from the very beginning of *Rope* what has happened to David would be the basic precondition for most of the story's subsequent dramatic irony. This decision allows the film, first, to stage numerous instances where irony 'catches a...figure unawares'. In particular, the movie's opening is indispensable for *Rope*'s ability to summon repeatedly a distinctive effect of dramatic irony from lines of dialogue, namely 'a strong contrast, unperceived by a character in a story, between the surface meaning of his [*sic*] words...and something else happening in the same story' (Dempster 1932: 7).

Such contrasts in *Rope* sometimes arise when a character's use of metaphorical language assumes disturbingly literal connotations in context. 'I could really strangle you', Janet says of Brandon while reprimanding him; elsewhere she asks frustratedly, 'Why can't he [Brandon] keep his hands off people?'; 'I hope you knock 'em dead', Kenneth tells Phillip, referring to the latter's upcoming piano recital. It is only thanks to the knowledge we have been granted by the film's opening that these moments become imbued with dramatic irony: without it, we would effectively share with these characters the more limited perspectives that cause them to use such metaphors unwittingly. Another consequence of our superior perspective is the privileged position it places us in regarding the matter that progressively preoccupies the guests: where is David? All those who have been invited to the party either already know he is expected to arrive or learn as much. David's absence thus becomes increasingly perplexing to everyone except Brandon and Phillip, prompting numerous questions as to his whereabouts, which become more pressing as the evening wears on. Occasionally, again, these questions acquire the dissonant double meanings of dramatic irony: 'Is David here?' asks his father upon arriving, unaware that, in fact, he is; 'I can't think what's keeping him,' offers Mr Kentley at another moment, not knowing that what is 'keeping' David is the chest beside which he is presently standing. This spectacle of confusion about David's location comes to feel, for us, like a perverse game of hide-and-seek, or a treasure hunt, which is designed to be fruitless even while its solution is always maddeningly close at hand.

We can account for the storytelling strategies necessary to create this basic, ongoing dramatic irony—and indeed *any* moment of dramatic irony—via theories of point of view. As we have already seen, one useful definition of point of view in film concerns 'an audience's overall epistemic access to narrative' (Wilson 1986: 3). Choices concerning how to manage our 'epistemic access'—what we are permitted to see and know, when, and how—are clearly bound to be pivotal to dramatic irony. To help deepen our conception of how *Rope* prepares for the ironies mentioned, we might turn to Douglas Pye's (2000) 'axes' of point of view. It is only because of how the film handles what Pye calls its *spatial* and *temporal* axes that we may perceive the doubled significance of all the dialogue mentioned previously. Bluntly put, at its opening, the film has allowed us access to the location in which, at the time *at* which, David's body was hidden. Decisions about the spatial and temporal dimensions of point of view will always be essential to creating dramatic irony in film. *Rope* in particular, though, also makes further decisions with very particular consequences for what Pye dubs the *cognitive* axis of point of view: what we know relative to what particular characters know. Dramatic irony may, of course, be conceived such that no characters share our more knowledgeable perspective. In *Rope*, however, we share our position of knowledge with Brandon and Phillip. One key outcome of this is to raise troubling questions concerning one further axis of point of view: Pye's *evaluative* axis, which involves a film's apparent degree of sympathy or admiration for its characters. There is no necessary correlation between our 'cognitive' alignment with a character and our feeling encouraged towards a positive 'evaluation' of them;[14] nonetheless, this does always remain a possibility, and I will return shortly to what that might mean for our relationship with Brandon in particular.

How might these matters of point of view be articulated in relation to the properties not of film but of drama? It has sometimes been argued that 'the problem of point of view is narrative art's own problem, one that it does not share with...dramatic literature' (Kellogg/Scholes 1966: 240). Theatre's status as a non-narrative medium has therefore meant that '*point of view* is consequently not usually thought to be of much interest in [dramatic] texts' (McIntyre 2006: 2). Yet many of the same strategies necessary to create dramatic irony in film will clearly also be important to a wholly dramatic medium like theatre. For instance: on stage too, comparable choices concerning our spatial and temporal access to a story's events will evidently have comparable effects on our degree of cognitive alignment with particular characters. Given this, even if we cannot speak of *point of view* in relation to theatre, it would nonetheless seem, as Manfred Pfister claims, that the concept of *perspective* can be 'as fruitful for the analysis of drama as…for the analysis of narrative' (1991: 58). Indeed, the 'discrepant awareness' associated with dramatic irony fundamentally relies on a theatrical production's ability to create what Pfister calls a particular 'perspective structure', wherein significant disparities are established between the perspectives of certain characters and those of the audience (ibid.: 58).[15] In principle, then, a wholly dramatic enactment of *Rope* too would be eminently capable of achieving the kinds of dramatic ironies itemised earlier (as Hamilton's play itself does). Indeed, granting the audience a superior degree of knowledge than a story's characters is clearly a prerequisite for dramatic irony *whatever* the medium. Let us thus now turn to ironies in *Rope* that owe more to film's dramatic properties specifically.

One moment mentioned earlier—David's father wondering what is 'keeping' his son while standing beside the chest—hints at possibilities for dramatic irony that seem available to dramatic and filmed media alone. The sound film, like drama, is simultaneously a visual and aural medium. This allows it to exploit the potential for dramatic irony inherent in (among other things) how a story's visual elements can be arranged, how its action can be staged, and how its words are heard. These properties can be key to dramatic irony, and they help create numerous ironic effects throughout *Rope*.

We might begin with perhaps the most notable feature of *Rope*'s mise-en-scène: the chest concealing David's body. First, the mere continued presence of this piece of furniture brings a sustained sense of dramatic irony to the very set itself. Not only those moments already cited but *any* moment spent in this room can effectively become infused with dramatic irony upon recalling this object's contents. Second, Brandon makes several morbidly comic decisions about how to dress the chest: it is decorated with a table cloth that is simultaneously like a coffin drape; it is bedecked with candlesticks that are also evocative of a funeral; and the buffet is served from it such that it resembles, as Brandon explains to Mrs Wilson, 'a ceremonial altar, which you can heap with the foods for our sacrificial feast'. Third, regarding the relationship between dialogue and mise-en-scène: the dramatic irony created by each line concerning David's whereabouts is heightened considerably by the chest's physical proximity. This stubbornly material reminder of the missing character's final resting place causes some lines' double meanings to reverberate more audibly while visually answering (for us) every confused utterance of 'where's David?' with a mute *'here'*. This, finally, also touches upon the medium's capacity to create significant relationships between performers and décor. We might consider here a disturbing moment when Janet and Kenneth converse about David while standing directly behind the chest. The self-deprecating smiles Janet gives when admitting how happy and relaxed she is with David, the far-off gazes she eases into while reflecting on how spending time with him has allowed her to reveal what she embarrassedly calls 'the real, real-me stuff': all are cast into tragically ironic relief by this staging decision. The culmination of this moment comes when Janet utters a final frustrated and concerned 'Oh, where's *David?*' while turning her neck and body *away* from the chest—the one object with the power to answer her.

This last moment suggests another pivotal ability that film shares with drama: creating irony through an actor's performance. Having already suggested several elements that contribute to *Rope*'s dramatic ironies, we might probe this particular capacity further in relation to another kind of irony common to drama, namely the possibility for 'irony [to] be conscious—as in the observations of a deliberate ironist' (Storm 2011: 4).

'The spoken ironic voice', argues Storm, 'is as old as the theatre' (2011: 214), and it offers a key means of ironic expression for both drama and film. It can, for instance, contribute to characterisation—both of individuals and of social environments. In *Rope*, nonchalantly communicating ironically is actually transformed into something of a social *shibboleth*. There are those characters whose cultural positions and tastes (among other things) are suggested by their expressing themselves ironically nearly constantly (Brandon and Rupert); those apparently familiar enough with such positions and tastes to speak ironically occasionally (Phillip, Janet, and Kenneth); and those who seem associated with the linguistic conventions of other social milieus, in which irony may play little to no part (Mr Kentley, Mrs Atwater, and Mrs Wilson). Sober plain-speaking, convivial credulousness, and pragmatic practicality are defining characteristics of Mr Kentley's, Mrs Atwater's, and Mrs Wilson's roles respectively, and irony is almost wholly alien to these (not coincidentally?) older characters' communications.[16] For the younger generation of hyper-educated urban socialites represented by Phillip, Janet, and Kenneth, ironic speech is more common, though not total. Phillip's taste for irony has perhaps been blunted by the evening's events, but he can still make use of withering sarcasm rhetorically ('Nothing matters, except that *Mister Brandon* liked the party...'). Janet too treads a particular line in ironic wordplay, though possibly a somewhat less ostentatiously 'sophisticated' one than some in her circle (complaining, for instance, that the unexpected presence of Kenneth, her former lover, 'makes everything just ginger-peachy').[17] For Brandon and Rupert, though, irony constitutes an overarching principle of communication, seemingly bespeaking simultaneously a high level of erudition and a philosophically informed—but culturally expressed—taste for condescension. Moments after David's murder, for instance, Brandon jokingly exonerates himself and Phillip in a manner suggesting his character's belief in a universal intellectual hierarchy, but via reference points betraying a very specific form of cultural snobbery: 'Of course, he *was* a Harvard undergraduate', he chuckles: 'that *might* make it justifiable homicide!'

It can be crucial for works in any fictional medium to use irony to assist characterisation. Yet only media with dramatic capacities—those in which 'the *dramatis personae*...are impersonated by actual flesh and blood' (Muecke 1970: 67)—can physically *embody* ironic characters. Rupert, for example, at one point feigns interest in Janet's professed 'passion' for the movie star James Mason by asking, 'Is he...good?' Here it is not the words but Stewart's delivery that expresses his character's disdain for this conversation's topic and terms: his little upwards flick of the eyes before uttering the line, as if pretending to struggle to formulate what he considers such a banal question; the tiny but barbed pause before 'good', audibly implying quotation marks; the furrowed brow that mildly over-eggs the seriousness of his desire for an answer; the slight twitch of his mouth, suggesting a suppressed grimace, after these words have passed his lips. Stewart's performance of Rupert's ironic temper here thus provides us with revealing insights into his character. Furthermore, by alerting the audience to the ironic tone behind a character's lines, an actor's performance can also subtly align us cognitively with that character—a fact made especially plain if, as here, the skill of a consummate performer allows the audience to grasp ironies that other characters in the story apparently miss.

In drama, then, 'so much is accomplished by verbal nuance and by gesture that it becomes...simple to express meaning that is contrary to saying, or to alter intent through pronunciation [and] behaviour' (Austern 1986: 476). The ironic potential of this dramatic possibility is frequently exploited by films too, and *Rope* puts it to several purposes—some of them not restricted to characterisation alone. For instance, as well as allowing us a better sense of Rupert's personality, Stewart's ironic performance also constitutes another means by which the film suggests his character's indirect complicity in David's murder. Rupert is implicated in part, of course, because he shared with Brandon and Philip the philosophical theory that 'the lives of inferior beings are unimportant'; but, as Perkins notes, 'Rupert's complicity...[is] underlined by a large number of correspondences between his actions and attitudes and those of Philip and Brandon' (1963: 13). Chief among those correspondences is, precisely, the loftily ironic attitude betrayed in his interactions with other guests all night—up to and including his inability to ask Janet 'is he...good?' without a telltale pause.

As the ironies of *Rope* considered thus far suggest, then, we might say that fiction films find many creative possibilities for irony within those properties also possessed by drama: its script, its staging, and its performances. Any theoretical account of irony in this medium must encompass these possibilities. Having stressed several debts that *Rope*'s ironies owe to film's nominally dramatic properties, though, let us now turn to debts owed to the fact that 'film is a narrative *and* a dramatic art' (Pye 2000: 3; emphasis mine).

Filming Dramatic Irony

In a valuable article about adapting literary ironies, David Roche proposes that much irony in film is 'not medium-specific' (2015: 9); more specifically, he argues that 'dramatic irony functions in a similar manner... whether it be prose, drama or film' (ibid.: 5). It is worth noting two things about these claims. First, as previously suggested, the fact that a given element may not be *exclusively* filmic need make it no less specifically so. It is a specific feature of the live-action fiction film that many of its properties bear partial resemblances to those of drama. As such, those many important ironies in *Rope* that are indebted to, say, staging or performance, or more generally to dramatic irony, represent inherent possibilities of this medium—possibilities belonging no less specifically to film than drama. The second thing to note, however, is that resemblances between such properties in drama and film, while important, are indeed destined to remain partial.

Although a particular moment of irony in a film may owe much to film's dramatic properties, it could never be precisely the same moment of irony in a wholly dramatic medium. We might demonstrate this, first, by returning to some moments of *Rope* already touched upon. I referred earlier, for instance, to the chest acting as a material agent of dramatic irony in *Rope*'s staging. This claim remains true, yet incomplete. Of course, in film, mise-en-scène is never merely a matter of staging. Although mise-en-scène '*includes* those aspects of film that overlap with the art of the theater: setting, lighting, costume, and the behavior of the figures' (Bordwell/Thompson 2008: 112; emphasis mine), more precisely, 'we may define [it] as "staging *for the camera*"' (Durgnat 1976: 34; emphasis mine). We thus must account, for instance, not only for the chest's relationship to the surrounding action, but also for both the chest's and that action's relationship to the camera. On stage, it would theoretically be possible to keep the chest forever in plain sight. This, indeed, is the decision taken by Hamilton's play, and it is one that is destined to have its own particular consequences for the story's dramatic ironies. However, short of keeping the camera extremely and perpetually distant, this option was effectively unavailable to *Rope*, the film. When considering the ironic effects the chest creates, then, we need plainly to ask when and how the camera permits us to see it, from what angle, and in relation to whom.

Take, for example, Mr Kentley's telling Brandon, 'I can't imagine what's keeping him'. This moment's irony is due partly both to dialogue and staging—specifically, Kentley's proximity to the chest as he utters these words. However, the line's dramatic irony would not be of the same order if no sign of the chest were visible at the moment he spoke it. Instead, though, the chest is indeed gestured towards here via the inclusion in the frame of four of the candles with which it has been sardonically decorated (Fig. 2.5). Furthermore, the fact that the filmmakers deem it significant that we should be allowed to see these aspects of mise-en-scène at just this moment is confirmed when, seconds later, the camera pushes in far enough that the candles become excluded entirely from the shot once Mr Kentley leaves the frame. We might equally consider Janet speaking lovingly of David to Kenneth, again while next to the chest. Once more, throughout this two-shot, three candles protrude prominently from the bottom of the frame, intervening softly but firmly between us and Janet. Moments like these suggest that we could be led astray by claims such as that 'dramatic irony functions in a similar manner in…drama or film' (Roche 2015: 5). 'Similar' may perhaps be correct, but we should never assume that it could be the same.

As noted earlier, dramatic irony refers not merely to the *fact* of 'discrepant awareness', but rather to *effects* it can create: in Storm's words, a sense of 'dissonance between what the audience may see and the limitations of

Fig. 2.5 *Rope*: Mr Kentley by the chest

the character's own self-awareness' (2011: 5–6). The specific dissonance created in the shots referred to above—that is, the dramatic irony itself—is due precisely to 'what the audience may see', and what we are able to see is determined precisely by the framing. This, of course, is because any image in film that creates dramatic irony relies upon the pictorial and perspectival qualities of the medium discussed in this chapter's first section, which must 'be referred to a choice [to] show…us the scene from this perspective for a reason' (Davies 2010: 178). Unlike on stage, then, in film our understanding of any ironies involving staging must contend with the fact that films express themselves 'through staging and performance and yet [also by] mediating our access to what is enacted through an extensive series of photographic shots' (Pye 2013: 133).

Elsewhere in his article, Roche acknowledges that 'an essential element of the narration, camerawork is, of course, instrumental in bringing out the irony of a given situation' (ibid.: 12). Given that only filmed media narrate (in part) by means of camerawork, in no other medium could the irony of a situation be brought out in this fashion and, thus, create this particular ironic effect. Roche's reference to narration, meanwhile, serves to remind us that what is clearly at stake here is precisely film's nature as both drama *and* narrative. We might thus deepen our account of dramatic irony in film by turning to concepts proposed by a key theorist of this aspect of our mongrel medium.

'Dramatic' and 'Narrative' Techniques: Ironic Points of View in Film

Gilberto Perez, as we have noted, believes that film is both a dramatic and narrative medium. However, he also argues that a film can choose to emphasise either its medium's dramatic or narrative properties. To help explain what this distinction might entail, he first offers a definition of the different ways stories are conveyed by narrative and drama:

> Words in a narrative...[give] us not what happened but an *account* of what happened.... A play enacted on the stage is not an account.... Of course, someone made the choice of what to put [on stage], but once it is actually there, before us without mediation, it becomes a fact, ...no longer a matter of choice. Narrative is always a matter of choice.[18] (1998: 64; emphasis mine)

Whether a film stresses more fully the medium's dramatic or narrative properties, meanwhile, depends for Perez on whether it encourages us to recognise the particularity of the photographic perspective we are being given. '*Dramatic* film technique', he argues, 'makes the perspective of that point in space, the angle and distance from which we are viewing the scene, seem motivated by dramatic necessity'—the camera's viewpoint appearing 'perfectly appropriate to the action, the best possible view of it...rather than *a point of view*' (1998: 90; emphasis mine). Such an approach is 'dramatic' because it effectively seeks to approximate the experience of viewing unfolding events 'without mediation', which drama provides (ibid.: 64). By contrast, 'for the camera's perspective to function as a *narrative* point of view...we must register the particularity of that point in space. We must note how that angle and distance...modifies our impression of things that would look different from a different perspective' (ibid.: 90; emphasis mine). This approach is closer to narrative since it offers something approximating how the words of a narrated fiction 'mediate between us and the world they tell us about' (ibid.: 64).

As Perez acknowledges, the difference between these approaches is necessarily always one of degree, and the mongrel nature of film ensures that in fact every shot of every movie is, in the final analysis, a composite of both narrative *and* drama. As Pye notes—far from being the exclusive preserve of the camera—in film, 'narration can in practice potentially involve any or all of the filmmakers' choices and strategies (colour, lighting, costume, performance, set design and dressing, as well as camera movement, framing and editing,' and so on (2013: 133–134). Why, Perez writes,

> distinguish between drama and narrative in film, it may be asked, if film is both a dramatic and a narrative medium? For a better understanding of how the thing works. For the same reason one distinguishes between a particle and a wave even if the kind of thing that skips around in quantum physics behaves like both. (ibid.: 64)

I take this to mean that '*dramatic*' and '*narrative*' techniques should not be treated as utterly distinct categories but should rather be used merely to aid our descriptions of the effects made possible by particular filmmaking strategies. Taken in this spirit, I believe that the terms are illuminating and that they can help us distinguish between different kinds of ironic effects available to film.

We might begin by reformulating Roche's claim about many filmic ironies being 'profilmic...[and] therefore not medium-specific' (2015: 9) as meaning instead that much irony in film could be described as more 'dramatic' than 'narrative' in its strategies and effects. I would agree with this and suggest that *Rope* has furnished us with many examples. It is true that moments such as when Mr Kentley wonders what could be 'keeping' his son or Janet rhapsodises about David would have different effects without the camera's framing. Nonetheless, making us *register* the partialness or particularity of their framings does not seem among these shots' key intended effects. Rather, these camera positions are meaningful in the manner of so many camera positions in 'classical' Hollywood films: their particular viewpoints will necessarily be instrumental in determining our experience of the moment, yet they do not appear to draw attention to their significance *as* particular viewpoints. There are, however, certainly instances in *Rope* of the camera behaving otherwise.

About a third of the way into the film, Phillip sits down at the piano towards the left-hand rear of living room; as he does so, the camera begins retreating. Into our view now gradually emerge several characters, but two in particular are lent prominence in the shot because they are speaking: Janet and Mr Kentley. 'Your wife sends her love,' Janet is saying, having arrived from Mr and Mrs Kentley's home; 'David wasn't there?' Mr Kentley replies; 'No', responds Janet, 'He'll probably be here in a minute though'. Two things happen simultaneously as Janet finishes these words. Phillip begins to play a pleasant tune on the piano; as he does so, the still-retreating camera pulls back far enough to reveal the chest prominently in the foreground, before stopping, and pausing long enough to allow us to take in this devastating composition: David's father and fiancée sitting in the background anticipating his arrival, while, closer to the camera, the now-visible chest announces for us—silently but firmly—the uncomfortable fact that David is already very much present (Fig. 2.6).

Two things are worth noting here. First, this is not merely another moment whose dramatic irony depends upon the camera's framing; rather, it depends upon our sensing that we are being invited to *notice* the framing, and its purpose. The camera here flaunts its mediating role, ostentatiously manoeuvring itself in such a way that the chest begins to

Fig. 2.6 *Rope*: The camera reframes to include the chest

emerge into frame at precisely the moment Janet predicts David's immi-nent arrival, then sitting on the resulting painful viewpoint long enough for its newly formed compositional irony to sink in. By adopting a far more 'narrative' than 'dramatic' technique, the shot creates an effect not only unavailable to drama but also unlike many other dramatic ironies in film. It is an example of filmic dramatic irony depending far less obvi-ously upon the medium's dramatic properties than upon a film's particular approach to narration.

The second point to make is how the 'narrative' qualities of this camera movement relate to the film's stylistic approach overall, and what this means for the film's strategies of point of view. The pointed deliberateness of this camera movement ensures its likeness to several other moments of what we might call forthrightly narrative camera technique in *Rope*. Individual instances where the camera adopts points of view stressing the partialness or particularity of our perspective are too numerous to itemise and have already received much valuable critical discussion.[19] Suffice it to say that the marked precision and self-consciousness of the camera in a moment such as this relates to a pattern of many comparable camera movements across the film—a pattern so extensive that, as William Rothman puts it, 'the deliberateness of every move that the camera makes...enhances our sense that it represents a palpable presence' (1982: 247). This sense of the camera's palpable presence is created partly through such conspicuously rhetorical tracking motions, but it is also rendered virtually all-pervasive by perhaps the most famous aspect of *Rope*, which my analysis has hitherto refrained from mentioning: the fact that the action is shot in unusually long takes—some up to ten minutes in length, with several cuts 'disguised' in an effort to make takes feel even longer.[20] In an important sense, of course, the long takes allow the film to exploit further the medium's dra-matic properties by ensuring that, for long stretches, our temporal and spatial experience of the action recalls the continuity afforded by theatrical performances. In another sense, however, the effects of the strategy are far more 'narrative' than 'dramatic'.

For one thing, this technique simply represents an extremely unusual way to shoot a film (Bordwell calls *Rope* 'the longest-take movie in stu-dio history' [2008: 41]), and the evidence of this remarkable strategy is necessarily visible and tangible throughout. This therefore encourages us, again, to be continually reminded of the mediating role of the camera. Additionally, whereas in the theatre the decision to let dramatic action continue uninterrupted for long periods permits us to feel we have a complete view of the action, in *Rope* it creates the opposite effect: it produces an unavoidable sense of ongoing action always occurring off screen, reminding us that we presently have a restricted view and that 'there is always more to see' (Perez 1998: 72). One key outcome of our continual awareness of the camera is that *Rope* is able to create moments of dramatic irony that rely ostentatiously on the medium's 'narrative' properties. Another outcome, though, relates to *Rope*'s ability to create the kind of irony Storm describes as 'authorial—in the sense of a mastered or overarching irony that marks the dramatic representation overall' (2011: 4).

In this respect, it is first vital to acknowledge that even a wholly dramatic enactment of *Rope* would be capable of implying significant connections between Brandon's ironic 'artistry' and the artistry of the creative figure(s) responsible for the artwork we are watching. As has often been noted, by manipulating the 'action', 'set', 'props', and 'players' of his 'masterpiece', Brandon behaves very much like the dramatist or 'metteur-en-scène' of a play (Wood 1989: 354). Furthermore, if Brandon effectively stages a drama, then its structuring principle is one of discrepant awareness. For virtually every detail of the party Phillip and Brandon are hosting, there are intentionally at least two perspectives available. This is sometimes explicitly noted: Brandon, for instance, initially jokes that the only excuse he and Phillip need for serving dinner from the chest is that 'We can't leave our guest of honour [David] alone during supper'; Phillip, though, insists: 'We've got to have an excuse for the *others*'. It is, moreover, this aspect of the party that brings Brandon the greatest joy, as evidenced by the many moments throughout the evening when he 'amuse[s] himself by making oblique references to the knowledge that [only] he and Phillip share' (Zborowski 2008: 31). For instance, speaking with Rupert, Brandon refers to himself and Phillip having earlier 'had our hands full getting ready for the party'; upon being asked whether the party is for someone's birthday, Brandon responds that actually it is 'almost the opposite'; Kenneth at another point asks whether Brandon would relish David walking in and catching him and Janet alone together, to which Brandon responds: 'No, that'd be *too* much of a shock…'. Brandon therefore not only effectively crafts a drama, but one whose primary pleasures (for him) are those of dramatic irony: witnessing actions and words assume different meanings depending on one's degree of knowledge.

For these reasons, even an entirely dramatic rendering of *Rope* would certainly be capable of implying a connection between Brandon-as-ironic-dramatist and the ironic dramatist of the action we are watching (as

Hamilton's play itself does). This in turn would allow it to exploit the uncomfortable possibility of a connection between our *cognitive* alignment with Brandon and our *evaluative* relationship to him (Pye 2000). After all, through its heavy reliance on dramatic irony, the film invites us to take a very similar kind of pleasure in the action as Brandon himself experiences: the pleasure of possessing an ironic perspective.[21] *Rope*'s abilities in the realm of point of view, however, also offer the film further possibilities in this regard. This is largely because, whereas Brandon may have effectively staged an ironic work of dramatic art, Hitchcock and his collaborators have staged instead an ironic work of both dramatic *and* narrative art.

Both the individual moments when dramatic irony is created via the camera and the long-take approach in general make possible additional layers of correspondence between the ironies that Brandon appreciates in his 'work of art' and those engineered by the figure(s) responsible for the 'work of art' that is *Rope*. Both strategies ensure that the artist behind the film not only 'imitates Brandon, the director of the party, by preparing an utterly controlled environment' (Toles 2001: 218), but also by stressing the exacting control that is being continually exerted by the meticulously plotted camera style through which that environment is being mediated. The audacity of the camera technique ensures that 'its execution [is] a virtuoso performance' (Rothman 1982: 247), thus making it possible for 'the flashy precision of the camera…[to become] a projection of Brandon's evil assurance and calculation' (Perkins 1972: 88–89). This feels especially true on some occasions—for instance, the aforementioned moment when the camera times its revelation of the chest with Janet's prediction of David's arrival. Via the calculated way the film's narrative technique undercuts Janet's words here, the style feels imbued with a kind of cruel mockery— an effect, of course, in whose service irony (dramatic or otherwise) may sometimes be used. In an influential early discussion of dramatic irony (or, as he preferred to call it, 'tragic irony'), Lewis Campbell pleaded that

> 'irony' in this connection should be stripped of some associations which ordinarily cleave to it; such as the smile of conscious superiority, the dissembled laugh, the secret mockery of the unfortunate—everything, in short, which impairs the fullness of emotional sympathy. (1904: 171)

It is certainly true that there is nothing *inherently* arrogant or unfeeling about dramatic irony; nonetheless, distanced, cruel laughter at those 'inferior in power or intelligence to ourselves' (Frye, 1957: 33) remains at least one possible outcome of the device. At times the dramatic ironies indebted to *Rope*'s 'narrative' technique seem to exploit this possibility, and so make us complicit in an experience rather akin to the kind of superior, derisive spirit in which Brandon has conceived his party's own dramatic ironies and with which he views the world in general. Yet there are also moments of dramatic irony in *Rope* that seem more removed from the kinds of lofty pleasures irony affords Brandon. We might think here, for instance, of when Janet speaks tenderly of her love for David while standing by the chest—a moment which, tellingly, goes unseen by Brandon. Here the film appears to be exploiting dramatic irony's more compassionate, or 'tragic', possibilities—allowing us, as Richard Allen puts it, to 'side with the victims of Brandon's machinations, ...which affords us a critical perspective on Brandon's behavior' (2007: 144). This might remind us that, depending on the way dramatic irony is handled, its implied 'attitude towards the victim of the irony...[may range] from a high degree of detachment to a high degree of sympathy' (Muecke 1970: 51).

Furthermore, at certain points, Brandon himself occasionally becomes a victim of *Rope*'s own dramatic ironies. This happens partly at the level of the script, via Brandon's over-confident proclamations about his plan's success. An early claim like 'Not a single, infinitesimal thing has gone wrong' or his later declaration that 'There's not a *chance* [of being caught]' seem designed to strike us as hubristic, given the likelihood that the audience will be anticipating the murderers' 'delayed but inevitable retribution' (Perkins 1963: 12).[22] To the extent that such ironies as these—or Janet's emotional speech—remain beyond Brandon's awareness, they therefore allow the film to distance its perspective (and ours) from Brandon's. An even more decisive distance is made possible, however, via that mediating, controlling—often ironic—presence of which Brandon too must remain forever unaware: the camera.

A key instance of this comes, in fact, just seconds after the camera has so pointedly tracked back to show the chest concurrently with Janet's prediction of David's arrival. Having lingered on the irony of this composition, a slow, deliberate pan then moves our view to the left, revealing Rupert standing silently in the doorway—this new arrival's entrance going momentarily unnoticed by everyone, except us. This camera movement thus stresses the utter superiority of the film's, and our, point of view over all characters present, including Brandon. Yet, as well as revealing the man who will ultimately solve Brandon's cruel puzzle, this new composition also maintains the chest prominently in the shot on the right-hand side

Fig. 2.7   *Rope*: The camera reframes to include an unnoticed Rupert and the chest

of the image (Fig. 2.7). This, as Thomas Bauso notes, has two consequences: 'Rupert is thus wed visually not simply to the eventual revelation of the murder but to the very fact of the crime' (1991: 235). We might explain the complexity of this moment in terms of the conflicted effects of dramatic irony made possible by the framing. On the one hand, the composition momentarily makes Brandon and Phillip the victims of *Rope*'s dramatic irony—the visual connection between the unnoticed Rupert and the chest creating anticipation for the moment when he will ultimately reveal its contents. Equally, though, the shot also creates dramatic irony at *Rupert*'s expense, stressing for us a connection that he does not yet see between himself and what the chest contains. Both of these consequences of the moment's irony are equally important for the film's overall ironic point of view, and neither could be created without this medium's ability to provide us with a mediating narrative viewpoint on its dramatic action.

As we have seen, then, dramatic irony in film is indebted, first, to the medium's ability to tell stories such that we are granted a perspective superior to those of certain characters. This is an ability it shares with all storytelling media. We have also seen that some of film's capacities for dramatic irony are especially indebted to the medium's dramatic properties. Increasingly, though, we have encountered dramatic ironies that owe their character to film's peculiar ability to combine both dramatic *and* narrative elements. It is the narrative possibilities of film that ultimately permit *Rope* to create the particular ironic perspective it does—the film's style seeming sometimes complicit with Brandon's cruelly ironic attitude, but also occasionally making this character himself a victim of the film's ironic viewpoint.[23] *Rope* is able to achieve this because fiction films in general can ironise characters and situations by mediating their action through a particular point of view, which can stress discrepant awareness in ways typically foreign to the dramatic arts. Before moving on to consider other consequences of film's narrative properties (as well as another kind of irony altogether), it is worth lingering for a moment on this capacity of the medium, since it represents such a key means for creating irony in film.

*

Identifying instances when films use their points of view to create dramatic irony in fact accounts for a great deal of critical discussion about irony in film studies. It is often essentially this that is being referred to, for example, when we speak of a film creating an ironic 'distance' between our perspectives or attitudes and those of its characters. Without wishing at all to reduce the value of their individual insights, I think it fair to claim that numerous critical accounts of particular filmmakers, styles, or cycles have been characterised by a concern with this capacity of the medium. Demonstrating the presence of ironic distance of this kind across a director's films, for instance, has been crucial to much work on figures like Max Ophuls, Douglas Sirk, Claude Chabrol, Eric Rohmer, and indeed Hitchcock.[24] The discussion of similar strategies was also for some time key to the critical literature on whole genres such as the family or domestic melodrama.[25] More recently, scholarship on cycles like the American indie 'smart film' and 'quirky' cinema has frequently concerned the kinds of 'detachment' (Sconce 2002: 352) or 'degrees of ironic distance' (King 2013: 39) such films adopt towards their characters.[26] And this, clearly, certainly does not exhaust the many (albeit often fleeting) engagements with irony that emphasise this particular possibility of the medium.

Whether irony in such critical accounts is attributed to a film's director, tone, point of view, or even its cultural context, very often it is the medium's ability to create a sense of ironic distance from fictional characters and events that is, aesthetically speaking, at stake. To the extent that these kinds of critical engagements with irony are often concerned with how a film 'provides a perception which is available only to the audience, who are privileged over the characters' (Gibbs 2002: 51), it is tempting to characterise much of such criticism as being ultimately concerned with dramatic irony as created by filmic means. To help briefly demonstrate this, we could do far worse than note some ways in which a justly celebrated moment from *Letter from an Unknown Woman* (Max Ophuls 1948) has been interpreted.

One especially memorable shot in *Letter from an Unknown Woman* is carefully designed to echo an earlier shot in terms of (among other things) the location of the camera, its angle, and the actions it depicts. This shot shows, from atop a spiral staircase, our protagonist, Lisa (Joan Fontaine), being led into the apartment of Stefan (Louis Jourdan) after their first romantic evening together. Lisa has long idealised and loved Stefan from afar, and this moment—which we presume marks a prelude to their relationship being physically consummated—constitutes for her in many ways a moment of romantic bliss. It is prevented from seeming uncomplicatedly romantic or blissful for us, however, in part because the earlier shot, which is so carefully echoed here, depicted a younger Lisa from behind, standing on this same staircase, as she sadly observed Stefan ushering in just one more of the numerous young women that this famous and seductive man has brought home. Virtually every critic who has considered this moment in any detail acknowledges that irony is created by the correspondence (even if that specific word is not used), with critical disagreements concerning mainly the degree and complexity of that irony.

Edward Branigan, for example, claims the stylistic echo guarantees that, to us, 'it is evident that Lisa has become that other woman she observed as an adolescent' (1992: 184). Lucy Fischer proposes that 'in filming her with Stefan, the identical camera stance is adopted, implying that there will be yet others' who will follow Lisa (1989: 104). Similarly, George Wilson suggests that we are invited to regard Lisa here 'as an element in a mere recurrence' (1986: 104) and that this repetition is one of several that 'give the viewer an insight into her condition that she never herself attains' (ibid.: 115). Dwelling instead on what distinguishes the paired moments, Robin Wood stresses that Lisa and Stefan have by this point achieved a degree of genuine intimacy seemingly lacking from the earlier seduction scene, meaning that, while our 'identification is...qualified—or counterpointed—by an ironic detachment', nevertheless, 'the twinning of the staircase shots is not, then, a matter of simple irony' (1998: 207, 213). Also keen not to oversimplify the ironic effect, Perkins emphasises that the 'radical change in tone' between the two scenes ('frivolous clatter and chatter' being replaced by 'solemn, considerate grace') means that, for us, the repetition also creates a pronounced 'sense of difference between this occasion and the one that its images repeat'—even if 'we do not know... whether [Lisa] recognises anything that unites her with Stefan's, and the film's, other women' (2000: 46). Finally, the matter of what precisely Lisa might know is given an intriguing inflection by Perez, who reads the later shot as being imbued with the perspective of the older Lisa who is recounting the events to Stefan in the titular letter, which serves as a framing device in the film: 'This may not be the way Lisa views herself in the scene', argues Perez, 'but it is the way the Lisa writing the letter would look back on herself and her experience on that enchanted evening'— able to recognise the irony, perhaps, while nonetheless still cherishing the moment (1998: 78).

What differentiates these accounts matters less for my purposes than what they share and on what we might say their disagreements depend. Key to all these interpretations is, first, the fact that we are provided with a distanced perspective on the action that Lisa, at least at this moment, cannot possess; indeed, the importance of her comparatively limited perspective is emphasised by the fact that, whereas in the first shot Lisa was depicted as an observer, the second sees 'the removal of Lisa's watching presence' (Perkins 2000: 44). Second, all agree that our privileged perspective is created by the stylistic echo, which is made possible in turn by the particular uses to which the film puts its medium's dramatic and narrative capacities—what Wood calls 'Ophuls' use of the technical specificities of mise-en-scène—camera placement, camera movement, decoupage. It is by these means that we are allowed a position of ironic detachment that is not available to Lisa' (1998: 212). Finally, the critical disagreements stem from different proposed answers to the question of precisely *how* distant from Lisa's perspective is the film's own point of view. Expressed in this fashion, it would thus seem that what is being demonstrated in all these cases is a movie creating dramatic irony by means unique to filmed fictions. The various interpretations, meanwhile, might therefore be characterised as debates about which possibilities of dramatic irony are, in this instance, stressed more strongly: its potential to imply 'the smile of conscious superiority', its ability to offer 'the fullness of emotional sympathy' (Campbell 1904: 171), or both?[27]

I suggest that many critical discussions of ironic distance in film could be described as being broadly of this kind, focusing on similar capacities of the medium and debating comparable questions.[28] Dramatic irony thus ironises situations or *dramatis personae* by stressing the 'discrepant awareness' between our point of view and those of characters. This is indeed an important, and common, kind of irony found in film. There is another kind of irony available to the medium, however, which can ironise something else entirely.

IRONIC NARRATION: PROSE FICTION, COMMUNICATIVE IRONY, AND FILM

Dramatic irony requires that our perspective be ironically distanced from the more limited perspectives of characters. One way a *narrative* medium can create such ironic distance is by mediating its story through a particular point of view. In discussing film, I have so far occasionally attributed this point of view to a work's narrative dimensions, or its narration. In prose fiction, however, a distanced, ironic point of view would tend to be attributed to a work's *narrator*—the agent or consciousness that we understand to be telling the story. This figure has long been acknowledged as key to the ways in which prose fiction can create irony; in Wayne Booth's words: 'the narrator may...be more or less distant from the characters in the story he [*sic*] tells' (1961: 156). However, the narrator has also been seen as fundamental to prose fiction's ability to create another kind of irony.

This form of irony has in fact received more scholarly attention than any other. The most common name for it is *verbal irony*[29]; however, since this term announces so loudly its inappropriateness to film, I shall hereafter refer to it by the still imperfect but infinitely preferable name *communicative* irony.[30] It is this kind of irony that, as seen earlier, Currie believes pictures characteristically have difficulty achieving. Similarly, when scholars express misgivings about film's ironic potential, it is usually not situational or dramatic irony to which they are referring but communicative irony specifically. Before comparing film's capacities in this respect to those of prose fiction, we must dwell for a moment on what exactly communicative irony is.

Communicative Irony, Pretence, and Narration

Ironic expression of all kinds involves juxtapositions between (what are offered as) limited and less limited points of view. In the case of communicative irony, this juxtaposition is achieved by feigning to possess precisely the limited point of view that is being ironised. Communicative irony can cover a great deal of what gets called irony, especially in linguistic situations—from Socratic irony, to a sarcastic verbal comment, to complex ironies in prose fiction. To help us understand it, we might return to the pretence theory of irony. I have already argued that this theory should not be the sole framework we use for conceptualising irony in film. And indeed, it is worth adding here that equipping ourselves only with this theory would also mean excluding dramatic irony entirely from our definition of ironic expression. Yet the pretence theory does nonetheless offer a convincing account of communicative irony specifically.[31]

Recall that the pretence theory contends that irony is 'the pretended adoption of a defective outlook' (Currie 2006: 121). Say, for instance, I turn to my friend in the middle of a rainstorm and declare, 'What lovely weather!' Assuming that I do not consider pouring rain lovely weather, the pretence theory gives a persuasive explanation of what is happening here. In speaking this way, I momentarily pretend to possess an outlook that, if sincerely held, would reveal my powers of perception to be (what *I* consider) deeply defective. I am also, furthermore, pretending to adopt this outlook with the aim of expressing an attitude towards an imagined person or kind of person, namely someone who might in this situation exclaim with sincerity, 'What lovely weather!' More than merely pretending to believe something one does not, then, communicative irony effectively involves pretending to possess a limited perspective in order to imply a judgement or attitude about that perspective, and perhaps anyone who might conceivably hold it (Clark/Gerrig 2007).

Prose fiction has developed numerous strategies for creating the kind of pretence necessary for communicative irony. One thing likely to be integral to all such strategies, though, is the figure of the narrator. The mediating 'voice' or 'consciousness' that 'speaks' a story, the narrator of prose fiction can be a character within it, giving an account of events witnessed or experienced (what Gérard Genette [1988] calls a *homodiegetic* narrator); equally, the narrator may be absent from the events of the story (for Genette, *heterodiegetic*). This is to note only two types of, and terms for, the host of different kinds of narrators prose fiction is able to create. Several strategies have also been suggested for how narrators can be used to create communicative irony. One common strategy, though, is for a story's narrator to pretend to adopt a certain point of view. As Currie notes, 'as exploiters of irony we engage in pretence. We pretend to congratulate, approve, admire,' and this can be '[as true of] narrators…as it is of casual contributors to a conversation.' (2010: 150). In such cases, then, the narrator establishes an ironic distance not necessarily from a story's characters (as in dramatic irony) but rather from certain perspectives that the narrator is pretending to express sincerely.

There is at least one reason why we might suspect that film could find it difficult to create irony in this way. I have already claimed that ironies can be created through a film's narration—or, rather, through film's characteristic combination of dramatic enactment *and* narration. This seems uncontroversial. Whether or not *narration* is an appropriate term for describing storytelling in film is close to being a settled matter: almost every scholar who has considered the question in any depth agrees that it is. Far more knotty, though, is whether the argument that fiction films are narrated necessarily assumes that they also possess *narrators*. The proposed answers range across arguments that films should always be assumed to have narrators (e.g. Browne 1975; Chatman 1980; Gunning 1991; Levinson 1996), that they should not be assumed to have narrators (Bordwell 1985; Branigan 1992; Currie 1995; Pye 2000; Gaut 2004), and positions lying somewhere between the two (Perez 1998; Thomson-Jones 2008). One seemingly good reason for avoiding the concept of the narrator in this medium altogether is that perhaps *the* most basic question we can ask of prose fiction—'Who speaks?' (Genette 1988: 64)—seems flatly inappropriate to film, in which 'there is no narrative "voice"' (Pye 2000: 13). Many theorists have attempted to posit terms that might serve something like the function the term *narrator* serves for prose fiction: the *grand imagier* (Metz 1974), *image-maker* (Kozloff 1989), *fundamental narrator* (Gaudreault 1987), *impersonal narrator* (Burgoyne 1990), or simply the *cinematic narrator* (Chatman 1990). All, however, appear vulnerable to a famous criticism offered by David Bordwell: whereas we have little trouble attributing a novel's words to some kind of human-like agent, 'in watching films, we are seldom aware of being told something by an entity resembling a human being' (1985: 62).

It is not possible or necessary for me to settle this controversial issue here. Suffice it to say, though, that I do not believe it productive to posit the existence of a narrator for most fiction films.[32] Thus, as George Wilson puts it, 'in the absence of reasons for inserting visual narrators..., we do best to explicate the needed categories in terms of the properties and relations of the narration itself' (1986: 136). These needed categories include the 'guiding intelligence' (Wilson 1986: 136) that is necessarily implied by the fact that a film's narration seems always constructed intentionally. It remains true that when watching a film 'we experience it as an intentional object, designed to have certain effects on us' (Gunning 1991: 24); indeed, the fact that films appear to be designed intentionally for particular purposes is crucial—especially in the case of irony—and will be explored in depth in Chapter 4. However, on this matter I am inclined to agree with those such as Bordwell (1985) and Branigan (1992) who believe we are better served by attributing the intentional qualities of film narration not to a narrator, but to the narration itself, or even 'the film itself' (Pye 2000: 14).[33]

What, if anything, might the apparent absence of a narrator mean for film's capacity to create communicative irony? Currie, for one, is sceptical about film's ability to create this kind of irony, arguing that 'it is much more difficult for a film-maker to achieve something that will be understood as "pretending to have a point of view" than it is for a writer' (2010: 169). Although he does not here link this claim to the nature of film narration *per se*, it seems likely that Currie's reservations stem from his belief that films do not possess narrators (Currie 1995). I say this partly because Currie (like others) understandably makes narrators key to his definition of communicative irony in prose fiction—submitting, for instance that, 'a narrator may adopt…the pretence of another point of view, and do so in an ironical way, intending to highlight the defects of that point of view' (2010: 164). Yet, even if films might not ordinarily possess narrators, should this necessarily make it difficult for them to pretend to adopt points of view and, thus, create communicative irony? I suggest that there are reasons for believing otherwise.

Pretence, Parody, and Tone

As acknowledged, prose fictions are capable of creating numerous kinds of narrator and numerous kinds of ironic pretence. However, I will restrict myself here to one common kind of narrator in particular: a heterodiegetic narrator who narrates the story using a 'free indirect style'. Free indirect style allows a narrator to incorporate into the narration attitudes, perspectives, and modes of address stemming from other sources—be that the story's characters or, for instance, other kinds of writing. Perhaps unsurprisingly, this approach to narration is especially useful for creating communicative irony. As Stefan Oltean puts it, the 'natural conjunction' of irony with free indirect style lies in the way that the latter creates a double significance produced by the contrast of values associated with... two positions. Depending on the distance of the ironist—most often the narrator—from the object of irony—a character, his/her attitudes or beliefs, or the discourse itself—..., several degrees of irony can be distinguished, ranging from subtle irony...to mockery or even to parody. (1993: 706–707)

Free indirect style is so well suited to communicative irony because it offers ample opportunities to contrast different positions, values, or points of view, while also allowing a narrator to pretend to adopt one of these positions, values or points of view. As already noted, communicative irony usually requires some real or imagined other figure associated with the point of view that one is pretending to express. In my 'lovely weather!' example, for instance, that other figure was a hypothetical person who might truly misinterpret pouring rain in this fashion. In free indirect prose, as Oltean notes, a narrator can pretend to adopt numerous kinds of other perspectives, perhaps those of a character in the story, but also potentially those of some other kind of 'discourse' entirely. Furthermore, as he intimates, the ironic effects created by pretending to adopt these perspectives may range from subtle irony to all-out parody. It will be instructive to begin with one of the less subtle possibilities before moving on to consider others. Let us thus start with prose fiction's capacities for parody.

Parody—that is, 'imitation characterised by ironic inversion' (Hutcheon 1985: 6)—is a concept whose own expansive theoretical history overlaps significantly with, yet is far from reducible to, that of irony itself.[34] Owing to the focus of this chapter, I am interested here in the practice of parody largely for what it may help us understand about ironic pretence and, therefore, communicative irony. Parody has been acknowledged as one important way in which ironic pretence can be created in linguistic situations (e.g. Rossen-Knill/Henry 1997). Prose fiction is a very complex linguistic situation indeed, but parody can prove just as useful to communicative irony here as in conversation. In this medium (and especially in cases of free indirect style), parody frequently involves a narrator pretending to adopt perspectives, attitudes, or values of a different *kind* of narrator. Often, this is achieved by using conventions from other kinds of fictions—for instance, those associated with specific genres. Take, for example, a famous moment from *Madame Bovary* (1857). At one point in this novel, the story's protagonist, Emma, is experiencing the thrill of illicit romantic joy because of an extramarital affair she has begun, prompting the narrator to offer the following:

So at last she was to know those joys of love, that fever of happiness of which she had despaired! She was entering upon marvels where all would be passion, ecstasy, delirium. An azure infinity encompassed her, the heights of sentiment sparkled under her thought, and ordinary existence appeared only afar off, down below in the shade, through the interspaces of these heights. (Flaubert 1994: 124)

In context, it is clear that this passage constitutes, among other things, a parody of the stylistic conventions of romance fiction, with all the narration's clichés, exaggerations, and hyperbolic metaphors contributing to this effect.[35] We can thus say the narrator here momentarily pretends to adopt aspects of the style of a different sort of narrator—specifically, the sort who might narrate the kinds of romantic novels that Emma herself reads, which are described elsewhere as being 'all love, lovers, sweethearts, persecuted ladies fainting in lonely pavilions, …gentlemen brave as lions, gentle as lambs, virtuous as no one ever is' (ibid.: 28). There are in fact important strategies at play in this passage other than the characteristically parodic gesture of 'wearing…a stylistic mask' (Jameson 1983: 114), and I will return to these shortly. But it is enough for now to acknowledge this as one strategy through which prose fiction can create ironic pretence and, thus, communicative irony.

The pretence involved in this instance of parody is considerably more complex than, but fundamentally comparable to, my 'lovely weather!' example: a point of view is adopted, but with an ironic distance. It is thus essential to note that 'the distance of the ironist' (Oltean 1993: 706) in a case like this must clearly be conceptualised differently than the distance involved in dramatic irony, which relates primarily to characters. Communicative irony *may* be used to create distance from the points of view of characters (more on this shortly), but it is not restricted to this purpose. Instead, this kind of irony involves striking an ironic attitude towards points of view that the work itself appears to be adopting. In that sense, it is also self-reflexive: it is irony at the expense of a discourse, style, or mode of expression that one is using.[36] In a passage like this from *Madame Bovary*, the narrator's communicative irony is thus, as Currie puts it, 'expressive of [an ironic] attitude towards the narration itself' (2010: 171). This phenomenon—narrators adopting a distanced attitude towards the perspectives they express or the style in which they do so—is one thing that we may mean when we say that a work of literature possesses an ironic tone.[37]

What, though, of film? When scholars discuss the adaptation of literary ironies to film, they often draw attention to film's lack of a narrator. Frequently, they do so in order to suggest that this lack may impede film's ability to create an ironic tone. For instance, writing of Conrad adaptations, Wallace S. Watson argues that 'it is difficult to sustain in cinema the point of view and tone of a dramatized narrator, who is frequently the agent of irony in Conrad's fiction' (1997: 18); equally, June Perry Levine expresses analogous concerns about adapting Forster, arguing that 'the tone [of Forster's fiction] is often ironic, which...is not a voice that comes easily to film, since its agency is so often the narrator' (1998: 205).[38] Could it be that, without a narrator to give voice to an ironic tone, communicative irony and ironic pretence need necessarily be difficult for film to achieve? I suggest that one reason to suspect not is the widespread presence of parody in other media that also lack narrators.

We have seen that one way prose fiction can create communicative irony is by having a narrator parody conventions: conventions that might be used sincerely are in fact being used with a distanced tone. Yet parody has also been recognised as a key means through which artistic works in numerous other media may create irony—not only linguistic art forms like prose fiction or poetry, but also those such as painting, photography, and music.[39] Media like these, then, appear to find the lack of a narrator no barrier to the creation of parody and, thus, ironic pretence. This would seem to be because all that is necessary in order for a medium to create parody is that it be capable of 'ironic imitation' (Bersier 1997: 34), and the only thing a work must do to imitate ironically is adopt particular aesthetic conventions with an ironically distanced tone. I suggest that this is something that is certainly achievable, and in fact relatively common, in film.

The first place we might expect to find parody in cinema is, of course, within that class of film comedy that is itself often called 'parody' (sometimes 'spoof' or 'travesty')—whether it be *Abbott and Costello Meet Frankenstein* (Charles Barton 1948), *Blazing Saddles* (Mel Brooks 1974), *Hot Shots!* (Jim Abrahams 1991), or *MacGruber* (Jorma Taccone 2010). Such films tend to be full of moments when aspects of the narration appear to create a pretence of straight-faced participation in a particular genre's conventions, often while some ludicrous comic business works simultaneously to undermine that façade. For instance, at one point in *The Naked Gun: From the Files of Police Squad* (David Zucker 1988), the sounds of a sleazy saxophone, swelling strings, tinkling piano, and jazzy high-hat cymbal accompany the introduction of the initially archetypal 'cool-blonde' character, Jane Spencer (Priscilla Presley). In addition to the film's score,[40] other aspects of dramatisation and narration here also help indicate the film's parodic intentions towards *film noir* specifically: Jane is introduced as being in the employ of a powerful older man; she is first seen standing atop a staircase in a wide-shot like the *femme fatale* of *Double Indemnity* (Billy Wilder 1944); and our protagonist, Lieutenant Frank Drebin (Leslie Nielsen), will soon begin a faux-*noir* voice-over, telling us: 'Her hair was the color of gold in old paintings; she had a full set of curves...' The targets of the film's ironic imitation thus established, Jane begins to descend the staircase, only to tumble head over heels all the way to the bottom, before swiftly righting herself, reassuming her affectedly nonchalant demeanour in readiness to glide by Frank with a sultry glance; throughout this, the *noir*-associated music continues undaunted.

It does not seem that we need to attribute the film's narration to an ironic narrator in order to conceptualise the ironic distance at which *Naked Gun*'s conventions are being held. Instead, distance is signalled through several incongruities. First, incongruities are established between certain conventions of narration (for instance, the music) and the dramatic material narrated (the pratfall); second, and as a consequence, incongruities also emerge between the kinds of attitudes that would usually be adopted towards such conventions in their original context, and the attitudes adopted towards them here. We have, I suggest, no need to speak of a narrator in order to identify and adequately describe the nature of these ironic incongruities and attitudes. Instead, we may say that the narration itself is 'pretending' to participate in the conventions of a certain genre, while much else alerts us to the film's contrary—ironic—intentions.

Pursuing this further, then, we might say that the pretence being undertaken by *The Naked Gun* ensures that the film makes use of certain conventions with what amounts, indeed, to an ironically distanced *tone*. As already noted, we can define a film's tone as its 'attitude to its material and the stylistic register it employs' (Pye 2007: 7). It is this focus on a film's attitude towards its own stylistic register (in addition to, say, its characters or fictional world) that makes tone indispensable as a concept—for film no less than prose fiction. Tone is the best available term capable of accounting for the fact that, for instance, films routinely 'take up varying relationships to generic conventions and norms, including parody' (Pye 2000: 12). As Pye suggests, 'a film's relationship to conventions of genre or film style can...be considered as questions of "distance": *generic distance* and *formal or stylistic distance*,' and it is one purpose of a film's tone to alert us to the degree of distance at which such conventions are being held, thereby 'signal[ing] how we are to *take* what we see and hear' (ibid.: 12; original emphases).[41] At a parodic moment like this one from *The Naked Gun*, huge incongruities between the conventions of a particular genre and the nature of the dramatic action signal that we should 'take' these conventions as being offered with a very high degree of distance indeed. It is this which alerts us to the fact that the film can only be 'pretending' to use these conventions of narration in a conventional manner. And again, I suggest that we have no need to posit a narrator in order to discern the narration's ironic tone and, thus, this film's ironic pretence.[42]

All-out parodies may seem to be where film engages in ironic pretence most pervasively. It is certainly true that the very existence of this class of film does at least testify to the medium's potential in this regard. Having made this case, however, we must acknowledge two things. First, this particular genre is relatively niche. Second, it could be argued that the ostentatious comic absurdity typical of such parodies may actually dampen these films' ability to practise pretence *per se*. A defining feature of communicative irony is usually taken to be its 'implicit' (Utsumi 1996) or 'covert' (Booth 1974: 6) character; Hutcheon goes so far as to suggest that irony's 'identifying rhetorical nature lies in its indirection' (1994: 146). Could it be that, although wholesale parodies might mock their narration, their characteristically broad humour is simply too overt to allow for ironic pretence? Whatever the answer, it seems reasonable to raise the question. This offers cause enough to look elsewhere for examples of communicative irony in film.

Ironic Narration, Conventions, and Tonal Distance in Film

Currie, as we have seen, believes that 'it is...difficult for a film-maker to achieve something that will be understood as "pretending to have a point of view"' (2010: 169); and, as he also goes on to note,

> this sort of pretence is central to ironic effect. So in the cinematic case, we have to look for those rare...indications that [communicative] irony is in play—though in film [the] representation of ironic situations is frequent and unremarkable. It is against the background of this limited palette that we should judge the extent to which a film achieves an ironic tone. (ibid.: 169)

Two key points are advanced here: first, the claim that ironic pretence is difficult and rare in film; second, the sharp distinction drawn between communicative irony and the representation of ironic situations. I will first address the former before raising some critical questions about the latter.

I have suggested that a movie like *The Naked Gun* allows us to see that one way films can '[pretend] to have a point of view' and thereby create communicative irony is to establish a distanced tone towards stylistic or generic conventions. If parodies such as this were the only place we found cases of ironic pretence in film, though, we might agree with Currie that communicative irony is indeed relatively rare in this medium. Yet it seems to me that 'pure' parodies are only where we find the most extreme uses of strategies that are rather more widespread. Moreover, it strikes me that Currie himself may inadvertently demonstrate this fact during his analysis of one film he claims *is* communicatively ironic: *The Birds* (Alfred Hitchcock 1963).

Currie's account of *The Birds* draws attention to what he takes to be moments at which this film subtly distances itself from horror-thriller conventions while giving the impression of deploying them 'straight'. For instance, he reads certain reaction shots of Melanie (Tippi Hedren) as being intended to undercut the emotional impact of the horrifying events to which her character is putatively reacting (fire and explosions ripping through a gas station); the interpretation he offers of this moment is worth quoting at some length:

> Her face in these shots is both static and composed into an oddly exaggerated expression....Often the function of reaction shots is to engage the viewer's emotions. These shots of Melanie's so *un*expressive face—a parody of emotion—are unlikely to contribute to making the viewer more involved with the scenes of mayhem than they would otherwise be. My claim is that these shots, by recording a face which fails, spectacularly, to pass the test of emotional verisimilitude, are an expression of the film-maker's ironic attitude to the project....These shots pretend to derive from an outlook which takes seriously the business of making a frightening movie, intending to instil in the audience an appropriate reaction of fear—but which, in reality, expresses an awareness of the deficiencies, or at least the limitations, of that outlook and purpose. (ibid.: 170)

Currie thus first draws attention to the film's relationship to several conventions: stylistic conventions (e.g. reaction shots), generic conventions ('a frightening movie'), and the emotional responses conventionally associated with them ('engage the viewer's emotions', 'an appropriate reaction of fear'). Second, he argues that, by distancing itself from these conventional materials in various ways (e.g. Hedren's 'parody of emotion'), *The Birds'* narration gives the appearance of employing them in purely conventional ways, when in fact it is doing so ironically. Currie thus essentially argues this film achieves subtly something that is being done more forthrightly by a film like *The Naked Gun*: it deploys stylistic and generic conventions with a distanced, ironic tone.

Whether or not one agrees with Currie's specific interpretation, I agree absolutely with the logic underpinning his argument. I agree, too, that the ironic pretence he argues for here would be more easily definable *as* pretence than in most cases of all-out parody since the signals as to the film's tone are more implicit. Finally, I also agree that noting the distance between two or more potential *emotional* responses is helpful since, as Currie argues elsewhere (in relation to conversational ironies), ironic pretence will usually imply 'a contrast between the kinds of *effects* one intends by one's ironic utterance and the effects one would probably intend if one were speaking seriously' (2006: 113; original emphasis). I fundamentally disagree, however, with Currie's use of this sort of account to argue that films find ironic pretence difficult to achieve.

One of the only existing in-depth explorations of irony in film, Mary Ann Doane's PhD thesis, 'The Dialogic Text: Filmic Irony and the Spectator' (1979), is dedicated to identifying instances of what Doane calls 'irony as a narrational strategy' (ibid.: 99). Though she does not use the term, we can say that the kind of irony she is concerned with (which she calls 'duality of narration' [ibid.: 291]) is primarily communicative irony. Moreover, the strategies she identifies in her chosen films (e.g. 'misuse or overuse of certain narrative devices', 'perverse rewriting of a genre', 'hyperbolization of gesture' [ibid.: 231, 262, 260]) can largely be characterised in terms of ironic pretence. For instance, a romantic scene in *Spellbound* (Alfred Hitchcock 1945) is highlighted for the way its characters discuss the conventionality of romantic imagery at the same time as 'the clichés of the love scene...are all present' (ibid.: 155); *Once Upon a Time in the West* (Sergio Leone 1968) is characterised as 'exploiting the genre's mechanisms for producing pleasure and simultaneously conducting an interrogation of that genre' (ibid.: 260), and so on. Expressed in Currie's terms, then, Doane identifies many moments that only *appear* 'to derive from an outlook which takes seriously' the conventions employed, when 'in reality, [the film] expresses an awareness of the deficiencies...of that outlook' (Currie 2010: 170). Expressed in my terms: her readings repeatedly demonstrate films adopting ironically distanced tones towards generic and stylistic conventions.

Beyond Doane's work, many other critical engagements with irony in film (however fleeting) have also been dedicated to demonstrating the relatively widespread nature of precisely such strategies. Although they may not mention 'tone', 'distance', or even 'irony' by name, scholars frequently claim to identify films that—via various approaches to intertextuality, self-reflexivity, self-consciousness, and so on—treat stylistic, generic, and representational conventions with ironic distance. Indeed, such strategies have, of course, long been associated with innumerable different periods, genres, movements, cycles, and modes of film: moments like modernism, postmodernism, and periods following the postmodern[43]; movements like the French New Wave, New German Cinema, or New Queer Cinema[44]; cycles within genres like the musical, romantic comedy, or the western[45]; directors like Lang or Minnelli, Lynch or Verhoeven, Godard or Kaurismäki[46]; particular stars such as Judy Garland, Marlene Dietrich, or Joan Crawford[47]; and styles or modes like camp, pastiche— and, of course, parody.[48] Analysing ways in which films ironise aesthetic conventions has therefore plainly been another way in which the field of film studies has—albeit often implicitly, without dwelling on the issue— thus far engaged with the topic of irony in film. We need not necessarily be convinced by all of these accounts in order to grant that they may nonetheless correctly diagnose one means of creating communicative irony in film. Furthermore, I think that the very prevalence of such accounts should give us pause before concluding that the medium necessarily has such a 'limited palette' for this kind of irony.

Before offering my own account of an instance of communicative irony in film, however, it is necessary to attend to Currie's second proposition mentioned earlier: that creating communicative irony and representing ironic situations always constitute discrete endeavours. Like most scholars, Currie regards dramatic irony as resulting from the depiction of a particular type of (fictional) ironic situation; as such, when he notes that 'in film [the] representation of ironic situations is frequent and unremarkable' (ibid.: 169), he can be understood as referring to the commonness of dramatic irony in this medium.[49] I would argue, however, that it is not always quite so easy to distinguish between dramatic and communicative irony, in this or other mediums.

We might begin to demonstrate this by returning to the previously quoted passage from *Madame Bovary*. We have seen that, by adopting certain conventions of style and language familiar from romance fiction, Flaubert's narrator can be described as briefly pretending to adopt the point of view of another kind of narrator—namely one who might use these conventions entirely *un*ironically. Yet there is also, of course, another point of view with great relevance to this passage: that of the novel's protagonist, Emma. As noted, Emma herself is an enthusiastic reader of romance novels, and we are told elsewhere that 'she recalled the heroines of the books that she had read, and...saw herself in this type of amorous woman whom she had so envied' (Flaubert 1994: 124). We are thus certainly able to take the romantic clichés in the passage as indications that the narrator is parodically adopting conventions we might find in a romance novel; however, since *Madame Bovary* as a whole is narrated in a 'free indirect' style, we can also take the clichés as expressing aspects of Emma's own point of view. The narrator momentarily describes Emma's experience as if she were the heroine of a more conventional romantic fiction, in part because that is precisely how Emma regards herself at this moment. Articulated in terms of different kinds of irony, then, the fact that the narrator pretends to adopt a limited point of view means that the moment is certainly a case of communicative irony; however, the fact that doing so also stresses the discrepant awareness between Emma's point of view and that of the narrator/reader means that the moment equally creates *dramatic* irony.

One outcome of combining communicative and dramatic irony in this way is that, not only are particular conventions employed with an ironic tone, but a character's point of view is also ironised. It seems to me that creating a similar interdependence between the effects of communicative and dramatic irony may also be common in film.[50] In this medium, too, then, the purpose of communicative irony need not be restricted purely to self-reflexively ironising conventions or styles (say, reaction shots, the horror film, the clichés of a love scene); rather, it may also contribute to the kind of distance from characters' actions and attitudes usually associated with dramatic irony. I will attempt to remain sensitive to this possibility in my closing analysis of communicative irony in the conclusion of a single film.

Communicative (and Dramatic) Irony in There's Always Tomorrow

It might have been noted that a significant number of the critical accounts of communicative irony that I cited earlier relate to popular American filmmaking. This may be due not merely to the relatively high proportion of scholarly engagement with Hollywood cinema relative to other filmmaking traditions, nor only to film studies' predilection for locating 'subversion' or 'rupture' in Hollywood films;[51] rather, I suspect that it may also be due partly to the very nature of Hollywood filmmaking as an aesthetic and industrial tradition.

Our discussions of *Madame Bovary* and of parody have suggested that familiar aesthetic conventions often offer fertile grounds for ironic pretence. Given this, it is perhaps unsurprising that Hollywood cinema in particular might frequently generate instances of the practice. As Bordwell, Staiger, and Thompson note, 'to a large extent...pervasive and persistent conventions of form, technique, and genre constitute the Hollywood tradition' (1985: 4); at the same time, Hollywood films are also, as Andrew Britton puts it, 'remarkable for the extraordinary diversity and heterogeneity...which is achieved within the tradition's conventional limits' (2009: 496). While hardly unique in either of these respects, Hollywood cinema is certainly a cinematic tradition associated especially closely with familiar generic and stylistic conventions. Yet this tradition is simultaneously apt to produce films in which one 'comes to recognise norm and deviation oscillating, perhaps wrestling, within the same artwork' (Bordwell et al. 1985: 82). Of course, employing familiar aesthetic conventions with ironic distance is a strategy perennially available to any artwork. Yet we might expect to find such approaches particularly frequently within aesthetic traditions whose generic and stylistic conventions are as familiar as those of Hollywood. Furthermore, we might particularly expect to encounter such strategies within traditions whose 'conventional limits' can be tightly policed, meaning that 'deviation' must sometimes be achieved implicitly rather than openly.

Such, I suggest, is at least true of *There's Always Tomorrow* (Douglas Sirk 1956). During the historical moment in which this film was made, the Production Code Administration dictated to Hollywood filmmakers that 'the sanctity of the institution of marriage and the home should be upheld. Adultery...must not be explicitly treated or justified or presented attractively' (in Maltby 2003: 595). While numerous films approved for release by the Production Code Administration did find ingenious ways of bending or working around this stipulation, its existence nonetheless contributed to the development of a widespread aesthetic convention: that films (often romantic melodramas) whose stories concern adulterous relationships would end with the return of errant married partners to their spouses, families, or homes.[52] This convention is adhered to at the conclusion of *There's Always Tomorrow*.

This adulterous melodrama's narrative culminates with Norma (Barbara Stanwyck) ending her affair with the married Cliff (Fred MacMurray) and finally with Cliff's return home. Cliff and Norma had enjoyed a brief (but, we may infer) unconsummated romantic relationship some twenty years ago. Early in the film, Norma reappears unexpectedly in Cliff's life; over the next few days their feelings for one another are reignited, and they eventually declare their love for each other. However, because of pressure from two of Cliff's teenage children, Ellen (Gigi Perreau) and Vinnie (William Reynolds), Norma abandons her and Cliff's plan of absconding together. During their painful final meeting, Norma tells Cliff she will be flying back to New York at six o'clock that evening. The film's last scene sees Cliff return home. Clearly despondent, he behaves distantly with his children in the family living room, before looking at his watch, moving to the window, and staring longingly at a plane moving across the sky. Here we cut to Norma onboard; she is also evidently distressed, also glancing at the window, tears streaking her face; on the soundtrack we hear a sombre orchestral arrangement of 'Blue Moon', a song with sentimental associations for the couple. As Cliff closes the shutters, his wife, Marion (Joan Bennett), who knows nothing of his affair, approaches him: 'Hello, dear', she says, 'Feeling better tonight?' 'What?' responds Cliff, initially distracted. 'I've been worried about you the last few days', she continues: 'it's not like you to be irritable and depressed.' 'I know', answers Cliff, 'but I'm all right now.' 'Good', she smiles, as the couple begin to move arm in arm into the house. 'You know me better than I know myself', Cliff tells Marion; 'I should, after a lifetime with you', she answers. The couple move off, and we now see their three children, who are watching their parents through the bars of stair balustrades that intervene between them and the camera. Frankie (Judy Nugent), the youngest child, sighs happily: 'They make a handsome couple, don't they?' The other children smile, and we fade to black.

It happens that I am touching here on two of the few phenomena that have prompted film scholars to address irony somewhat consistently: Douglas Sirk, and Hollywood happy endings. In both cases (as for many critical arguments about 'classical' Hollywood generally), irony has often been treated as a saving grace: sometimes as something that manages to rescue Sirk's films from being the 'standard women's magazine weepie—mawkish, mindless, and reactionary' (Halliday 1972: 10), and frequently as the only thing ensuring that a happy ending might represent anything other than a mere 'ideological straightjacket' (Wood 1998: 37).[53] I am in fact sceptical of both of these critical orthodoxies. I have argued elsewhere that, although Sirk 'has been predominantly discussed as an ironist' (Babington/Evans 1990: 48), this aspect of his work has often been overstated, especially as it pertains to his movies' endings. Indeed, I have argued that many scholarly accounts of his film *All That Heaven Allows* (1955) demonstrate 'the trouble critics often have discussing happy endings in anything other than binary terms: either as unproblematically celebratory or seditiously subversive' (MacDowell 2013: 161). Nevertheless, I have also suggested that the conclusion of *There's Always Tomorrow*, at least, can indeed justifiably be called ironic (ibid.: 155–159). That argument, however, now strikes me as notably incomplete (like many film studies engagements with irony) because it neglects to interrogate where precisely this irony lies and what it consists of. In particular, I failed to discriminate between different kinds of irony that film can create: specifically, between *dramatic* and *communicative* irony. I return to this ending here partly to clarify this matter since I think that looking closely at the conclusion of *There's Always Tomorrow* will allow us to see both how dramatic and communicative irony in film can be distinguished, while also demonstrating succinctly some ways in which one can be made to interpenetrate the other.

The kind of irony that is usually attributed to both Hollywood happy endings and to Sirk is essentially *communicative*, which is to say that it is characteristically claimed to rely on ironic pretence. We frequently find iterations of the happy ending in general being described as, say, a 'happy ending in which the mechanics of cinema are exposed' (Geraghty 2009: 106) or as 'virtual self-parody' (Armes 1994: 75).[54] And, despite Sirk himself having more commonly discussed dramatic or tragic irony in interviews,[55] for several decades he has far more often been deemed a filmmaker whose 'ironies [are] playing on the conventions' his films are employing (Babington/Evans 1990: 58); in other words, he effectively pretends to use certain Hollywood conventions 'straight' yet in fact uses them only with a self-conscious, ironic distance.[56] This claim is made particularly frequently about his endings: 'the happy endings of his melodramas were self-consciously artificial', John Mercer and Martin Shingler tell us (2004: 60), while Richard Neupert argues of *All That Heaven Allows* that the 'ironic addition of an unwarranted happy ending foregrounds the rules and restrictions of both the classical melodrama and audience expectations' (1995: 72). All such characterisations, then, can reasonably be understood as claims for the communicatively ironic nature of certain happy endings. There could seem, however, to be a problem with the proposition that *There's Always Tomorrow* might be ironising its happy ending: can we even say that this film *pretends* to have a happy ending at all?

Described cursorily, the conclusion of this film could sound like an affirmatively moralistic, Production Code-approved resolution. However, that description would have to be extremely cursory indeed, since it would need to ignore many significantly less affirmative aspects of the conclusion, which receive considerably more emphasis. First, there is the simple fact that Cliff and Norma's relationship, in which we have been encouraged to invest emotionally throughout, has been required to end. There is also the great attention granted by the film to Cliff's desolation, especially as he stands at the window, where the camera lingers on him staring at Norma's plane while enclosed by the window's frame, swallowing back his emotions with a suppressed gasp before he closes the shutters. Equally, rather than sidelining Norma so as to give the film a chance of focusing on the potential consolations of domesticity, she is made emphatically present by the cut to the plane's interior—again, granting intense access to her experience via Stanwyck's tear-stained face. In addition, the sad reprise of 'Blue Moon', which plays over these shots of Cliff and Norma, reminds us forcefully that his homecoming represents the tragic loss of the future that this couple might have built upon their happy past.

It does indeed seem that the emphasis granted these elements ensures that, for most of its length, the final scene makes no efforts to treat Cliff's return as a happy ending at all. This is to say, in part, that much of the conclusion gives little sense that conventional materials are being treated with the kind of distanced tone that could indicate ironic pretence. Irony is a word scholars tend to reach for too readily when faced with happy endings featuring any degree of ambiguity or irresolution whatsoever, and it initially seems tempting to say that *There's Always Tomorrow* too has fallen afoul of this critical tendency. However, the film's tone appears to change in the final shot, which depicts Cliff's conversation with Marion, as well as the final tableau of the children. Several incongruities of viewpoints and attitudes are stressed within the span of this shot. Some are best described as instances of dramatic irony and most easily explained in terms of point of view; others, however, are better defined in terms of ironic pretence and demand explanation in terms of the tone the film is adopting towards its conventions. Let us consider first the scene's dramatic ironies before exploring how these relate to ironic pretence.

We might begin with Cliff's last line: 'You know me better than I know myself.' Hardly ironic in itself, this line becomes dramatically ironic in the context of Marion's far more limited viewpoint, and has been prepared for in quite particular ways. Marion is currently unaware of what ails Cliff, but the film has also repeatedly established that, in general, she does not seem to know him well at all. Her comparatively limited insights into her husband have been dramatised not merely through her continual ignorance of the affair but also in her consistent inability—or, perhaps more charitably, unwillingness—to intuit the very meaning of Cliff's words, even when he tries to speak with her comparatively openly. In an earlier scene, Cliff attempted to communicate what he feels to be the constricting nature of family life, and she persistently appeared to misinterpret his complaints as pertaining only to 'expenses'—finally prompting Cliff to exclaim, 'You *know* that isn't what I mean!' It seems, though, that she truly does not, and that she remains similarly in the dark about what Cliff's words mean in the final scene; the film, however, ensures that we have no such illusions. For Cliff, saying 'You know me better than I know myself' thus constitutes merely a deception of Marion, an attempt at deceiving himself, or both; for the film, though, within the particular pattern of perspectives established for them, these words become dramatically ironic.

It is not only Cliff's words but also those of characters who possess more limited perspectives that contribute to the ending's dramatic irony. First, Marion's pronouncement 'I *should* [know you], after a lifetime with you', clearly assumes a troubling double meaning in light of all that we know that she does not. Equally, Frankie's last question, 'They make a handsome couple, don't they?', intended by her as rhetorical, seems intended by the film to encourage us to respond in the negative. Perhaps this couple are 'attractive', but this is plainly not all that Frankie or the film wishes her observation to convey, and the audience have been well prepared to reject the phrase's more metaphorical connotations. More important still is the fact that Frankie possesses a literally naïve perspective—not only due to her young age, but also because, unlike her brother and sister, she has no inkling of Cliff's affair.

The film's final words are thus already lent dramatic irony, but in addition there is also, of course, the stylistic gesture of finally framing Frankie and her siblings through the stairs' balustrades—an image unavailable from their perspective but emphatically present for us (Fig. 2.8). A comparable composition has actually been seen elsewhere in the film when, in an earlier scene, Cliff's feelings of constriction were suggested by his being framed through these same bars during a phone call to Norma. In that scene this composition offered little dramatic irony since its point of view chimed rather precisely with Cliff's own perspectives and feelings: later he describes having felt 'desperate sitting in my own living room. I felt as though I were trapped in a tomb of my own making'. In this final shot, though, the film adopts a similar point of view, yet ensures it clashes greatly with the contrary perspectives and feelings of the characters.[57] For the film to enclose Frankie's optimistic pronouncement behind bars is thus to end by creating dramatic irony by specifically filmic means.

These, then, constitute some of the ending's dramatic ironies. While crucial to the scene's overall ironic effects, these elements certainly do not by themselves amount to cases of communicative irony. This, of course, requires that a film adopt an ironic attitude towards its own narration, which is by far the most common kind of irony attributed to Sirk's endings. I suggest that this is also something offered by this conclusion, however, and that this can be discerned in the various ways the film seems to *pretend to try* to make this feel, despite everything, like a 'happy ending' after all.

As we enter the film's final shot, Marion approaches Cliff by the window and asks him, 'feeling better tonight?' While she does so, the sombre, minor-key version of 'Blue Moon' is segueing—not without a little strain—into the far more major-key, far more reassuring and hopeful melody of an original piece by composers Heinz Roemheld and Herman

Fig. 2.8 *There's Always Tomorrow*: the children enclosed by the stairs' balustrades

Stein. This considerably more cheering score continues throughout the remainder of the ending, as Marion leads Cliff away, arm in arm, and as we focus on the children. As it plays, there is an unmistakable incongruity between its mood and the mood of both the dramatic action (especially what has taken place just moments before) and the film's style (especially the final composition). This shift in the music, and the fact that the latter piece accompanies all that follows, makes perhaps the most decisive contribution to the sense of ironic pretence pervading this ending's tone. It creates a sustained suggestion that the film's narration is urging us to take this ending as significantly more 'happy' than numerous other aspects of the scene will permit us to feel is warranted.[58] Also pivotal is how the score changes from the mournful rendition of 'Blue Moon' to this more upbeat music at precisely the moment Marion enquires whether Cliff is 'feeling better'. The effect of the concurrence is almost to give an impression of the lighter music being conjured into existence by this hopeful question—or, perhaps more reasonably, that the score may be beginning to align itself with perspectives and feelings other than Cliff's (more on this shortly).

There are aspects of the dramatic action too, though, that conspire in what we might call a strained attempt to make this feel more like a happy ending than it credibly can. Marion's face while leading Cliff into the house—and away from the window—betrays no lingering worries she might have, but rather projects calm and (in context) poignant credulousness (Fig. 2.9). It would have been easy, perhaps even dramatically logical, for Bennett to play Marion here with some suggestion of uncertainty about Cliff's (and thus their marriage's) wellbeing: she notes, after all, his recently having seemed 'depressed', and he responds to her first question here with a distracted 'What...?' that might have caused her concern. Yet there is no hint of this; instead, she smiles contentedly in response to his reassurances, looks up at him trustingly, and speaks confidently of knowing him well. Continuing the pattern, Frankie's smile is broader still than her mother's, and the sigh she gives before extolling the couple's handsomeness is of the kind a lovesick fan might let out while watching their favourite matinee idol. On one level these performances of happiness are merely expressive again of these characters' limited viewpoints. Yet they also have a major effect on the tone of the scene—as if to nudge us, in a more subtle but comparable way to the music, into an untenable emotional response. This sense becomes considerably stronger, though, with the final grins of Vinnie and Ellen. Far more than Marion's, these smiles (especially that of

Fig. 2.9 *There's Always Tomorrow*: Marion leads Cliff into the house

Ellen, who is closer to us) seem notably wider and easier than we might expect given the circumstances: unlike their sister, they *do* know about their father's relationship with Norma; furthermore, by this point they in fact still do *not* know that the affair has even been ended. Given this, and especially in combination with the music, the fact that these characters too should ultimately be required to seem so happy—Ellen even laughs— makes this happiness feel in part precisely a requirement, their smiles contributing to a convention that is uneasily half-performing its function as a resolution to this story and scene.

The decision finally to move our viewpoint to the children is itself highly significant. The concluding shot first pans to follow Cliff and Marion as they walk away from the window; soon, though, they leave the left-hand side of the frame and we come to a rest on the children behind the balustrades, remaining with them until the fade to black. This decision seems to me to make at least two distinct but interrelated contributions to the ending's irony. In one respect, the irony of the gesture lies in ensuring that these characters' limited perspectives characterise our final experience of the film: we fade out on this spectacle of blindness, as well as on a shot expressly composed so as to emphasise that blindness. At the same time as meaning the film concludes with these multiplied dramatic ironies, however, the gesture also finally directs us towards these multiplied happy, smiling faces. It does so, furthermore, by excluding other possible final views we might have been given—especially, of course, any concluding view of Cliff, which would have guaranteed a much more forthrightly disquieting final image. Particularly when combined, again, with the emotional tenor of the comforting score, for the film to force our gaze in its final seconds onto these apparently recklessly happy characters also constitutes, I maintain, a thin but nonetheless palpable pretence of trying to salvage a conventionally 'happy' concluding image from the meagre materials available. On this view, the bars not only create a dramatically ironic effect but also offer a tonal commentary on the ironic pretence that is also taking place. Thanks especially to the fact that they seal in the entire space of the frame, they seem to lock in not only the characters but also the unconvincingly conventional cinematic image itself, which this film has nonetheless elected—seemingly against its better judgement—to leave us with.

Turning once more, finally, to the relationship between ironic pretence in film and prose fiction, it is tempting to imagine how the ending of *There's Always Tomorrow* could be handled by a novel narrated in free indirect style. Throughout most of such a hypothetical novel's conclusion, the narration might incorporate aspects of Cliff's thoughts and feelings in order to make clear his despondent state while returning home and staring at Norma's plane. Having allowed us to share in his experience, however, the novel might nonetheless conclude with a brief final paragraph that could read something like this:

> Frankie watched her parents as they walked arm-in-arm into the house. She sighed happily; they made a handsome couple.

Treated in such a way, in this medium, we would be inclined to say that Frankie's perspective was absorbed into the voice of the narration, meaning that the novel ends with words unmistakably infused with her innocently trusting attitudes towards the events of the story. The final clause could only be uttered from a limited perspective; since we would know that the narrator's own perspective is far from limited in this fashion, we would thus understand that the narrator was ultimately adopting a naïve viewpoint for poignantly ironic effect. That irony, moreover, would be both dramatic and communicative: based on discrepant awareness, but also constituting a pretence.

Clearly, a comparison between this hypothetical conclusion and the actual conclusion of Sirk's film can only be partial—just as any comparison of any two different media must always be partial. Yet this does not mean that it cannot also be suggestive. The final composition of *There's*

Always Tomorrow both emphasises the characters' limited points of view *and* appears to undercut a convention that the film is employing; equally, the exaggerated happiness of Marion and the children both emphasises their narrow perspectives *and* contributes to the pretence of enacting a happy ending by populating the screen with images of smiles. Even clearer in this respect is the use of the affirmative score, which, as noted, seems in some sense to be aligned with the feelings and point of view of Marion—and perhaps those of the children, too. We might say that, in something like the way Flaubert's narrator seems to adopt Emma's naïve perspective in order to ironise both her and the narration's use of romantic language, this music suggests the film's narration becoming infused with—or belatedly attending more closely to—the feelings and limited perspectives of the more contented characters in the scene, who can only see the happiness in this homecoming.

There is no need to claim that this film or any other somehow finds a cinematic equivalent for free indirect style in order to argue that it is nonetheless able to make dramatic and communicative irony interdependent.[59] Indeed, as we have seen repeatedly—despite film's manifold debts to other media—no correlation between the ironic capacities of film and those of any other art form can ever be precise. I suggest, though, that it may be this very fact that means that our medium's prospects for ironic expression prove, upon inspection, to be nowhere near as meagre as many have supposed.

*

As has been stressed throughout this chapter, irony in film is irony as created by a mongrel medium. Doubtless, this art form's mongrel nature may assure losses as well as gains in ironic potential: there will certainly exist ironic approaches that are available to some media that film is likely to find more challenging.[60] However, given the frequent critical misgivings about film's capacities in this respect, it has seemed necessary for one of the first extended theories of irony in this medium to stress possibilities rather than limitations. My theorising has itself necessarily been somewhat mongrel in character. I have not offered an overarching theory of what types of irony might be 'specifically "filmic"' (Elleström 2002: 147) since film's specificity seems to lie precisely in its hybrid nature. Rather, I have offered a somewhat piecemeal, but evidenced, theoretical account of certain kinds of irony that film seems capable of creating. The results of my theorising and analyses suggest to me that, despite many pronouncements to the contrary, it would appear that this medium's very hybridity ensures its ironic palette is by no means excessively 'limited' (Currie 2010: 169).

We have seen that film possesses photography's ability to construct and depict ironic situations or adopt a visual perspective from which a situation might appear ironic; yet it also supplements these abilities in many ways: it can create multiple such images, combine them with the ironic possibilities of sound, elect to have ironic situations unfold over time, or provide additional ironic context for images through their placement within a story. In a number of these respects, film may draw upon the ironic capacities of theatre—primarily, the capacity to create dramatic irony—but it is also able to take advantage of other ironic possibilities common to dramatic media, resulting from actors' performances, staging, mise-en-scène, dialogue, music, and so on. Film then augments these possibilities, however, with its capacities of photographic visual perspective and through its abilities in the realm of narrative point of view, which it shares to some extent with prose fiction. Yet, of course, this important overlap with the ironic potential of prose fiction is complemented in the case of film by all the abilities it shares with photography and the theatre, as well as by its entirely unique capacities: editing, camera movement, and—most significantly of all—its routine ability to combine all these features within the space of a single scene.

Given these possibilities, this medium's ironic capacities seem, in fact, to be considerable. Far from being stymied by its similarity or dissimilarity to this or that other medium, film's ability to create various kinds of irony would appear rather to benefit from its 'impure' (Perkins 1972: 151) admixture of expressive properties. Having argued for our medium's potential to create these varied kinds of irony, then, the question becomes: what particular filmic properties, techniques, and conventions can be and have been put to such purposes? It is this question that is taken up in Chapter 3.

NOTES

1. As such, I also reject claims such as Örjan Roth-Lindberg's that only ironies created through editing, for instance, can constitute 'pure' filmic irony (1995: 158–165).
2. While it is not clear from the photograph itself, the poster was commissioned by the National Association of Manufacturers—a political advocacy group representing the business interests of manufacturing companies.

3. Currie in fact acknowledges at least one example of photography achieving ironic pretence (2010: 149).

4. This is certainly how Bourke-White has described the circumstances of the picture's genesis; in her words: 'There was the irony of the relief line standing against the incongruous background of a NAM [National Association of Manufacturers] poster showing a contented family complete with cherubic children, dog and car' (1963: 150).

5. *Dr. Strangelove*'s use of a convention also found in a journalistic photograph like *Kentucky Flood* may not be entirely coincidental. Kubrick worked as a photojournalist at *Look* magazine from 1945 to 1951, and Philippe Mather argues Kubrick seems to have internalised during this period at least one 'staple of photojournalistic practice': namely, 'including signs in...compositions, using them as built-in captions that comment on the action' (2013: 39). This, he suggests, may have influenced his later 'longstanding habit of including signs as commentary' (ibid.: 193).

6. Elsewhere and in another context, Currie himself in fact comes close to offering a similar formulation, proposing that a novel can be ironic by 'describ[ing] situations in ways which make their irony evident, ...exhibiting its ironic nature in this case by its manifest sensitivity to the irony of situations' (2010: 175). I will return to this point later in the chapter.

7. See Pye's definition of tone in film as the ways in which a movie 'implicitly invites us to understand its attitude to its material and the stylistic register it employs' (2007: 7); I will be returning to this definition later.

8. See, for instance, Rick Altman's *Silent Film Sound* (2004).

9. Relevant here, of course, is the fact that in 1964 'Peace Is Our Profession' really *was* the motto of Strategic Air Command.

10. Making wry use of various documentary, newsreel, and 'direct cinema' aesthetic conventions is something *Dr. Strangelove* does throughout: an authoritative voice-over detailing facts about the United States' nuclear capabilities at the opening, handheld camera during some cockpit scenes, and so on; see Wallace (2011: 52–56) for a discussion of some of the parodic uses to which these strategies are put. I will discuss parody at greater length later in this chapter.

11. See, for instance, Kellogg/Scholes (1966: 240) or Genette (1988: 164).
12. Storm (2011) offers a useful overview of different kinds of irony available to a dramatic medium.
13. Thirlwall's article 'On the Irony of Sophocles' (1833) is usually cited as the genesis of the concept, although, as often noted, that article does not in fact feature the term 'dramatic irony' itself (Dane 1991: 126–130). In tribute to Thirlwall's definition, dramatic irony is sometimes referred to as 'Sophoclean irony' or 'tragic irony' (Campbell 1904).
14. See also Murray Smith's (1994) useful distinction between narrative 'alignment' (our relative 'access to [characters'] actions and to what they know and feel') and moral 'allegiance' (our relative 'moral and ideological evaluation of characters') (ibid.: 41).
15. A term often used to describe similar matters concerning our knowledge relative to that of characters is 'focalisation'; see Genette (1988) in relation to literature and Branigan (1992) and Deleyto (1991) in relation to film. Given its close conceptual ties to narrative and narration, however, I would resist applying such terminology to drama; I am also unsure that it would necessarily bring much to our present discussion of filmic storytelling that the more familiar concepts of 'perspective' and 'point of view' cannot already offer.
16. This can be seen especially clearly in Mrs Atwater's remaining unaware of being mocked while Rupert is poking fun at her twin passions of cinema and astrology, as well as in Mr Kentley's taking offence at a darkly comic conversation about the benefits of murder ('I must confess: I really don't appreciate this morbid humour').
17. For further explorations of how such characters' ironic tastes might contribute to characterisation, see, for instance, Elsaesser (1999) on the figure of the 'dandy' in Hitchcock; Allen (2007) too refers to this aspect of Brandon in his analyses of *Rope*. Susan Smith (2000) also offers valuable reflections on *Rope*'s thematic preoccupation with the workings of humour and irony.
18. This distinction may, incidentally, offer us a way of understanding the difference between a *perspective*, which is available to drama, and a *point of view*, which is available only to narrative. As I have noted, even on stage, dramatic irony always depends upon and highlights the fact that 'someone made [a] choice'—in this case,

the choice to grant us a perspective that is superior to certain characters. Nonetheless, as Perez notes, in drama such choices are made prior to the action's unfolding; once the action is actually happening before us there is no further 'mediation' between us and the world of the story that might attest to further choices. In a written narrative, however, every word attests to choices, and together these choices constitute the point of view through which the story is mediated: the ways in which our 'overall epistemic access' is structured by the particular account of the story we are being given (Wilson 1986: 3).

19. See in particular Perkins (1963, 1972: 116–118).

20. This is notwithstanding, of course, the five 'undisguised' cuts in the film and also ignoring for our purposes some scepticism regarding quite how 'disguised' the other cuts really are; George Toles, for instance, wittily suggests that Hitchcock '[draws] as much attention to the act of editing as Brandon draws to David's corpse' (2001: 218).

21. Bauso (1991) offers an illuminating analysis of this aspect of the film.

22. Of course, a prime reason for anticipating that Brandon and Phillip's murder will ultimately be uncovered is *Rope*'s necessary adherence—as a 1948 Hollywood film—to the prescriptions of the Production Code. We shall be returning to the Code later in this chapter.

23. Zborowski notes such ambivalence in the film's style in his description of the famous moment when the camera lets us glimpse through a swinging door Brandon dropping the rope into a drawer: 'it remains an open question whether the camera here aligns itself with Brandon, undercuts him with a display of superior power, or does both' (2008: 32).

24. See, for instance, Wood (1998: 198–224), Babington/Evans (1990), Thomas (2005), Leigh (2012), and Allen (2007) respectively.

25. See Klinger (1994) for an overview.

26. See, for example, Sconce (2002), Thomas (2009), Perkins (2011), MacDowell (2012b), Gibbs (2012), Brown (2012: 169–175), and King (2013: 23–76).

27. If the answer must surely be to some extent 'both', then we might think here of Bruce Babington and Peter Evans' useful term 'criti-

cal pathos', coined to account for the fact that 'empathy and detachment [can] exist in a mutually qualifying relationship,' wherein 'empathy [is] qualified but not destroyed by critical understanding' (1990: 50).

28. In terms of critical accounts that suggest the centrality of dramatic irony without necessarily naming it as such, we might think, for instance, of George M. Wilson's acknowledgement that all of the films he analyses in *Narration in Light* feature 'characters whose perception and comprehension of their personal circumstances are shown to be dim, distorted, and severely restricted' (1986: 191). For two other more recent explorations of comparable forms of distance in film, see Plantinga (2009) and Zborowski (2015).

29. Dynel (2014) offers a good recent overview.

30. In this, I follow Currie, who uses the term *communicative irony* to refer to this form of irony in his aforementioned 'The Irony in Pictures' (2011). Currie (2010) and others have also called the phenomenon *representational irony*, but this term seems vulnerable to confusion with other practices such as the representation of situational or dramatic ironies.

31. Though see also, for instance, the 'echoic-mention' or 'relevance-theory' account (Sperber/Wilson 2007).

32. It may be worth making explicit here that I follow virtually all other theorists of the subject in drawing a sharp distinction between the concept of a filmic narrator and that of a voice-over narrator. As Brian Henderson argues, 'voiceover narration…has little in common with character narration in fiction' (1983: 15); this is because, as Roche puts it, 'a voice-over is…just another element of the narration' (2015: 9)—along with the film's image track, other aspects of the soundtrack, and so on—and so this voice cannot be understood as narrating the film as a whole. Incidentally, this is not to say that voice-over narration cannot be used to ironic effect; indeed, we will encounter examples of this in Chapter 3.

33. Though I should say I also remain open to the usefulness of the concept of an 'implied filmmaker', as used by theorists like Wilson (1986), Robertson (1990), and Currie (1995). I will return to this matter in Chapter 4.

34. See Hutcheon (1985); on film parody, see Harries (2000).

35. On parody and pastiche in *Madame Bovary* see, for instance, Warning (1982), Lloyd (2014: 85–89), or Dyer (2007: 158–163).

36. See Stam (1992: 127–166) on the relationship between strategies of self-reflexivity and parody in literature and film.
37. See, for instance, Van Deusen (1966), Fleming (1971), or Watts (1981: 96–180).
38. Likewise, Nora Nachumi suggests that the 'crucial problem' for Jane Austen adaptations is 'the loss of the ironic third-person narrator' (2001: 130). Of course, any film may elect (as do several Austen adaptations) to include an ironic *voice-over*; however, as noted previously, this is by no means the same thing as possessing a narrator understood to be responsible for the tone of the film's narration as a whole.
39. Muecke, for instance, notes that a painting can '"comment" ironically upon other works or upon a style or convention' (1970: 6); see too Currie on parodic photography (2011: 52–53) and Dutton (1987: 200) on 'sendups' in music.
40. Though see Richard Dyer (2007: 124) on the intriguing film-historical anomaly wherein saxophones tend to feature far more frequently on the soundtrack of later iterations, pastiches, and parodies of *films noirs* than they ever did in the original 1940s/1950s cycle of films themselves.
41. Pye proposes in this particular article that 'tone, I think, is...[not] a form of distance' (ibid.: 12). However, while tone certainly cannot be reduced to merely 'a form of distance' alone, implying degrees of distance (or indeed 'closeness') of various kinds can nonetheless be a crucial part of what a film's tone does. This can be seen in Pye's numerous uses of the term *distance* in his later 'Movies and Tone' (2007) to describe a film's implied relationships both to characters and to its stylistic or generic conventions.
42. Again, we do nonetheless need to posit an *intention* to adopt such a tone—whether we attribute that intention to an 'implied film maker' (Wilson 1986: 134/5), to the text itself (Eco 1992a), or otherwise. I will be returning to this issue in Chapter 4.
43. For example, Fredericksen (1979), Collins (1993), and Rombes (2005) respectively.
44. For example, Kline (2002), Kinder (1990), and Rich (1992) respectively.
45. For example, Feuer (1993), Garrett (2007: 92–125), and Knight/McKnight (2010) respectively.

46. For example, Martin (2011), McElhaney (2006: 141–200), Mulvey (1996: 187–209), Hunter (1999), Bordwell (1985: 311–224), and Garin (2014) respectively.
47. For example, Cohan (2005: 24–32), Constable (2005), and Robertson (1996: 85–114) respectively.
48. For example, Tinkcom (2002), Dyer (2007), and Harries (2000) respectively.
49. Currie argues that 'the representation of [situational irony] in performance or literature would count as dramatic irony (2006: 129).
50. Currie himself comes close to acknowledging this in his analysis of *The Birds* when he briefly suggests that 'for all the distinctness of situational and [communicative] irony, a tendency on the part of [the narration] to describe situations in ways which make their irony evident seems to me a further indication of a narrative point of view which is itself [communicatively] ironic' (2010: 175).
51. See Klinger (1984) for an overview.
52. See, for instance, *Intermezzo* (Gregory Ratoff 1939), *Casablanca* (1942), *September Affair* (William Dieterle 1950), or *Strangers When We Meet* (Richard Quine 1960).
53. See Klinger (1994: 1–36) for an overview of such arguments about Sirk; see MacDowell (2013: 5–7) for an overview of such arguments about the 'happy ending'.
54. See MacDowell (2013: 153–154) for an overview of such critical pronouncements about Sirk's endings.
55. Halliday (1972: 93–96, 119, 132).
56. Again see Klinger (1994: 1–36).
57. This, incidentally, is why I would refrain from describing as ironic the putatively similar concluding shot of *The Reckless Moment* (Max Ophuls 1949): unlike the smiling characters framed behind balustrades at the end of *There's Always Tomorrow*, I would maintain that the feelings and perspective of Ophuls' protagonist, Lucia (Joan Bennett), find rather apt expression in the prison-like bars that contain her in that film's final image.
58. It is worth noting that (other than the opening credits) this piece's main melody was first heard in the scene in which Norma first appeared. While it is by no means exclusively associated with Norma (it is used in several scenes from which she is absent), it does thus carry associations of her, thereby increasing subtly the irony of its use here.

59. Some theorists have advanced claims of this kind about film; see Schwartz (2005) for an overview of such debates.

60. For instance, if, as I have suggested, films cannot easily be described as possessing narrators, we might argue that this medium would find it hard to ironise narrators, as the novel does so frequently (Booth 1961: 156); however, see Brütsch (2015) for an exploration of this possibility.

BIBLIOGRAPHY

Allen, Richard. (2007). *Hitchcock's Romantic Irony*. New York: Columbia University Press.

Altman, Rick. (2004). *Silent Film Sound*. New York: Columbia University Press.

Aristotle. (1961). *Poetics* (Translated by S. H. Butcher). New York: Hill & Wang.

Armes, Roy. (1994). *Action and Image: Dramatic Structure in Cinema*. Manchester: Manchester University Press.

Arnheim, Rudolf. (1957). *Film As Art*. London: University of California Press.

Austern, Linda Phyllis. (1986). 'Sweet Meats with Sour Sauce: The Genesis of Musical Irony in English Drama after 1600', *The Journal of Musicology*, 4: 4, 472–490.

Babington, Bruce & Peter Evans. (1990). 'Another Look at Sirkian Irony', *Movie* 34/35, 47–58.

Barthes, Roland. (1977). *Image, Music, Text*. (Translated and edited by Stephen Heath). New York: Hill and Wang.

Bauso, Thomas M. (1991). '*Rope*: Hitchcock's Unkindest Cut', in Raubicheck, Walter & Walter Srebnick (eds), *Hitchcock's Rereleased Films: From Rope to Vertigo*. Detroit: Wayne State University Press, 226–239.

Bersier, Gabrielle. (1997). 'A Metamorphic Mode of Literary Reflexivity: Parody in Early Germany Romanticism', in Muller, Beate (ed), *Parody: Dimensions and Perspectives*, Atlanta, G A: Ropoi, 27–46.

Booth, Wayne C. (1961). *The Rhetoric of Fiction*. Chicago: University of Chicago Press.

Booth, Wayne C. (1974). *A Rhetoric of Irony*. Chicago: University of Chicago Press.

Bordwell, David. (1985). *Narration in the Fiction Film*. New York: Routledge.

Bordwell, David. (2008). *Poetics of Cinema*. New York: Routledge.

Bordwell, David, Janet Staiger, & Kristin Thompson. (1985). *The Classical Hollywood Cinema: Film Style and Mode of Production to 1960*. New York: Columbia University Press.

Bordwell, David & Kristin Thompson. (2008). *Film Art: An Introduction* (Eighth Edition). New York: McGraw-Hill.

Bourke-White, Margaret. (1963). *Portrait of Myself.* New York: Simon and Schuster.

Branigan, Edward. (1992). *Narrative Comprehension and Film.* New York: Routledge.

Brown, Tom. (2012). *Breaking the Fourth Wall: Direct Address in the Cinema.* Edinburgh: Edinburgh University Press.

Browne, Nick. (1975). 'The Spectator-in-the-Text: The Rhetoric of *Stagecoach*', *Film Quarterly* 29: 2, 26–38.

Britton, Andrew. (2009). *Britton on Film: The Complete Film Criticism of Andrew Britton*, Barry Keith Grant (ed). Detroit: Wayne State University Press.

Brütsch, Matthias. (2015). 'Irony, Retroactivity, and Ambiguity: Three Kinds of "Unreliable Narration" in Film', in Nünning, Vera (ed), *Unreliable Narration and Trustworthiness: Intermedial and Interdisciplinary Approaches.* Berling: De Gruyter, 221–244.

Burgoyne, Robert. (1990). 'The Cinematic Narrator: The Logic and Pragmatics of Impersonal Narration', *Journal of Film and Video*, 42: 1, 3–16.

Campbell, Lewis. (1904). *Tragic Drama in Aeschylus, Sophocles, and Shakespeare.* London: Smith, Elder and Co.

Chatman, Seymour. (1980). *Story and Discourse: Narrative structure in Fiction and Film.* Ithaca: Cornell University.

Chatman, Seymour. (1990). *Coming to Terms: The Rhetoric of Narrative in Fiction and Film.* Ithaca: Cornell University Press.

Clark, Herbert H. & Richard J. Gerrig. (2007). 'On the Pretense Theory of Irony', in Gibbs, Raymond W. & Herbert L. Colston (eds), *Irony in Language and Thought: A Cognitive Science Reader.* London: Lawrence Erlbaum, 25–34.

Collins, Jim. (1993). 'Genericity in the 90s: Eclectic Irony and the New Sincerity', in Collins, Jim, Hilary Radner & Ava Preacher (eds), *Film Theory Goes to the Movies.* New York: Routledge, 242–264.

Cohan, Steven. (2005). *Incongruous Entertainment: Camp, Cultural Value, and the MGM Musical.* London: Duke University Press.

Constable, Catherine. (2005). *Thinking in Images: Film Theory, Feminist Philosophy and Marlene Dietrich.* London: British Film Institute.

Currie, Gregory. (1995). *Image and Mind: Film, Philosophy and Cognitive Science.* Cambridge: Cambridge University Press.

Currie, Gregory. (2010). *Narratives and Narrators: A Philosophy of Stories.* Oxford: Oxford University Press.

Currie, Gregory. (2006). 'Why Irony is Pretence', in Nichols, Shaun (ed), *The Architecture of the Imagination: New Essays on Pretence, Possibility, and Fiction.* Oxford: Oxford University Press, 111–133.

Currie, Gregory. (2011). 'The Irony in Pictures', *The British Journal of Aesthetics*, 51: 2, 149–167.

Dane, Joseph A. (1991). *The Critical Mythology of Irony*. Athens: University of Georgia Press.

Davies, David. (2010). 'How Photographs "Signify": Henri Cartier Bresson's "Reply" to Scruton', in Walden Scott (ed), *Photography and Philosophy*. Oxford: Blackwell, 167–186.

Deleyto, Celestino. (1991). 'Focalization in Narrative Film', *Atlantis* 8: 1/2, 159–177.

Dempster, Germaine Collette. (1932). *Dramatic Irony in Chaucer*. Stanford: Stanford University Press.

Doane, Mary Ann. (1979). *'The Dialogic Text: Filmic Irony and the Spectator'*. PhD Thesis, University of Iowa.

Durgnat, Raymond. (1976). 'The Mongrel Muse', in *Durgnat on Film*. London: Faber & Faber, 17–28.

Dutton, Dennis. (1987). 'Why Intentionalism Won't Go Away', in Cascardi, A. J. (ed), *Literature and the Question of Philosophy*. Baltimore: Johns Hopkins University Press, 194–209.

Dyer, Richard. (2007). *Pastiche*. New York: Routledge.

Dynel, Marta. (2014). 'Linguistic Approaches to (Non)humorous Irony', *Humor* 27: 4, 537–550.

Eco, Umberto. (1992a). 'Between Author and Text', in Collini, Stefan (ed), *Interpretation and Overinterpretation*. Cambridge: Cambridge University Press, 67–88.

Elleström, Lars. (1996). 'Some Notes on Irony in the Visual Arts and Music: The Examples of Magritte and Shostakovich', *Word & Image* 12: 2, 197–208.

Elleström, Lars. (2002). *Divine Madness: On Interpreting Literature, Music, and the Visual Arts Ironically*. London: Bucknell University Press.

Elsaesser, Thomas. (1999). 'The Dandy in Hitchcock', in Allen, Richard & Sam Ishii-Gonzales (eds), *Alfred Hitchcock: Centenary Essays*. London: British Film Institute, 3–13.

Evans, Bertrand. (1960). *Shakespeare's Comedies*. Oxford: Clarendon Press.

Feuer, Jane. (1993). *The Hollywood Musical*, Second Edition. Bloomington: Indiana University Press.

Fischer, Lucy. (1989). *Shot/Countershot: Film Tradition and Women's Cinema*. Princeton: Princeton University Press.

Flaubert, Gustave. (1994). *Madame Bovary* (Translated by Eleanor Marx Aveling). Ware: Wordsworth Editions.

Fleming, Robert E. (1971). 'Irony as a Key to Johnson's the Autobiography of an Ex-Coloured Man', *American Literature* 43: 1, 83–96.

Fredericksen, Don. (1979). 'Modes of Reflexive Film', *Quarterly Review of Film Studies*, 4: 3, 299–320.

Garrett, Roberta. (2007). *Postmodern Chick Flicks: The Return of the Woman's Film*. New York: Palgrave Macmillan.

Gaudreault, André. (1987). 'Narration and Monstration in the Cinema', *Journal of Film and Video* 39 (Spring), 29–36.

Gaut, Berys. (2004). 'The Philosophy of the Movies: Cinematic Narration', in Kivy, Peter (ed), *The Blackwell Guide to Aesthetics*. London: Blackwell, 230–253.

Garin, Manuel. (2014). 'Drifting Deaths and Happy Endings: Paradoxical Irony in the Films of Aki Kaurismäki', conference paper delivered at *Irony: Framing (Post)modernity*, January 23/24, Catholic University of Portugal.

Genette, Gérard. (1988). *Narrative Discourse Revisited*. Ithaca: Cornell University Press.

Geraghty, Christine. (2009). 'Foregrounding the Media: *Atonement* (2007) as an Adaptation', *Adaptation* 2: 2, 91–109.

Gibbs, John. (2002). *Mise-en-Scène: Film Style and Interpretation*. London: Wallflower Press.

Gibbs, John. (2012). 'Balancing Act: Exploring the Tone of *The Life Aquatic with Steve Zissou*', *New Review of Film and Television Studies* 10: 1, 132–151.

Gunning, Tom. (1991). *D. W. Griffith and the Origins of American Narrative Film: The Early Years at Biograph*. Chicago: University of Illinois Press.

Halliday, Jon. (1972). *Sirk on Sirk*. London: Seeker & Warburg.

Harries, Dan. (2000). *Film Parody*. London: BFI.

Henderson, Brian. (1983). 'Tense, Mood, and Voice in Film (Notes after Genette)', *Film Quarterly*, 36: 4, 4–17.

Hunter, I. Q. (1999). 'From SF to Sci-Fi: Paul Verhoeven's *Starship Troopers*', in Bignell, Jonathan (ed), *Writing and Cinema*. New York: Routledge, 179–192.

Hutcheon, Linda. (1985). *A Theory of Parody: The Teachings of Twentieth-Century Art Forms*. Chicago: University of Illinois Press.

Hutcheon, Linda. (1994). *Irony's Edge: The Theory and Politics of Irony*. New York: Routledge.

Hutcheon, Linda. (2006). *A Theory of Adaptation*. New York: Routledge.

Jameson, Fredric. (1983). 'Postmodernism and Consumer Capitalism', in Foster, Hal (ed), *The Anti-Aesthetic: Essays on Postmodern Culture*. Seattle: Bay Press, 111–125.

Kellogg, Robert & Robert Scholes. (1966). *The Nature of Narrative*. New York: Oxford University Press.

Kennedy, John M. (2008). 'Metaphor and Art', in Gibbs, Raymond W. Jr. (ed), *The Cambridge Handbook of Metaphor and Thought*. Cambridge: Cambridge University Press.

Kinder, Marsha. (1990). 'Ideological Parody in the New German Cinema', *Quarterly Review of Film & Video* 12: 1/2, 73–103.

King, Geoff. (2013). *'Indie 2.0: Change and Continuity in Contemporary American Indie Film'*, New York: I. B. Tauris.

Kline, T. Jefferson. (2002). *Screening the Text: Intertextuality in New Wave French Cinema*. Baltimore: Johns Hopkins University Press.

Klinger, Barbara. (1984). '"Cinema/Ideology/Criticism" Revisited: The Progressive Text', *Screen*, 25: 1, 30–44.

Klinger, Barbara. (1994). *Melodrama and Meaning: History, Culture and the films of Douglas Sirk*. Bloomington: Indiana University Press.

Knight, Deborah & George McKnight. (2010). 'The Northwestern: *McCabe and Mrs. Miller*', in McMahon, Jennifer L. and Csaki, Steve B (eds), *The Philosophy of the Western*. Lexington: University Press of Kentucky, 241–257.

Kozloff, Sarah. (1989). *Invisible Storytellers: Voice-over Narration in American Fiction Film*. Los Angeles: University of California Press.

Kroeber, Karl. (2006). *Make Believe in Film and Fiction: Visual vs. Verbal Storytelling*. London: Palgrave Macmillan.

Leigh, Jacob. (2012). *The Cinema of Eric Rohmer: Irony, Imagination, and the Social World*. London: Continuum.

Levine, June Perry. (1998). 'Two Rooms With a View: An Inquiry in Film Adaptation', in Stape, John Henry (ed), *E. M. Forster: Critical Assessments*. Volume IV, Bodmin: MPG, 202–224.

Levinson, Jerrold. (1996). 'Film Music and Narrative Agency', in Bordwell, David & Noël Carroll (eds), *Post-Theory: Reconstructing Film Studies*. Madison: University of Wisconsin Press, 248–282.

Lloyd, Rosemary. (2014). *Madame Bovary (Routledge Revivals)*. New York: Routledge.

MacDowell, James. (2012b). 'Wes Anderson, Tone and the Quirky Sensibility', *New Review of Film and Television Studies*, 10:1, 6–27.

MacDowell, James. (2013). *Happy Endings in Hollywood Cinema: Cliché, Convention and the Final Couple*. Edinburgh: Edinburgh University Press.

Malcolm, Janet. (1980). *Diana & Nikon: Essays on the Aesthetic of Photography*. Boston: David R. Godine Publisher.

Maltby, Richard. (2003). *Hollywood Cinema* (Second Edition). London: Blackwell.

Martin, Adrian. (2011). 'Guess-Work: *Scarlet Street*', *Movie: A Journal of Film Criticism*, Issue 3, 35–42. Available at: http://www2.warwick.ac.uk/fac/arts/film/movie/contents/scarlet_st._final.2.pdf (Accessed 20 January 2016).

Mather, Phillipe. (2013). *Stanley Kubrick at Look Magazine: Authorship and Genre*. London: Intellect.

McElhaney, Joe. (2006). *The Death of Classical Cinema: Hitchcock, Lang, Minnelli*. Albany: State University of New York Press.

McIntyre, Dan. (2006). *Point of View in Plays: A Cognitive Stylistic Approach to Viewpoint in Drama*. Philadelphia: John Benjamins.

Mercer, John & Martin Shingler. (2004). *Melodrama: Genre, Style, Sensibility*. London: Wallflower.

Metz, Christian. (1974). *Film Language: A Semiotics of Cinema*. Oxford: Oxford University Press.

Monaco, James. (2009). *How to Read a Film: Movies, Media, and Beyond*. Oxford: Oxford University Press.

Muecke, Douglas Colin. (1970). *Irony and the Ironic*. London: Methuen.

Mulvey, Laura. (1996). *Fetishism and Curiosity*. London: BFI.

Nachumi, Nora. (2001). '"As if!" Translating Austen's Ironic Narrator to Film', in Troost, Linda & Sayne Greenfield (eds), *Jane Austen in Hollywood*. Lexington: University of Kentucky Press, 130–139.

Neupert, Richard. (1995). *The End: Narration and Closure in the Cinema*. Detroit: Wayne State University Press.

Oltean, Stefan. (1993). 'A Survey of the Pragmatic and Referential Functions of Free Indirect Discourse', *Poetics Today*, 14: 4, 691–714.

Ong, Walter J. (1976). 'From Mimesis to Irony: the Distancing of Voice', *The Bulletin of the Midwest Modern Language Association*, 9: 1/2, 1–24.

Perez, Gilberto. (1998). *The Material Ghost: Films and Their Medium*. Baltimore: Johns Hopkins University Press.

Perkins, Claire. (2011). *American Smart Cinema*. Edinburgh: Edinburgh University Press.

Perkins, V. F. (1963). '*Rope*', *Movie*, 7, 11–13.

Perkins, V. F. (1972). *Film as Film: Understanding and Judging Movies*. London: Penguin Books.

Perkins, V. F. (2000). 'Same Tune Again! Repetition and Framing in *Letter From an Unknown Woman*', *CineAction*, 52, June, 40–48.

Pfister, Manfred. (1991). *The Theory and Analysis of Drama*. Cambridge: Cambridge University Press.

Plantinga, Carl. (2009). *Moving Viewers: American Film and the Spectator's Experience*. Los Angeles: University of California Press.

Pye, Douglas. (2000). 'Movies and Point of View', *Movie*, 36, 2–34.

Pye, Douglas. (2007). 'Movies and Tone', in Gibbs, John & Douglas Pye (eds), *Close-Up 02: Movies and Tone/Reading Rohmer/Voices in Film*. London: Wallflower Press, 1–80.

Pye, Douglas. (2013). 'Seeing Fictions in Film', *Projections* 7: 1, 131–38.

Rich, B. Ruby. (1992). 'New Queer Cinema', *Sight and Sound* 2: 5, 30–34.

Robertson, Pamela. (1990). 'Structural Irony in *Mildred Pierce*, or How Mildred Lost Her Tongue', *Cinema Journal* 30: 1, 42–54.

Robertson, Pamela. (1996). *Guilty Pleasures: Feminist Camp from Mae West to Madonna*. London: I. B. Tauris.

Roche, David. (2015). 'Irony in *The Sweet Hereafter* by Russell Banks (1991) and Atom Egoyan (1997)', *Adaptation* 8: 2, 237–253.

Rodriguez, Natalie. (2010). 'On Particle-Waves, a Mediating Gaze and the Narrative Sequence', *Prometheus Journal*. Available at: http://prometheus-journal.com/2010/12/30/on-particle-waves-a-mediating-gaze-and-the-narrative-sequence/# (Accessed 5 March 2015).

Rombes, Nicholas. (2005). *New Punk Cinema*. Edinburgh: Edinburgh University Press.

Rossen-Knill, Deborah F. & Richard Henry. (1997). 'The Pragmatics of Verbal Parody', *Journal of Pragmatics*, 27: 719–751.

Roth-Lindberg, Örjan. (1995). 'Skuggan av ett Leende: Omfilmisk Ironi och den Ironiska Berättelsen', PhD Thesis, University of Stockholm: Bokförlaget T. Fischer & Co.

Rothman, William. (1982). *Hitchcock: The Murderous Gaze*. Cambridge: Harvard University Press.

Schwartz, Louis-Georges. (2005). 'Typewriter: Free Indirect Discourse in Deleuze's *Cinema*', *SubStance*, 34: 3, 107–135.

Sconce, Jeffrey. (2002). 'Irony, Nihilism and the New American "Smart" Film', *Screen* 43: 4, 349–369.

Sedgewick, Garrett Gladwin. (1948). *Of Irony, Especially in Drama*. Toronto: Toronto University Press.

Smith, Murray. (1994). 'Altered States: Character and Emotional Response in Cinema', *Cinema Journal*, 33: 4, 34–56.

Smith, Susan. (2000). *Hitchcock: Suspense, Humour and Tone*. London: BFI.

Sperber, Dan & Deirdre Wilson. (2007). 'On Verbal Irony', in Gibbs, Raymond W. & Herbert L. Colston (eds), *Irony in Language and Thought: A Cognitive Science Reader*. New York: Lawrence Erlbaum Associates, 35–55.

Stam, Robert. (1992). *Reflexivity in Film and Literature: From* Don Quixote *to* Jean-Luc Godard. New York: Columbia University Press.

Storm, William. (2011). *Irony and the Modern Theatre*. Cambridge: Cambridge University Press.

Tagg, John. (2009). *The Disciplinary Frame: Photographic Truths and the Capture of Meaning*. Minneapolis: University of Minnesota.

Thirlwall, C. T. (1833). 'On the Irony of Sophocles', *The Philological Museum*, II, 483–537.

Thomas, Deborah. (2005). '"Knowing One's Place": Frame-breaking, Embarrassment and Irony in *La Cérémonie*', *Style and Meaning: Studies in the Detailed Analysis of Film*. Manchester: Manchester University Press, 167–178.

Thomas, Deborah J. (2009). *Ambivalent Fictions: Youth, Irony and Affect in American Smart Film*. PhD Thesis, The University of Queensland.

Thomson-Jones, Katherine. (2008). *Aesthetics and Film*. London: Continuum.

Tinkcom, Matthew. (2002). *Working Like a Homosexual: Camp, Capital, Cinema*. Durham: Duke University Press.

Toles, George. (2001). *A House Made of Light: Essays on the Art of Film*. Detroit: Wayne State University Press.

Utsumi, Akira. (1996). 'Implicit Display Theory of Verbal Irony: Towards a Computational Model of Irony', in Hulstijn, Joris & Anton Nijholt (eds), *Automatic Interpretation and Generation of Verbal Humor*. Enschede: University of Twente, 29–38.

Van Deusen, Marshall. (1966). 'Narrative Tone in *The Custom House* and *The Scarlet Letter*', *Nineteenth-Century Fiction* 21: 1, 61–71.

Wallace, Richard. (2011). 'The Fine Line Between Stupid and Clever: Re-thinking the Comic Mockumentary', PhD Thesis, University of Warwick.

Warning, Rainer. (1982). 'Irony and the "Order of Discourse" in Flaubert', *New Literary History*, 13: 2, 253–286.

Watson, Wallace S. (1997). 'Conradian Ironies in the Conrad Films', in Moore, Gene M. (ed), *Conrad on Film*. Cambridge: Cambridge University Press, 16–30.

Watts, Richard J. (1981). *The Pragmalinguistic Analysis of Narrative Texts: Narrative Co-operation in Charles Dickens's* Hard Times. Tubingen: G. Narr Verlag.

Wilson, George M. (1986). *Narration in Light: Studies in Cinematic Point of View*. Baltimore: John Hopkins University Press.

Wood, Robin. (1989). *Hitchcock's Films Revisited*. New York: Columbia University Press.

Wood, Robin. (1998). *Sexual Politics and Narrative Film, Hollywood and Beyond*. New York: Columbia University Press.

Zborowski, James. (2008). '"Between Sympathy and Detachment": Point of View and Distance in Movies Directed by Alfred Hitchcock, Otto Preminger and Max Ophuls', PhD Thesis, University of Warwick.

Zborowski, James. (2015). *Classical Hollywood Cinema: Point of View and Communication*. Manchester: Manchester University Press.

CHAPTER 3

Ironic Filmmaking: Properties, Devices, and Conventions

In the previous chapter I argued that there is nothing intrinsic to the film medium that should necessarily inhibit movies from creating irony. This chapter moves our focus from general questions concerning the possibility and nature of irony in film towards more specific questions about how particular aspects of, and approaches to, filmmaking can and have been used to create ironic effects. Needless to say, I am able to address here only a handful of the countless questions potentially relevant to such a discussion. Innumerable features of style and dramatisation may contribute to even the most fleeting moment of filmic irony. As David Roche notes, 'the fact that film is a "multitrack" medium' enables ironic clashes and incongruities 'between words, between images, between various areas of a composition, between sounds, as well as between word and image, word and sound, and image and sound' (2015: 3). This brief list, which hardly exhausts the facets of the fiction film that can be put to ironic purposes, begins to indicate the potential enormity of the topic this chapter broaches.

To structure my inquiry, I have chosen to focus primarily on five elements of film art: sound, editing, mise-en-scène, the camera, and performance. The apparent ironic potential of each these features will be explored through moments from films which span almost the whole history of U.S. fiction filmmaking. Of course, this can by no means hope to produce a comprehensive account of all the myriad ways these components might be used

© The Author(s) 2016
J. MacDowell, *Irony in Film*, DOI 10.1057/978-1-137-32993-6_3

ironically. Yet, taken together, the investigation should amount at least to a suggestive critical survey of some of the ironic devices, techniques, and conventions that these various aspects of film style have helped to create. Before we begin, though, a few comments are in order about my focus, aims, and concerns in this chapter.

One obvious risk of compartmentalising discrete elements of filmmaking is to imply that irony can be created by any element of filmmaking in isolation, when in fact each individual element is always working in synthesis with every other. 'Film,' as V.F. Perkins famously put it, is indeed 'a matter of relationships' (1972: 101); this holds true for every effect that films might create, and perhaps none more so than irony, which itself inherently relies upon the construction of (usually contrasting) aesthetic relationships. The constituent features of a film that make up these relationships can be various, potentially encompassing every weapon in the filmmaker's dramatic and stylistic arsenal. As such, none of the ironic moments considered in this chapter depends wholly upon one aspect of filmmaking in isolation, regardless of the subheading under which it falls. This will become self-evident in the course of my discussions and will occasionally be a focus of the accounts themselves. It nonetheless seems necessary for the first book on irony in film to attempt to consider the ironic potential of some distinct features of the medium—even at the risk of appearing to prise apart in the name of critical clarity what in practice remains inseparable.

My focus on individual moments, meanwhile, means that one kind of irony that I am able to address here less explicitly than others is what we might call a film's global ironic perspective or tone, which can be built up over its entirety. Sometimes this might be the result of the particular story a film is telling, and sometimes it may be the result of large-scale patterns of style or dramatisation. Yet I would suggest, first, that any such global ironic perspective or tone will usually be—in part—an outcome of a film accumulating many more local moments of irony. At the same time, simply because the majority of my examples are drawn from narrative cinema, virtually all of the ironies I will address here only become ironic in the first place (or at least only become *recognisable* as ironic) in the context of the stories in which they appear. Each moment considered in this chapter will therefore be placed as far as possible in the context of its broader film. Indeed, doing so will frequently be essential, since the ironic effects of any single moment will tend always to rely precisely upon that moment's relationship to other surrounding features of the movie—whether because of its placement within a narrative or its relationship to other elements of the film's style.

Finally, this chapter draws upon certain conceptual tools and terminology established in Chapter 2. In particular, I will frequently have cause to note the different *kinds* of irony that a moment seems to create. I suggested in the previous chapter that films may be both *dramatically* and *communicatively* ironic. Dramatic irony involves films distancing our perspective from those of characters for ironic effect. Communicative irony involves *ironic pretence*—films 'pretending' to employ certain styles or conventions 'straight' when in fact they are adopting a distanced tone towards them. Yet I have also suggested that, while it is useful to be able to distinguish between these kinds of irony, films may in fact combine them in a single moment, making one dependent upon the other. It will be necessary to keep these lessons in mind throughout the discussions that follow.

In the course of my investigations I will also, needless to say, continue to make use of insights offered by other critics and scholars, drawing upon and attempting to synthesise some of the most helpful existing work on filmic irony. I begin, in fact, with an aspect of the medium that (rather unusually for film scholarship) has received more sustained attention in connection with irony than any other: sound.

IRONY AND FILM SOUND

Ironic expression characteristically involves establishing incongruities, meaning that it usually requires two or more phenomena to be placed into particular kinds of relationships with one another. One especially noticeable way in which a (sound) film's address establishes relationships between two or more phenomena is through its combination of sound- and image-tracks. Given this, it is perhaps unsurprising that the interaction between film's sonic and visual elements has been regularly recognised as a key potential source of cinematic irony. The two main topics usually addressed in this fashion—and the two considered here—relate to music and voice-over narration.

Music: Pre-existing and Scored

One consequence of film's nature as a 'multi-track' medium is, as Robert Stam notes, that this allows movies to 'stage ironic contradictions between music and image' (2005: 20). This possibility is acknowledged relatively often by scholars, meaning that—more than for many other aspects of filmmaking—'music is frequently cited as a source of irony in film' (Roche

2015: 4). It seems safe to say that engineering musical incongruities is indeed one of the most common—and certainly among the most immediately obvious—ways that films express themselves ironically. Often associated with the terms 'counterpoint' or 'contrapuntal',[1] such an approach has also been associated with both diegetic music (music emanating from the fictional world) and non-diegetic music (which issues from outside that world), as well as with both pre-existing music and film scores; in what follows I shall address each of these permutations.

The very fact that a 'contrapuntal' use of film music has been identified as a distinctive approach at all relies, of course, on a far more widespread conventional *congruence* between music and dramatic action in fiction filmmaking. At least in 'classical' or 'popular' cinema, strong assumptions exist on the part of both filmmakers and audiences that the emotional register of a piece of music is expected, conventionally speaking, to align to some degree with the emotional register suggested by the dramatic events on screen—especially as regards the feelings of protagonists.[2] Bucking this convention via 'music which "goes against" the emotional dominant of the sequence' (Stam 2005: 64) may thus frequently create an effect of, essentially, dramatic irony: rather than serving to align our feelings and perspectives with those of the characters, emotionally incongruent music may rather seek to distance us from them. Equally, though, precisely because emotionally congruent music *is* such a widespread convention, drawing attention to that convention by flouting it may also assist in creating ironic pretence.

Given the long association of avant-garde art with aesthetic juxtaposition of all kinds, it is perhaps unsurprising that avant-garde and experimental filmmaking should have produced some especially notable and influential examples of contrapuntal music. To name only two high-profile instances from the United States: in films like Jack Smith's *Flaming Creatures* (1963) and Kenneth Anger's *Scorpio Rising* (1963), for instance, popular music 'operates in ironic counterpoint to the visual text, which subverts the hackneyed sentiments of the music (1930s Tin Pan Alley songs in Smith's case, 1960s bubblegum pop for Anger)' (Hatch 2012: 145). In addition to the practice's frequent association with the avant-garde, it may also be that contrapuntal approaches to film music have become somewhat more conventional from the latter half of the twentieth century onwards (even if certain pronouncements to this effect can seem rather overconfident).[3] However, as T. Austin Graham notes, in fact even mainstream 'silent film…had made musical-visual dissonance an everyday trope by 1922' (2013: 102) through the convention of 'funning', wherein accompanists would play tonally incongruous music over particular sequences (Lastra 2000: 111–114). Furthermore, it is also certainly not difficult to find instances of musical counterpoint in popular Hollywood films made soon after the advent of synchronised sound. I begin my exploration of why and how musical approaches of this kind might possess ironic potential with one such relatively early example.

The final scene of *The Public Enemy* (William A. Wellman, 1931) famously makes particularly pointed use of—in this case, diegetic—contrapuntal music. Tom Powers (James Cagney) is a Prohibition-era gangster who has risen high in the ranks of Chicago's criminal underworld, all the while endeavouring to keep his gang activities a secret from his adoring but overcredulous mother (Beryl Mercer). By the end of the film, Tom has been badly injured in a shootout and kidnapped by a rival gang; in the concluding sequence, his law-abiding brother, Mike (Donald Cook), waits with their sister (Rita Flynn) and mother in the latter's home, all of them anxiously hoping for Tom's safe return. Throughout this two-minute sequence we hear on the soundtrack an instrumental version of the contemporaneous hit song 'I'm Forever Blowing Bubbles', a record of which we have seen being placed onto a Victrola player in close-up at the scene's opening. This song's sweet, bouncy melody keeps playing softly in the background during a tense family dinner; it continues playing as Mike receives an anonymous phone call telling him to expect Tom's imminent arrival home, which prompts their overjoyed mother to begin preparing a bed for him upstairs. It also carries on through the climactic moment when Mike hears a knock at the door and rushes to open it, only to discover on the threshold Tom's bloodied corpse, standing upright and trussed-up in ropes and a blanket. His body stands swaying for a moment in long shot before toppling forward into the hallway with a heavy, unceremonious thud; at this point, we cut to an upstairs room to see Tom's mother still contentedly preparing his bedding, humming happily to herself as she changes a pillowcase; we then cut back to the hall where Mike crouches by his murdered brother (Figs. 3.1 and 3.2). The film ends on a close-up of the phonograph, the song now finished, the player's needle juddering aimlessly back and forth at the centre of the still-spinning record.

To help appreciate this moment, it is worth invoking Michel Chion's concept of *anempathetic sound*. Anempathetic sound refers to a diegetic element of a soundtrack that seems to exhibit 'conspicuous indifference to the situation, by progressing in a steady, undaunted, and ineluctable

Fig. 3.1 *The Public Enemy.* Tom's trussed-up corpse in the doorway

manner' (1994: 8), despite any emotionally contrasting dramatic events against which it is juxtaposed. Often, suggests Chion, this will involve music possessed of a 'studied frivolity and naivety', with this mood standing in opposition to—and yet paradoxically helping to heighten—the usually more sombre emotional register of the action it accompanies (1994: 8–9). The effect of *The Public Enemy*'s use of this concluding song depends absolutely upon the sense of 'indifference' Chion describes. The fact that the song spans a couple of different phases in the sequence—taking us from the dinner to the discovery—increases our awareness of its relentless, undeterred progress, mordantly unresponsive to the events in its vicinity. Equally, it is not only the song's upbeat tenor that helps create a sense of juxtaposition, but also its (inferred) lyrics, which concern 'pretty bubbles' which 'fly so high, nearly reach the sky, / Then like my dreams they fade and die.'[4] These implied words reverberate ironically not only for Tom, whose grandiose dreams of greatness have led literally to his death, but also his guileless mother, whose own contrary dreams of returning her son to the bosom of the family are now destined to fade just as quickly.

Fig. 3.2 *The Public Enemy.* Tom's mother hums happily to herself

This last observation suggests that the reason anempathetic music offers such possibilities for irony is less because it allows for clashes in moods and more because it makes possible clashes of implied *perspectives*. The conclusion of *The Public Enemy* offers us a bald opposition between 'dreams', variously conceived, and a comparatively far more tragic reality—a fact reinforced by the cut from Tom's dead body to the shot of his mother, still happily preparing his bed, her bubbly humming harmonising with the tune's melody. Used in this fashion, the song is thus made to appear to embody a naïve or limited perspective on life when contrasted against the putatively more disabused perspective presented to us by the film's action. Clearly, few songs could serve this function more completely than one that affirms the appeal of 'pretty bubbles', which may be beautiful but which—if existing in the real world—must eventually burst.

The diegetic status of anempathetic music is also clearly important to its particular ironic potential. We are—or should be—perpetually aware that a film's point of view and tone will always be implicitly striking various attitudes towards all diegetic phenomena. Actions may be presented as being more or less admirable, characters made to seem more or less sympathetic, their emotions implied to be more or less germane to the emotional experiences the film is encouraging from its audience, and so on. The same is true for diegetic music, which—simply by virtue of being a part of the fictional world—seems forever vulnerable to being treated by films with a wide range of implied perspectives and attitudes. In other words: the emotional appeals and implied perspectives of such music may always be qualified, questioned, or even undermined through the way in which a film elects to use it. Might the situation be any different, though, for non-diegetic music? To help answer this question, it will be instructive to consider a use of music that crosses the diegetic boundary.

About three-quarters of the way through *Good Morning, Vietnam* (Barry Levinson, 1987)—a wartime comedy-drama about a US Armed Services radio disc jockey stationed in Saigon in 1965—Louis Armstrong's recording of 'What a Wonderful World' is initially played as a part of a radio broadcast by our protagonist, Adrian Cronauer (Robin Williams). We soon move out of his radio studio, however, and into a montage that Armstrong's song is now effectively forced to score. This montage initially features calm shots of Vietnamese landscapes and daily life but quickly segues into dramatisations of various distressing sights associated with the war: bombing raids on villages, buildings on fire, the executions of Vietnamese men by gunfire, the violent police dispersal of protesters, and so on. At one moment, the lines 'I see friends shaking hands, saying "how do you do?" / They're really saying "I love you"', are made to accompany shots of police officers beating young men and women with truncheons.

As employed here, this song appears in some sense anempathetic, especially given that it begins (and in fact ends) as diegetic.[5] Yet the difference in effect between this film's approach and that of, say, *The Public Enemy* is nonetheless stark. Not only is very precise linguistic irony created out of these lyrics, but the filmmakers' decision to cut away from the radio booth and into the montage constitutes an extremely forceful rhetorical gesture when compared to 'I'm Forever Blowing Bubbles' impassively soundtracking its immediate surroundings. It seems important in this respect that Cronauer's playing of 'What a Wonderful World' itself constitutes something like an ironic gesture: he has been facing censorship from superior officers owing to his irreverent taste in comedy and rock-and-roll records, and so we can infer that he has selected this tune partly for satirical purposes—probably in the hopes that it will clash in his listeners' minds with their awareness of exactly the kinds of atrocities featured in the montage. The filmmakers here effectively choose, then, to literalise the significance of Cronauer's ironic gesture by stylistic means.

This sequence serves well to demonstrate that ironically incongruous musical cues will tend to function somewhat differently when the relevant contrast is created through non-diegetic rather than diegetic music. I think we might account for that difference in two broad ways. First, I referred earlier to the Louis Armstrong track appearing 'forced' to score its montage, and this hints at one major characteristic of the sequence's address. *The Public Enemy* is concerned to create the appearance that it merely allows its pop song to accompany whatever dramatic action takes place around it—be that a dinner or the delivery of the lifeless corpse of our antihero. *Good Morning, Vietnam*, on the other hand, creates its juxtaposition only by cutting away from the space in which the music plays,[6] then fashioning through its style a montage whose whole purpose, we cannot help but feel, is first and foremost to provide us with images that will jar against the song's sentiments. This ironic effect is, then, ostentatiously a product of the film's narration. As such, it alerts us emphatically to the presence of creative figures who have compiled and inserted this footage to accompany this music and who have done so with a certain attitude and for certain rhetorical purposes. We might express this, then, simply in terms of non-diegetic music offering opportunities for creating particularly assertive or 'direct, self-conscious, heavy-handed irony' (Gorbman 2006: 6) between sound- and image-tracks.[7]

Another way of accounting for the difference between diegetic and non-diegetic uses of incongruous music, though, may be to invoke the distinction between dramatic irony and ironic pretence (Chapter 2). In a discussion of tone as it relates to film music, Pye first considers the ability of films to establish a tonal distance from diegetic music, before suggesting that 'non-diegetic music tends to be different: we are used to it carrying, as it were, "editorial" authority...as setter of mood and dramatic register' (2007: 13). As already acknowledged, non-diegetic music does carry particularly powerful conventional expectations that it will serve as an indication as to the spirit in which we might respond to a scene. When the mood and perspectives implied by a piece of non-diegetic music seem manifestly inappropriate to the dramatic register of the material, we are thus made acutely aware not only of the creative choices involved in constructing the contrast but also that a convention is being intentionally 'misused'. Those responsible for crafting this sequence surely *cannot*, we feel, believe that this music represents a fitting emotional accompaniment to this action.

Given this, rather than merely distancing us from the perspectives and experiences of characters (as does *The Public Enemy*'s closing song), an ironic use of non-diegetic music like that in *Good Morning, Vietnam* seems to involve a film adopting an ironic tone towards its own conventions of narration—a practice we have previously defined as ironic pretence.

Pretence also seems one possible ironic effect of musical *scoring*, though by no means the only one. In a useful article concerned partly with ironic uses of popular music in film, Ian Garwood suggests that 'it may be the case that it is more common to create irony…by using an "imported" pop song, rather than through [a] specially composed score' (2000: 290–291). It is certainly easy to see why we might expect irony to be found less frequently in film scores. Pre-existing music affords films particular opportunities to create perspectival clashes through appropriation. Because we can usually assume that such music was not created with this particular film—let alone this particular scene—in mind, there is the immediate possibility of a gap existing between the sentiments and perspectives expressed by the song and those expressed by the film that uses it.[8] Since a film's score, by contrast, will usually have been written specifically for the film, its perspective seems incapable of being appropriated for purposes other than those imagined by its composer. Of course, a score may be made up entirely of existing pieces and may also 'quote' other recognisable pieces of music for ironic purposes;[9] but these practices too clearly involve making use of existing pieces, or at least their melodies. Even if films cannot ironically appropriate their own scores, though, this hardly exhausts the ironic purposes to which music may be put. I will again consider here just two broad ways in which scores might create irony: by contributing to dramatic irony and by assisting in ironic pretence.

We might quickly recognise how commonly film scores contribute to dramatic irony if we think of conventions within genre filmmaking. Drawing a parallel between tendencies of film scoring and dramatic irony in opera, Eddy Zemach and Tamara Balter suggest that 'in every B-movie the music forewarns the spectators, before the hero has any inkling of it, that the new man is the villain, or that the heroine is about to fall in love' (2007: 188). Although this observation may be somewhat sweeping, it does acknowledge something important: the potentially symbiotic relationship between dramatic irony and genre conventions. As we will see repeatedly throughout this chapter, genre films frequently exploit their audience's assumed familiarity with generic conventions to create dramatic irony by forewarning us of events to come. The very conventionality—and thus, frequently, predictability—of genre narratives ensures that viewers conversant with the genre in question are routinely placed in a position of superior knowledge over films' protagonists. In fact, we might risk saying that in this respect the assumed relationship between genre films and their audiences frequently resembles the relationship assumed by those ancient Greek dramas that first prompted critics to speak of dramatic (or 'tragic') irony.[10] And one common way in which a genre film may flaunt the kind of 'discrepant awareness' (Evans 1960) necessary for dramatic irony is through music.

Consider, for example, just a few seconds from *Halloween* (John Carpenter, 1978). At the end of the school day, Laurie Strode (Jamie Lee Curtis) is walking home through the sunny streets of her suburban neighbourhood with two of her friends; they are clutching bags and books, chatting and joking, passing by well-kept houses, manicured lawns, and rows of symmetrically planted saplings. Despite the sanguine nature of the image, though, a feeling of anticipatory dread permeates the moment. We can attribute this partly to the Steadicam shot that frames the characters—a stylistic choice likely to remind us of the film's opening sequence, in which a similar visual style was used to represent the point of view of the psychopathic murderer Michael Myers. Far more decisive, though, is the presence on the soundtrack of John Carpenter's dark synthesised score. This too carries associations of the murders we witnessed in the film's first scene; however, even if we had not heard it previously, its ominous, minor-key drone would be enough to alert us to the probability that these three girls are not nearly so safe, and cannot safely be so carefree, as they presently appear. Furthermore, this piece's intrinsically menacing musical qualities also interweave, of course, with our knowledge of the conventions of the horror film. Together, this creates a near-certain expectation that the crazed killer, whom we know to be on the loose, will soon be terrorising, and perhaps killing, one or all of these currently unsuspecting characters. Genre films habitually use their scores in such a fashion: effectively, to remind us of characters' blindness to, and our contrary awareness of, the genres that the characters exist within.

Yet film scores may also be used to create ironic pretence. Chapter 2 already touched on certain cases of this—*The Naked Gun*, for instance, momentarily adopting conventions associated with the music of *film noir*. Certainly, the most blatant way a film score can practise ironic pretence is via parody. However, I also touched in that chapter upon the importance of scored music to ironic pretence in *There's Always Tomorrow*. There, I suggested that this film's score appeared to strive to create a sense that the movie's ending was 'happier' than other aspects of the conclusion would allow us to believe. Also key to my argument, though, was the proposition that this music appeared to align itself with the feelings of certain characters in the scene whose perspectives on the dramatic events were far more limited than our own. This gesture, I argued, combines the typical effects of dramatic irony (stressing discrepant awareness) with those of ironic pretence (a tonal distance towards aesthetic conventions). I suggest that such a holistic technique is another common way in which film scores may help create irony.

Take, for example, a moment in the romantic comedy *Pillow Talk* (Michael Gordon, 1959). Interior decorator Jan Morrow (Doris Day) believes herself to be in the early stages of a romantic relationship with an old-fashioned, gentlemanly, and wealthy Texan rancher called Rex Stetson, with whom she is falling rapidly in love. What she does not know—but we do—is that 'Rex Stetson' is in fact an entirely fictitious character: an identity assumed for the purposes of seduction by her rude and lecherous playboy neighbour, Brad Allen (Rock Hudson). After a flirtatious goodnight phone call in which she has been wooed with clichéd approximations of Southern chivalry ('Bein' near you, ma'am; it's like, like—bein' round a pot belly stove on a frosty mornin'...'), Jan smilingly replaces the phone by her bed and settles down on her pillow. Grinning and sighing as she snuggles into the sheets, we hear her thoughts in voice-over: 'Mmmm— he *does* like you...'. We also hear the film's score, composed by Frank De Vol: a swooningly romantic arrangement for (initially) brass, strings, and harp. The harp ripples a glissando as the phone is put down and continues to bubble away beneath a soft, yearning, major-chord four-note melody played by brass, then by strings. Soon, two additional instruments edge their way in: a plucked nylon-stringed guitar and a melodious harmonica, which together unmistakably evoke (and mildly parody) the conventional sound and mood of the quieter moments of many Hollywood westerns. Conveying both Jan's amorous feelings and the fact that they have been conjured by Brad's performance of Western manliness, this music is, first, dramatically ironic: we know these feelings to be built upon an illusion of which Jan must eventually be disabused. The music here also, though, constitutes an act of pretence on the part of the film: *Pillow Talk*'s narration almost seems momentarily to pretend to forget all it knows about Brad's scheme. Via its music, the film appears to behave as if it shared

Jan's severely limited perspective on events, which allows her to smile so beatifically.

This final technique, then, uses the conventional purposes of film scoring—deepening our understanding of a protagonist's emotional experience—to ironic effect. Another aural technique that helps in this particular effect here, which is also frequently used to create irony, is voice-over.

Voice-over: Ironised and Ironic

Sarah Kozloff suggests two ways that films may use voice-over narration to ironic effect: either (1) 'throw the narrator's telling into question, make him or her out to be more or less unreliable'; or (2) 'give [the] narrator an ironic temperament' (1989: 110). I agree that these categories—we might call them variously *ironised* and *ironic* voice-overs—represent the most conventional ways in which voice-over narrators are used to create irony in film. *Pillow Talk* has already provided us with a brief example of the former, but let us explore this strategy a little further.

As with musical irony, the strategy of ironising voice-over narrators is acknowledged fairly frequently by scholars; Roche even suggests that this may be 'the form of irony in film that has been the most commented on' (ibid.: 4). The relative prevalence of critical observations on this subject may be due to its being a form of irony to which film seems especially suited. Seymour Chatman suggests that such an approach (which he calls 'partial unreliability') is 'unique to two-track media such as the cinema' (1990: 136), while Roche goes so far as to argue that this 'privileged mode of irony...is specific to film' (2015: 14). Whether or not we agree about film's uniqueness in this respect (clearly the strategy is possible in other screen media and also seems theoretically available to theatre), it certainly demands addressing.

Let us consider, then, a sequence of voice-over from *Election* (Alexander Payne, 1999) delivered by the unnervingly ambitious high school student Tracy Flick (Reese Witherspoon). At this early stage of the film, we have already been made aware that Tracy was recently briefly involved in a sexual relationship with one of her (married) male teachers, Dave Novotny (Mark Harelik); the main purpose of this stretch of voice-over and the montage it accompanies is to make clear Tracy's retrospective feelings about this affair. As Jeffrey Sconce notes in his discussion of *Election* as a paradigmatic example of 1990s/2000s American indie 'smart cinema', this is a film in which 'voiceover and image are often in direct conflict'

(2002: 361). Yet some ironies in Tracy's speech here do not in fact rely on contrasts between voice and image but rather consist of this character unintentionally ironising herself via her own words. For example, we are told earnestly that 'Since I grew up without a dad, you might assume psychologically I was looking for a father figure, but that had nothing to do with it at all: it was just that Dave was so strong, and he made me feel so safe and protected...'. Accompanied by a shot that does nothing particularly to heighten the self-betraying irony of Tracy's description (she and Dave making out in the school darkroom), these words themselves contain the juxtapositions necessary to ironise their speaker.[11]

Later in the same passage of voice-over, though, Tracy claims that 'When I look back on my relationship with Mister Novotny, what I miss most is our talks.' As we hear this line Tracy is advancing away from the camera up a hallway of Dave's house, before pausing at the door of (what we can presume is) Dave and his wife's bedroom[12]; a single arm then extends through the doorway; Dave places his hand on his student's shoulder and draws her across the threshold. Not necessarily contradicting the truth of Tracy's statement exactly (she may indeed remember their talks more fondly than their lovemaking), the decision to combine this proclamation with this image nonetheless ironises her for her naïveté—a quality also highlighted by how small and childlike she is made to seem in this long shot, in contrast to the height of Dave's protruding arm. The disjunction also ironises the naïveté driving the entire affair: while both Tracy and Dave may claim to have been truly in love, it is not their talks but what is about to happen beyond that door that will soon cause Mr Novotny's firing.

As this moment suggests, by effectively offering us two separate narratives of events simultaneously—one verbal, one visual—voice-over narration offers what Kozloff calls 'a pliable, double-layered structure, perfect for creating ironic disparities or contradictions' (1989: 110). And, although ironised narrators may not always be characters in the film's story,[13] when they *are*, this strategy represents another means by which the medium can create the kind of discrepant awareness between character and viewer— between their perspectives and our own—necessary for dramatic irony.[14]

Another way in which voice-over narration is conventionally used to ironic effect, though, is via 'intentional irony on the part of...narrators speaking in voice-over' (Roche 2015: 9). This overarching convention encompasses a multitude of different possible approaches—from the narrator being a sardonic character in the story (say, Dedee [Christina Ricci] in *The Opposite of Sex* [Don Roos, 1998]), to his or her voice representing an ironically amused author (for instance, Guy de Maupassant [Jean Servais] in *Le Plaisir* [Max Ophuls, 1952]), to the detached intrusions of an indeterminate voice, perhaps intended to stand in for that of the director (say, Godard's voice in *Two or Three Things I Know About Her* [Jean-Luc Godard, 1967]). I shall remain here, however, with narrators who constitute fictional characters.

One place we quite commonly find ironic voice-overs in cinema is *film noir*; indeed, as Pamela Robertson argues, 'the narrator's ironic temperament is almost as much a *noir* convention as the use of voice-over itself' (1990: 44). Consider, for example, the opening of *Sunset Boulevard* (Billy Wilder, 1950). As we watch police cars rip down a road in the titular upscale Los Angeles neighbourhood, a male voice (William Holden) begins to inform us of a murder that has taken place. He tells us, somewhat wearily, that we will probably soon read about these events in the papers, since they involve an old Hollywood star, but that we might be interested to learn the facts 'before you hear it all distorted and blown out of proportion'. Already, then, there is cynicism in his words and tone: not only does he imply the inevitability of sensationalised reporting on the lives of celebrities, but he also introduces the police cars by saying, 'That's the Homicide Squad, complete with detectives and newspaper men'— his 'complete with' suggesting a sneering acceptance that the business of police work and that of selling papers go hand-in-glove in a case like this. The ironic temperament suggested by this man's voice-over increases, however, when he begins to elaborate on the crime itself. If we do indeed wish to know the truth about the case, he tells us, then,

> you've come to the right party. You see, the body of a young man was found floating in the pool of a mansion, with two shots in his back and one in his stomach. Nobody important, really. Just a movie writer with a couple of B-pictures to his credit. The poor dope. He always wanted a pool. Well in the end he got himself a pool. Only the price turned out to be a little high.

As we hear these words, the film's images are advancing into the grounds of the mansion in question—past a wide shot overlooking its walls, through a distant shot allowing us to see the body floating face down in the outdoor pool, and finally arriving at a shot taken from within the pool itself, looking up at the floating man.

Both in themselves and in combination with the images, the narrator's lines here strike several ironic notes. There is the detached coolness with which he relates these grisly details and the intrinsic irony of the under-statement 'a *little* high' (the incongruity of both being intensified by the gruesome sight of the dead man's face and splayed bobbing body). There is also the observer's decision effectively to frame *as* ironic the fate of this deluded figure who had always desired a swimming pool. The irony of the voice-over is heightened several degrees, though, by the fact that the reason this man is 'the right party' to tell this story is that he himself *is* the dead man in the pool, Joe Gillis, speaking to us from beyond the grave. While not made explicit in the opening voice-over itself, this will soon become evident, and we might also say that it will be immediately plain to anyone capable of recognising William Holden's voice and face. Given this, the perspective offered by the irony here thus becomes not merely wearily cynical, but virtually existential in character. Hearing a man look back with detached amusement at his dead body, describing himself calmly after the fact as 'nobody important' and a 'poor dope', has the feel almost of Romantic irony—the philosophical view that 'the basic metaphysically ironic situation of man [*sic*] is that he is a finite being striving to compre-hend an infinite, hence incomprehensible, reality' (Muecke 1970: 23). The ambiguous metaphysical (and diegetic) position from which Joe is addressing us seems to have granted him the vision necessary to compre-hend and accept what he now considers the ironic nature of his existence. He was perhaps blinded to this irony in life, but he now seems to be taking some perverse pleasure in expressing it to us with rueful fatalism in this voice-over.

As often claimed, then, film sound clearly offers much ironic potential (and we will in fact passingly encounter this potential being fulfilled fur-ther elsewhere in this chapter). Unsurprisingly, key to many of the ironic effects I have focused on in this section has been the establishment of discrepancies, juxtapositions, or incongruities between soundtracks and image tracks. Another characteristic aspect of film style that seems intui-tively to carry significant potential in this regard is, of course, editing.

IRONY AND EDITING

Editing is fundamentally, as Valerie Orpen calls it, 'a connective process' (2003: 1). In this sense, it resembles film sound—representing a possibility of the medium whose effects depend innately upon combining constituent parts. Simply owing to its most common function of successively conjoin-ing two or more shots or images, then, editing too would seem to have something of an inbuilt potential for creating the kinds of juxtapositions necessary for irony.[15]

We might begin to explore the ironic potential of contrasting discrete visual elements by considering a device that does not quite constitute editing *per se* but that is nonetheless equally reliant on the medium's 'connective' capacities: the 'process' or 'composite' shot. Designed to allow more than one portion of film to be combined within a single image, process shots too are specific to filmed media and plainly offer significant opportunities for ironic contrasts. One memorable composite in *Sunrise: A Song of Two Humans* (F.W. Murnau, 1927) exploits this potential to striking effect. The two protagonists of this expressionistic melodrama— a married couple known only as 'Man' (George O'Brien) and 'Woman' (Janet Gaynor)—are managing to rebuild trust and love in their relationship following a harrowing event: the man having been tempted to the brink of drowning his wife on the advice of the treacherous 'Woman from the City' (Margaret Livingston), with whom he was having an affair. At one point during the husband and wife's tentative reconciliation, we follow the Man and Woman from behind as they walk across a busy city street, his arm enfolded round her. As they continue to walk, the backdrop of the surrounding buildings and roads begins to fade away, and in their place emerges into view a new background: a soft-focus image of a beautiful natural scene depicting a gentle, grassy slope covered in scores of flowers and framed by hanging willows. For a few moments the Man and Woman continue to appear to walk towards this idyllic vision, seemingly able to see it, basking in its verdant beauty; eventually they embrace in a passionate kiss. Now, however, the pastoral image fades, only to reveal behind it again the sights of the city—specifically: a traffic jam caused by the couple having wandered blindly out into the middle of a road while distracted by their shared daydream. Numerous disgruntled motorists yell and gesture angrily at the pair as the husband and wife embarrassedly flee the melee.

One effect of this moment is its dramatic irony: clearly, gentle fun is being had at the expense of our earnest couple's love-blinded reverie. Another, though, is ironic pretence, which is created via the satiric tone that is retrospectively cast upon the clichéd romantic imagery, as well as upon the very device of the process-shot itself. Indeed, this stylistic flourish offers in part a virtual parody of a visual convention that the preceding film has already established. Earlier, the 'Woman from the City' had tried to convince the Man to run away with her to the metropolis—her words at this moment becoming illustrated by a similarly handled composite image, which caused a vista of alluring neon lights and buildings to hover in front of the adulterous pair. The later composite thus gains a crucial part of its significance by repeating and inverting a convention to which the film has by this point accustomed us, but now with an ironic tone.

As in the case of many of the examples of film sound considered earlier, what makes the ironies of this moment possible is that different aspects of *Sunrise*'s address are being associated with different perspectives—in this case, the two different backdrops achieved through the process shot. Also, as for most of the sound examples, by juxtaposing these two per-spectives, the film uses one to undercut the other. It is this which permits our ironic distance from the film's characters and, thus, the moment's dramatic irony: the romantic view characterising the couple's perspective is withdrawn as easily as it initially materialised, emphasising its illusory nature and our protagonists' clouded vision. Yet it is important that the clichéd imagery also momentarily clouds *our* vision, briefly misleading us as to the tone with which the film is offering it. This is what allows the ironic pretence: *Sunrise* effectively pretends to employ the convention in earnest, only to reveal that it was really being offered ironically. I suggest that editing in film can also be used to generate both these kinds of ironic effects and that varying the timing or tonal handling of cuts is equally capable of signalling a film's ironic distance from characters, from stylistic conventions, or indeed from both at once.

It may be worth beginning our discussion of irony in editing with an extreme example in order to establish a context for more familiar uses. The genre of filmmaking that perhaps makes editing more crucial to its effects than any other is the 'found footage' or 'collage' film. I say this because the practical labour involved in making this type of film consists almost entirely of editing (plus sourcing, and possibly scoring or titling): a film is assembled by cutting together portions of other audiovisual material, with no original footage being shot. Given that this practice inevitably involves appropriation, it is unsurprising that irony is a relatively privileged term in discussions of such cinema; Sitney, for example, even goes so far as to refer to 'the natural irony of the collage film' (2002: 298). It is certainly true, at least, that such films can frequently exploit the 'connective' properties of editing to ironic effect.

At one point in Bruce Conner's short collage film *A Movie* (1958), for example, we are presented with two sequential shots: from a sailor onboard a submarine operating a periscope, we cut to an image of a young woman lounging on a bed in her underwear, posed with her left arm behind her head, looking seductively down the camera lens. An unlikely continuity thus suggested between the woman and what the sailor sees, we now cut to a different sailor also looking through a periscope, who calls out excitedly; we cut from this to a close-up of a hand squeezing a trigger, from that to an underwater shot of a torpedo being launched, and from this to a gigantic explosion seen expanding from a distance across a tranquil sea. The impossibility of these implied continuities lies, clearly, not merely in their diegetic improbability but in the fact that they do not seek to add up to a coherent diegetic world at all. Instead, these images have been assembled from a variety of sources: some (we are likely to presume, rightly) from documentary film reels, some from 'stag' movies, and so on. This has the effect of making this short sequence amount not simply to a surreal sexual joke but rather an ironic commentary on common conventions of cinematic editing themselves—as well as perhaps on (what the film appears to imply are) some of the characteristic clichés and pleasures of mainstream moviemaking. We seem entitled to say that the film here pretends to present us with a series of events connected by 'continuity editing', when it is instead using our familiarity with that convention to parody and satirise it.[16]

Sitney argues that irony is inherent to collage filmmaking because this form 'calls attention to the fact that each element…was once a part of another whole, thereby underlining its status as a piece of film,' which creates 'a distance between the image depicted and our experience of it' (ibid.: 298). Whether one agrees that this distance should always be defined as producing irony exactly, it is absolutely true that irony—and specifically ironic pretence—is one possible result of the kind of distance this approach to editing characteristically provokes. Yet it is by no means only through avant-garde cutting practices such as these that editing may help create ironic distance in general, nor ironic pretence in particular.

It seems reasonable to presume, in fact, that *any* style of editing is theoretically capable of contributing to ironic pretence—even perhaps the most familiar cutting technique of all: shot/reverse-shot continuity editing.[17] About a third of the way into *Happiness* (Todd Solondz, 1998) one of this film's lead characters, Bill (Dylan Baker), is cheering on his son from the sidelines of a Little League baseball game. While doing so, he notices one of his son's teammates, 11-year-old Johnny (Evan Silverberg), stepping up to bat. Bill currently seems to those around him to be an upstanding if unremarkable member of his suburban New Jersey community; we, however, know him to be a paedophile—a fact that was revealed to us in an earlier scene which showed him furtively masturbating in his car to images of pre-teen boys in a kids' magazine. Upon spying Johnny, Bill performs a double-take, following which his eyes remain glued to this child. He slowly moves towards and rests one hand on a nearby fence, this gesture combining with his dumbstruck expression (as well as with the lush romantic strings and flutes that have been brought in on the soundtrack) to dramatise his longing. We now cut back and forth between shots of Bill's face and reverse shots of an oblivious Johnny that suggest (while not precisely recreating) the former's desiring gaze; each time we return to Bill we have moved in slightly closer to him. Given the conventions of staging, shooting, scoring—but especially editing—employed here, one storytelling function of the moment is clear: Bill has seemingly fallen in 'love' at first sight with Johnny.

Happiness here thus employs an extremely conventional editing pattern to extremely unconventional, disturbing—and, I suggest, ironic—effect.[18] Used in combination with one character gazing towards another in this way, wordless shot/reverse-shot cutting between the faces of two parties has traditionally been associated not only with conveying but also inviting our investment in a protagonist's blossoming romantic feelings. Since this film is not truly encouraging us to invest emotionally in or sympathise with Bill's 'romantic' feelings, for *Happiness* to use this editing convention here constitutes an act of pretence. The narration pretends to try to elicit the responses commonly associated with this technique, when in fact we are being invited to register the use of the convention with irony, as well as perhaps with shock, or even revulsion. This moment thus serves as an especially stark reminder that the most familiar stylistic devices may create wildly different effects depending on the tone with which they are employed. And, as Pye argues, even 'angle/reverse angle cutting...*may* be a mechanical response to the problem of how to film the scene, or [it might be] a highly self-conscious strategy'—one which can, indeed, 'take on ironic force' (1989: 48).

While it is likely to be true that editing strategies of all kinds may be put in the service of ironic pretence, they are perhaps more commonly used in fiction filmmaking to create dramatic irony. 'Whatever else it may do,' writes Gilberto Perez, 'editing enables showing' (1998: 57). When put in the service of dramatic irony, editing will show us aspects of the fictional world to highlight an ironic state of affairs or pointedly reveal a character's limited perspective. Cutting might grant us such an ironic point of view by innumerable means. One possible approach, for instance, would be to present us with sustained, back-and-forth contrasts between two or more viewpoints on an unfolding story. Variously termed *crosscutting*, *intercutting*, or *parallel editing* (often depending on the temporal relationships implied), all such techniques can be used to create dramatic irony and have long been employed to this effect.

In the Keystone-Mutual short *Hide and Seek* (George Nichols, 1913), a mother who is visiting a bank believes that her young girl has become accidentally locked in its vault. In fact, however, we know her daughter to have merely wandered off and out of the building. While an increasingly hysterical group of family members, bank staff, and (eventually) firemen try frantically to break into the vault, we keep cutting away to see the little girl enjoying a series of perfectly pleasant experiences elsewhere: in one shot she finds a dog, in another she is shown playing in some sand, and so on. Each cut away from the bank only increases the potential for laughter upon returning to the gaggle of cartoonish characters trying progressively more desperate measures to open the door. As is true of dramatic irony generally, however, the same basic editing principle may create a range of effects—from low comedy of this kind to high tragedy. D.W. Griffith's eleven-minute melodrama *Lines of White on a Sullen Sea* (1909), for instance, creates a very tonally different kind of dramatic irony through fundamentally similar stylistic means. Bill (James Kirkwood), a fisherman, has promised to marry Emily (Linda Arvidson) when he returns from his upcoming voyage. However, upon reaching a foreign port, he has met, fallen for, and married another young woman (Marion Leonard). While the naïvely trusting Emma waits for Bill's return, we cut several times between Bill's carryings-on abroad and her hopeful performances of steadfastness (and declining health) back home. Just as in the comic iteration, the superior perspective afforded by the editing heightens our awareness of a character's comparative blindness, but the irony here is made to feel not fun or light but poignant, even cruel. Both examples nonetheless demonstrate that establishing sustained juxtapositions represents one way in which cutting can be useful to the creation of dramatic irony in film (Gunning 1991: 234–235).

Another possibility of editing—used less frequently than many, but hardly aberrant—is to cut, just once or twice, both away from and then back to an unfolding scene. Used ironically, what that cut-away reveals can function to contextualise pointedly facts about the scene that is in progress. Consider, for example, a moment in the romantic comedy *Puccini for Beginners* (Maria Maggenti, 2007). Allegra (Elizabeth Reaser), who defines herself as a lesbian, has surprised herself by having slept with a man for the first time in years and is now in bed discussing with him (Phillip, played by Justin Kirk) the differences between gay and straight relationships. She expresses surprise that Phillip has not yet proposed to the woman he is in a long-term relationship with, going on to offer the generalisation that, for straight couples, 'it's always the long-suffering woman who wants to do it, and the man who can't make the commitment—it's always the woman who wants the "Big Day" in her life'. Attempting to express annoyance calmly, Phillip shoots back, 'That's the most ridiculous, crass generalisation I've ever heard: that's completely and utterly specious.' From a close-up on his dismissive face, however, we now cut to a scene set some time previously. Phillip sits in a restaurant with his inquiring girlfriend, Grace (Gretchen Mol), who is seemingly initiating precisely this kind of conversation: 'So what about *us*, Phillip?' Grace demands, 'What are our plans? We've been together *six years…*' When, seconds later, we jump back to Phillip and Allegra in bed, Phillip now attempts to deflect the accusation: 'Right—*your* relationships are completely different: no pressure, no communication problems, no acting out, right?' 'Completely, are you *kidding* me!' Allegra answers with a self-satisfied smile, 'Lesbian relationships are *totally* different.' Yet as we stay close on her face, the established editing pattern now repeats: we cut into the midst of a fractious moment from Allegra's recent past, in which she is in the process of being dumped by her ex, Samantha (Julianne Nicholson): 'Just listen to that word—"*commit*"!' Allegra is yelling: 'That's what you do when you go to an insane asylum: they *commit* you!' 'Commitment', counters Samantha loudly, 'is the end of high romance and the beginning of day-to-day *closeness*…!' Cutting here thus intervenes to offer us privileged perspectives on the fictional world—the effect of which, within this pattern of shots, is to ironise these characters' hypocrises.

Probably rather more conventional than cut-aways of this kind, though, is for films to create comparable effects simply through when and how they choose to cut from one scene to the next. As Tom Brown observes, a film may create irony by 'the way it conjoins…scenes or characters in order to articulate a point to the audience about the actions in those scenes or of those characters' (2012: 172). One scene in *Annie Hall* (Woody Allen,

1977), for instance, ends with Alvy (Allen) defending himself against the accusation that he considers his girlfriend Annie (Diane Keaton) his intellectual inferior: 'Why?' he asks her defensively, 'Because I encourage you to take adult education courses? I think it's a wonderful thing! You meet wonderful, interesting professors...'. Immediately following Alvy's delivery of this line, we cut to a scene set some considerable time later, in which Alvy is revealed (in long shot) berating Annie outside of the college at which she is now enrolled: 'Adult education is such junk!' he protests vehemently, using a similar hand gesture. 'The professors are so phony! How can you do it?!' (Figs. 3.3 and 3.4). The rhetorical point of the edit is clear: adult education remains a 'wonderful thing' for Alvy so long as his holding this view mitigates a criticism being levelled at him; but it may become 'junk' in the blink of an eye when expressing this contrary assessment will help him justify a different argument (we soon learn he now wants Annie to quit the course because he believes one of her professors to be a rival for Annie's affections). This cut thus elegantly ironises Alvy by creating a concise cross-scene dramatisation of self-serving duplicity.

It is important to acknowledge at this point that it does indeed seem appropriate to describe a stylistic gesture such as this edit from *Annie Hall* as actually *creating* dramatic irony. We might imagine an alternative handling of this (relatively minor) plotline, wherein Alvy's opposing estimations of the value of Annie's studies were contrasted not by a sharp cut but separated from one another by numerous intervening scenes.

Fig. 3.3 *Annie Hall*: Alvy praises adult education

Fig. 3.4 *Annie Hall*: Alvy denounces adult education

While such an approach would still certainly ensure that we were granted the chance to register Alvy's self-contradiction, it would, first of all, assuredly decrease the emphasis granted it. In addition, I suggest that we would also lose the sense of the dramatic material having been assembled in just this way for specifically ironic purposes. We might say this about the aforementioned moment from *Puccini for Beginners*, too. Even without the cutaways, it is clear that the basic fact of these characters' duplicities would still exist within the story's world: by this point we already know, for instance, that Allegra's relationship with Samantha was very far from being free from 'communication problems', 'acting out', and so on. However, I suggest that it is only the editing that transforms Allegra's claim about the nature of her relationships from a dramatically revealing white lie, which we might discern, into an irony that we sense the film creating and inviting us to register as such. And indeed, something comparable is likely to be the case for most effects that we wish to call dramatically ironic. Recognising that a film is adopting an ironic perspective towards characters usually amounts to sensing our attention being directed towards certain ironic facts about their actions or about the fictional world. This, incidentally, is as true for other aspects of style as for editing: the use of music examined in *Halloween*, say, or the combination of voice-over and images in *Election*. Both these moments present or mediate the fictional world in such a way that we are granted perspectives that effectively confirm (*Halloween*) or reveal to us (*Election*) ironically telling facts about characters' fates or actions.[19] In this sense, the connective properties of editing merely offer film a particular range of expressive possibilities for creating the sorts of superior points of view necessary for dramatic irony in general.

We should keep this in mind while considering another technique. An additional ironic possibility of cutting plainly lies in its ability to create instant contrasts *within* a scene. Often, this might consist of juxtaposing what happens in one shot against a subsequent shot that serves to contextualise it in an ironic fashion. An example of this can be found in Todd Haynes' 1950s-set, Sirk-inspired romantic melodrama *Far from Heaven* (Todd Haynes, 2002). At a cocktail party taking place in the home of Cathy and Frank Whittaker (Julianne Moore and Dennis Quaid)—pillars of their suburban Connecticut community—a cluster of guests are discussing the issue of contemporary race relations in the United States. One male guest haughtily dismisses the possibility that Connecticut could ever experience serious racial unrest because, in this state, 'there are *no negroes!*' Following this line—and as the assembled group chuckle at the observation—we cut to a shot that tilts up from a plate of hors d'oeuvres to reveal, in a medium in-profile close-up, a nearby African American waiter, stooping slightly as he proffers canapés around the crowd (plus two more African American caterers, visible in the background). This waiter is not shown reacting obviously to the comment, but both the balance of the sound design (we hear the resulting laughter still rippling away off screen) and a slight severity in his expression suggest that he would have heard it. Again, the film has actually already furnished us with enough knowledge to distrust the truth of the guest's statement even without this stark edit: by this point the existence of African Americans within this town has been firmly established, partly via Cathy and Frank's maid Sybil (Viola Davis), but also through the still more prominent character of Raymond (Dennis Haysbert), their gardener. With the addition of the cut, though, the rhetorical weight accorded the pronouncement's spuriousness is increased several degrees—the film immediately thrusting into the foreground of our visual perspective all the evidence required to emphasise this character's comparative ignorance. It is therefore the edit that causes the line to be positioned not merely as dubious or deplorable, but as ironic.

The last example I wish to consider seems to me to find ways, once more, of actually blurring the lines between dramatic irony and ironic pretence. In *Clueless* (Amy Heckerling, 1995), a rich Los Angeles high school student named Cher (Alicia Silverstone) is lamenting some bad grades she has received. We move in closer to her distressed face as she looks heavenwards for inspiration, Cher telling us in voice-over that 'I felt impotent and out of control, which I *really* hate. I needed to find sanctuary in a place where I could gather my thoughts and regain my strength...'. At this point, we cut with a brief triumphant fanfare of strings and brass to an establishing shot of the rather grand Westside Pavilion—a popular mall in Los Angeles—and then to Cher and her friend Dionne (Stacey Dash) departing a store counter, several designer shopping bags hanging off their arms. Unlike the transition from *Annie Hall* considered earlier, editing here does not quite reveal a character to be contradicting him- or herself; rather, it surprises us by revealing the site of Cher's sanctuary and contemplation to be (what we are encouraged to feel is) an unlikely candidate for such a reverent description. The cut is thus dramatically ironic in the sense that it distances us comically from Cher's perspective: we are invited to understand that this connection is intended by the film as humorously incongruous, whereas Cher considers making this link between hallowed language and retail therapy entirely reasonable. Yet there nonetheless also appears to be a kind of ironic pretence at play here. Especially when accompanied by the quick blast of celebratory music, the cut creates a sense of acting as a flourish—the edit giving the impression that the film is pretending to take seriously Cher's attitude towards the mall as a restorative sanctuary. The movie associates the sanctified description with the mall in a parody of the spirit with which Cher associates these things, with the new shot being offered to us as if it represented the logical fulfilment of Cher's hyperbolic words, rather than something like their antithesis. Just as for other elements of film expression, it thus seems that, in the case of editing too, dramatic irony and ironic pretence need not be mutually exclusive.

As I have noted—and as in the case of sound-/image-track relationships—the ability of editing to combine two or more elements of a film together seems automatically to grant this aspect of the medium great ironic potential. These filmmaking devices may indeed frequently demonstrate particularly plainly the fact that 'the cinema offers synergistic possibilities of disunity and disjunction' (Stam 2005: 20). Yet it is by no means only such ostentatiously 'connective' (Orpen 2003: 1) properties of film that may contribute to ironic effects in this medium.

IRONY AND MISE-EN-SCÈNE

Mise-en-scène has frequently, famously, served as an extraordinarily elastic term when applied to cinema. The question of which aspects of the film-maker's craft it can reasonably be said to describe is still a matter of considerable debate.[20] Robin Wood offers one especially inclusive definition of the concept:

> A director is about to make a film. He [*sic*] has before him a script, camera, lights, décor, actors. What he does with them is mise-en-scène....The director's business is to get the actors (with their co-operation and advice) to move, speak, gesture, register expressions in a certain manner, with certain inflections, at a certain tempo....It is his business to place the actors significantly within the décor, so that the décor itself becomes an actor; with the advice and co-operation of a cameraman [*sic*], to compose and frame the shots; regulate the tempo of rhythm and movement within the frame and of the movement of the camera; to determine the lighting of the scene.... The movement of the film from shot to shot, the relation of one shot to all the other shots already taken or not, which will make up the finished film, cutting, montage, all this is mise-en-scène....And still more....The tone and atmosphere of the film, visual metaphor, the establishment of relationships between characters, the relation of all parts to the whole: all this is mise-en-scène.' (1961: 9–11)

As suggested by the fact that this chapter has already discussed editing, unlike Wood, I am choosing to consider this aspect of filmmaking apart from mise-en-scène. Equally, that I have previously discussed sound indicates that I am engaging here primarily with the term's visual connotations; I will soon also be devoting other sections to the camera and performance. These choices are not intended to amount to an implicit, restrictive definition of 'mise-en-scène'. Rather, I have elected to dedicate a discrete section to mise-en-scène in order to give attention to certain expressive properties that are most fruitfully thought of in relation to this concept before any other. I suggest that—no less than editing or sound—these properties can be made vital to both ironic pretence and dramatic irony in film.

'If we ever need a decent, English translation for mise-en-scène', Adrian Martin argues, 'staging is not bad' (2014: 15). Staging does indeed, at least, capture much of what I shall be considering in this particular section: costume, lighting, blocking, props, décor, and so on.[21] As well as being able to help create dramatic irony—and thus being relevant to a consideration of point of view (more on this shortly)—all these elements of mise-en-scène can also, as Wood suggests, contribute significantly to a film's tone. As Pye notes:

> Tone seems intuitively to belong to the 'how' of any discourse, the manner in which a story is told or an experience related, yet in analysis it rapidly becomes evident that the distinction between 'how' and 'what' is unsustainable. The choice of subject matter and all the specific decisions taken in creating every aspect of the fictional world, its characters and events, inevitably have effects on...tone. (2007: 29)

One way in which the creation of the fictional world itself may affect tone is by helping us to register that a film is engaging in ironic pretence. This is to say, in part, that mise-en-scène can play a fundamental role in a film establishing a distanced tone towards its own generic, narrative, or stylistic conventions.

As so often, it is in examples of film parody that we are likely to see this kind of irony demonstrated most unambiguously. For instance, the ending of *Play it Again, Sam* (Herbert Ross, 1972) is concerned to imitate ironically the climactic scene of *Casablanca* (Michael Curtiz, 1942). As Wes Gehring suggests of the sequence, 'both the situation (romantic triangle preparing for airport farewell) and the mis-en-scène (incoming fog and the separate starting of the plane's engines)...recreate *Casablanca*' (1999: 121). However, this being a parodic moment, the mise-en-scène of Ross' film does not merely recreate that of Curtiz's but rather *exaggerates* it for comic effect. Diane Keaton's canvas fedora-style hat, for example, is not a replica of the one worn by Ingrid Bergman but instead features a brim that is several degrees larger and droopier—both these qualities also heightening the clash between the film's early-1970s setting and the fashions of the period evoked via the parody. Equally, the fog in this scene is significantly thicker than that seen in *Casablanca*'s conclusion, also rolling in more suddenly and intervening more ostentatiously between the actors and the camera. The imitative qualities of these features of mise-en-scène thus help specify the target of the parody, while their amplification indicates the ironic distance at which they are being held. Yet it is not only by parodying specific movies that mise-en-scène can help a film establish an ironic distance from its conventions.

At one point in *Blue Velvet* (David Lynch, 1986), Jeffrey (Kyle MacLachlan), a college student, meets one of his small-town neighbours. Having been dismissed from the home of a detective who is handling a criminal case Jeffrey brought to the police's attention, Jeffrey walks down the policeman's drive into the nighttime streets. When he reaches the end of the path, he hears a female voice call to him from the shadows. As Jeffrey looks in the voice's direction, we cut to a shot consisting initially of total darkness, remaining on this undifferentiated blackness for several seconds. Already, this utter lack of light feels distinctly odd since the previous shot established several dim but definite light sources in this location. Eventually, out of the darkness emerges Sandy (Laura Dern), the detective's daughter. She moves slowly, slightly too slowly, into a medium shot; as she does, and accompanied by suddenly swelling romantic strings, she is gradually illuminated by a very precisely placed light—seeming almost to be a spotlight—which means that only she, and none of her impenetrably black surrounds, is lit, and lit brilliantly (Fig. 3.5). She is wearing a distinctly old-fashioned bright pink dress that appears (like her hairstyle) to belong to the 1950s rather than the contemporary 1980s. Together, these decisions concerning costume, lighting, and blocking create a sense that this moment is intentionally exaggerating to the point of strangeness the convention of the introduction of the 'girl next door' or 'good girl' character, readily associated in the popular imagination with (among other things) *films noirs*. Specifically, the scene seems almost to literalise what is more often a metaphorical suggestion: that such a character's 'innocence' might set her starkly apart from the plot's darker machinations.

Quite *how* ironically we should take a moment like this, and Lynch more generally, is open for debate,[22] but to consider it entirely *un*ironic

Fig. 3.5 *Blue Velvet*: Sandy spot-lit in the darkness

seems unfeasible. Ever since it plunged us into insect-infested depths beneath a white-picket-fenced small-town lawn in its first sequence, *Blue Velvet* has announced its concern with both presenting and disrupting highly conventionalised images. In particular, numerous aspects of the film are unmistakably interested in imitating, mixing, juxtaposing, and subverting materials associated with various popular American genres (Berry 1988). Much of this appropriation of familiar cultural imagery (and sounds) involves making the over-determinedly 'wholesome' feel uncanny by giving it, as Laura Mulvey puts it, 'the immaterial...quality of a cliché which speaks of appearance and nothing else'—a strategy she describes as 'almost comic' in effect (1996: 151). 'Almost' seems right, and parody would here be too blunt a word for the attitudes this moment strikes towards its conventions. Nonetheless, it seems accurate to describe this film as employing with a pointedly distanced tone a convention that other movies might use comparatively 'straight'. Furthermore, it is in large part *Blue Velvet*'s mise-en-scène that creates the impression that it is engaging in what we can reasonably call this act of ironic pretence.

Heightened moments such as those considered so far use an exaggerated mise-en-scène to help indicate a film's tonal distance from virtually every aspect of its address. Perhaps more common, though, is for mise-en-scène to assist in creating ironically exaggerated depictions of particular character-types or cultural milieus. The first scene of *Singin' in the Rain* (Gene Kelly and Stanley Donen, 1952), for instance, takes place outside a movie premiere at Grauman's Chinese Theatre in Los Angeles. A gushing radio show announcer (Madge Blake) is in full swing, describing for her listeners the arrival of 'every star in Hollywood's heaven' onto the red carpet. As a chauffeured limousine draws up, she excitedly reports that it contains 'that famous "zip" girl of the screen, the darling of the flapper set: Zelda Zanders!' Stepping from the car as these words finish, the young Zelda (Rita Moreno) is indeed likely to strike us as embodying a particularly pointed stereotype of an especially successful 1920s 'flapper': hair glamorously dolled up in tight red curls, wearing a black straight-cut dress, white fur wrap, silver headband, silver high heels, and so on. She also seems nearly impossibly vivacious, playing enthusiastically to the assembled crowds by opening her mouth widely in an ecstatic grin one moment, quickly affecting demure over-the-shoulder glances the next. The announcer goes on to explain that Zelda is accompanied by 'her new red-hot pash: J. Cumberland Spendrill III—that well-known eligible bachelor'. As this description is spoken, we get a good look at Zelda's date: a man seemingly at least in his late seventies, with white hair and moustache, decked out in top hat and impeccably conservative evening-wear. Now walking stiffly down the carpet towards us next to the relentlessly bobbing Zelda, he looks far more like her grandfather than a man who might be the object of her 'red hot' passion. As they pause for a gaggle of photographers—the flashes of their cameras apparently somewhat disorienting the decrepit Spendrill (Stuart Holmes)—the announcer informs her audience with a smile that 'Zelda's had so much unhappiness, I hope this time it's really love...'.

Numerous aspects of mise-en-scène combine to create irony here. First there is the flat contradiction between the way Zelda's new beau is described (thus, how he might be imagined by a radio audience) and what we see of him, which is due to various elements of performance, costuming, and staging. Second, there is the way this pair's appearance prepares us (though not, it seems, other characters) to take as ironic the announcer's incredibly optimistic hope that—Zelda having experienced much 'unhappiness' (hinting at former Spendrill-like figures in her life)—'this time it's really love'. Finally, there is the considerable sense of exaggeration that permeates the moment. This is created not just by the absurdly on-the-nose nature of the couple's names (the doubled-zeds of Zelda's name over-egging her effervescent bubbliness, '*Spendrill*' unambiguously spelling out what makes him 'eligible'), but also by how immediately and utterly—virtually parodically—they must visually embody their familiar character types in order for this gag to work in the time allotted it. Within approximately twenty seconds, these excessive visual embodiments of various cultural clichés prepare us for the affectionately satirical ironic tone with which *Singin' in the Rain* will treat many (though not all) aspects of the 1920s Hollywood it depicts.[23]

One kind of irony that mise-en-scène can help create, then, often depends upon excess and exaggeration. Encountering such pointed visual hyperbole within a film's mise-en-scène is frequently key in alerting us to the possibility that certain conventional materials are being treated with an ironic tone—be that generically familiar plot beats (e.g. *Blue Velvet*) or particular cultural stereotypes (e.g. *Singin' in the Rain*). To the extent that such approaches indicate a film using particular representational conventions ironically, we might define them as constituting different forms of ironic pretence.[24] As I have already suggested, however, mise-en-scène can be equally helpful in the creation of dramatic irony.

Robert Stam suggests that 'every film track and procedure…can convey a point of view': not only the visual or aural perspectives we are granted on the fictional world, but also all the elements that make up that world in the first instance, including 'performance, mise-en-scène', and so on (2005: 39). Just as a film's mise-en-scène may contribute to the creation of its tone, then, we also frequently become aware that it is 'touching on potentially complex patterns of point of view' (Gibbs 2002: 51). The particular points of view that it helps create can, moreover, grant us the kinds of superior perspectives on characters' actions and behaviour characteristic of dramatic irony. The aspects of mise-en-scène that films may use to such ends are potentially limitless, but I will focus here on three in particular: props, blocking, and décor.

Gibbs offers one useful definition of mise-en-scène as 'the contents of the frame and the way that they are organised' (2002: 5). In a live-action film, one type of contents that a frame will usually contain is props, and the ways in which they are organised may well stress for us pivotal facts of which characters are presently unaware. In *The Clock* (Vincente Minnelli, 1945), New York secretary Alice (Judy Garland) has enjoyed a brief flirtation with Joe (Robert Walker), a G.I. on two-day leave, whom she met earlier today at Grand Central Station. They have thus far spent a pleasant few hours together, visiting Central Park Zoo and the Metropolitan Museum of Art, and Joe has shown his appreciation by gifting Alice his lighter. He has asked Alice to see him again later that day, and, despite initially declining due to a planned date, Joe has managed to persuade her to meet him that evening. When Alice arrives home at her apartment, though, her mind is changed about the rendezvous by her streetwise roommate Helen (Ruth Brady). Helen advises Alice against letting herself be 'picked up' by a soldier, and Alice ultimately agrees that she cannot in good conscience keep the appointment. Left alone, Alice now receives a call from the man with whom she had originally planned a date for this evening, Freddy. She is sat in an armchair and filmed initially in a medium shot that allows both her arms to remain in frame. As she picks up the receiver, we notice that Alice holds in her right hand the lighter Joe gave her earlier that day. She balances the arm with the lighter at a right angle from the chair arm on which her elbow rests, holding the phone to her ear with her other hand. Before she even asks, 'Hello?', Alice has flicked the lighter on, with both the resulting flame and the sound of the flint drawing our attention to the prop. She then proceeds to extinguish and reignite the flame six times as she finalises the arrangements for her date with

Freddy—'I'm almost ready,' she says, 'What time...?'—until the screen fades out. We lose sight of the lighter itself after the second time it is lit, the camera pushing in so that we can see only the bottom of the thumb that flicks it off and on; the repeated noises made by its flint, though, are kept loud enough for its presence in the scene to be continually reasserted. The dramatic irony this prop helps create depends in part (again) on our knowledge of generic convention: this is a romance, a fact making it more than likely that Alice is going to form a relationship with the man who we have seen give her this quasi-romantic gift—as opposed to with Freddy, whom we have never even met. It also depends on our sense that Alice's repeated action seems quite unconscious, an absent-minded fiddling: she never looks at the lighter, keeping the hand holding it at some distance from the rest of her body, while she continues making plans to see this boy who (we are now likely to be certain) she will soon cast aside.

As well as concerning inanimate objects, mise-en-scène also encompasses 'the precise placement of actors...before the camera in various spatial, pictorial and rhythmic combinations' (Hodsdon 1992: 74). Given this, a key component of mise-en-scène is blocking: the positioning of performers relative to their surroundings (and the camera). This area of decision-making, too, can be used to dramatically ironic effect. In *Back to the Future* (Robert Zemeckis, 1985), Marty McFly (Michael J. Fox) has accidentally travelled back in time to 1955. Soon after his arrival in this period he visits a café and tries to calm his nerves. Throughout a shot/reverse-shot exchange with the grouchy Lou (Norman Alden), who runs the establishment, over-the-shoulder shots of Marty from Lou's side of the café's counter have been framed so that Lou's back and head take up virtually the whole right-hand side of the image; this has the effect of obscuring from view a figure who is sitting next to Marty on an adjacent stool. While Marty and Lou's conversation reaches its end, Marty slouches forward over the counter, placing his right hand to the back of his head in a worried posture; as he does so, Lou vacates the right side of the frame, revealing the man who is sitting beside Marty. Marty and this previously unseen figure are now framed in a symmetrical two shot. Two things are striking about this: first, this man's body is currently formed into the same posture as Marty's—slouched, right hand raised to the back of his skull; second, this man is played by Crispin Glover, whom we have previously seen portraying Marty's father in the earlier present-day portions of the film. We remain on this balanced arrangement for a few seconds, with neither character being aware of the other, before hearing the sound of the café door being pushed open and an exasperated voice saying, 'Hey, McFly...'. Hearing the voice, both Marty and the man beside him turn around simultaneously and at precisely the same pace, with Glover's left arm now also assuming a position very like that of Fox's, making their echo of one another even more complete. During the course of what follows—as the new arrival (Biff, Thomas F. Wilson) begins addressing not Marty but the stranger next to him—Marty comes to realise what will already doubtless be clear to us: that this man is a youthful George McFly, Marty's dad. The reason we are entitled to feel the film has already informed us of this is due partly, of course, to Glover. It is due also, though, to the particulars of staging and blocking, which have drawn our attention emphatically to the correspondences between the two figures, of which Marty has remained ignorant.

The final aspect of mise-en-scène I will consider here is décor. Specifically, I turn to how a moment in *The Best Years of Our Lives* (William Wyler, 1946) exploits an element of décor in the apartment of the uneasily married Fred (Dana Andrews) and Marie (Virginia Mayo). This scene, which will dramatise the explosive conclusion of this couple's perennially troubled marriage, begins on the profile of a man we have not met before; we soon learn his name is Cliff Scully (Steve Cochran) and that he is here for a tryst with Marie. Cliff is chewing gum and inspecting with a blank expression a framed portrait of Fred and Marie that hangs in the couple's living room. We saw this portrait several times in the background during previous scenes, but this is the first time we have been allowed to inspect it up close. The picture is clearly the work of a commercial photographer: well-lit, somewhat stiffly posed against a blank backdrop, it projects a flatteringly happy image of a smiling Fred and Marie. This professionally staged image of just-married bliss will reappear in the background many times throughout the rest of this scene, in which Fred arrives home sooner than Marie had predicted. When Fred first enters the room, the portrait hangs almost precisely half-way between him and Cliff as Fred stiffens at the sight of Marie's guest, and Cliff utters a cocksure 'How do you do?' Having cut a few seconds later to a closer three shot in which Marie attempts to smooth over the situation, the picture is re-revealed from behind Cliff as he gets ushered to one side by Marie with instructions to wait downstairs; when he then pauses on the right of the frame to put on his jacket, the portrait is again made to occupy a spot between him and Fred, as well as now Marie (Fig. 3.6). This aspect of the set design assumes perhaps its most fully ironic function, however, after

Fig. 3.6 *The Best Years of Our Lives*: Fred, Marie, and Cliff flanked by the wedding portrait

Cliff has exited, and Fred and Marie are left by themselves to thrash out what this discovery means for their marriage. After Marie announces her intention to file for divorce, Fred begins hastily preparing a suitcase to leave. The portrait hovers, unostentatiously but perpetually, in the background throughout the couple's final, bitter exchange, which is concluded by Marie's especially barbed parting riposte to Fred's announcement that he intends to leave town: 'That's a good idea', she says dryly as she heads out the door, 'You'll get a good job someplace else—there are *drugstores* everywhere...'. Set against a scene depicting this marriage's breakdown, the glamorous image of posed post-nuptial happiness serves as a visual counterpoint that is to some extent wistful; but, perhaps more significantly, its stubborn presence feels also somewhat mocking, especially in combination with Marie's own facetious and ironic tone upon leaving. It is almost as if we are finally invited to view the portrait with something approaching the same sceptical, ruefully amused—if not jaundiced—attitude with which the gum-chewing Cliff surely regarded it at the scene's opening.

We have thus seen that various aspects of mise-en-scène—specifically those that we might place under the general bracket of staging—are able to assist in creating both ironic pretence and dramatic irony of several kinds. I have not, however, yet dwelt upon one crucial fact about mise-en-scène: that, as Martin puts it, 'everything that is designed, staged, lit, dressed and so forth, is done with a particular vantage point, a particular angle—or rather, a concatenation of various perspectives and angles—in mind' (2014: 14). This naturally brings us, then, to the ironic capacities of the camera.

IRONY AND THE CAMERA

In addition to demonstrating the ironic potential of décor, the previously described scene from *The Best Years of Our Lives* also makes especially clear the necessary interrelationship between the ironic significance accorded any individual aspect of mise-en-scène and the ironic contributions of the camera. Since our attention has been drawn forcefully to Fred and Marie's portrait at the scene's opening, we are certainly more primed than we might otherwise be to register its presence in the background throughout what follows. However, it is also clearly and carefully (though not obtrusively) highlighted within shots. As Fred first enters the room, for example, the camera is positioned such that the door he opens concludes its swing just in front of the picture within the composition. As Fred then momentarily stands stock-still in the doorway, staring squarely at Cliff, Wyler and Toland's decision to maintain this (deep-focus) wide shot ensures that the portrait is placed directly in the centre of the diagonal eyeline established between the two men, occupying a middle ground in terms of height between Fred and Cliff. To acknowledge this is to acknowledge that no element of mise-en-scène can achieve ironic significance independently of its relationship to the camera.

Of all the subheadings offered by this chapter (perhaps even including 'mise-en-scène'), 'irony and the camera' is thus perhaps the most ostentatiously ludicrous in its attempt to designate a discrete topic. Very obviously, few ironies of any kind that are achieved in a live-action movie will fail to depend upon the camera for their very existence. Yet, just as obviously, the ironic potential of this foundational constituent of film style does seem to demand distinct consideration. I suggest that camerawork, like most dramatic and stylistic materials available to filmmakers, can be used (in combination with numerous other elements) to create both ironic pretence and dramatic irony. I will consider the former topic briefly before returning to the latter, which I believe will allow us to pose the most interesting questions about the ironic capacities of camerawork.

As in the case of sound, editing, and mise-en-scène, almost any act the camera can perform may appear ironic if undertaken with a distanced tone. Often, this will arise in combination with the use of a familiar stylistic convention. Again, parodies seem to be where are likely to find camera style being ironised most pervasively. In a meticulously precise parody like *Black Dynamite* (Scott Sanders, 2009), for example, virtually every camera placement and movement constitutes an ironic pretence on the part of the film that its narration might be participating sincerely in the visual style associated with 1970s blaxploitation filmmaking. Every crash-zoom into a face, every slow-motion shot of a character mid-fight, every shaky long shot during an action sequence—all represent the adoption of a generic visual convention with a high degree of ironic distance.

Beyond the realm of parody specifically, comedies in general—perhaps especially in the last few decades—quite frequently generate gags by using camera styles and effects in a manner that could easily be described in terms of ironic pretence. This will often involve the appropriation or 'misusing' of a stylistic convention traditionally associated with one genre or type of narrative event, incongruously applying it instead to a very different kind of generic or narrative moment. For a particularly clear-cut device, we could think of comic uses of the notorious 'dolly-zoom' effect, in which a camera's simultaneous zooming and tracking in or out unnervingly warps a shot's representation of space. A stylistic technique most conventionally associated with moments of drama, tension, and danger due to its famous uses in films like *Vertigo* (Alfred Hitchcock, 1958) and *Jaws* (Steven Spielberg, 1975), in *The Mask* (Chuck Russell, 1994) the effect is instead adopted to represent two sad-sack male bank tellers lustfully gawking at the appearance of Cameron Diaz's 'blonde bombshell' - its employment here both sending up the men's exaggerated ogling and the device itself. We could think equally of slow motion; in *Office Space* (Mike Judge, 1999), for instance, when a group of disgruntled corporate drones take out their frustrations on a perennially malfunctioning printer by smashing it to pieces with unbridled aggression and a baseball bat, their violent attack is depicted in a slow-motion style (and with a hip-hop soundtrack), which seems to grant their petty, minor rebellion the intensity and momentousness of a gangland murder. Or we might consider uses of handheld cameras; take, for example, *Wet Hot American Summer* (David Wain, 2001). This film's largely unobtrusive visual style undergoes a sudden, temporary shift during one sequence in which characters melodramatically and absurdly overplay their desperation while hunting through a building to find a telephone; as they scream histrionically, needlessly emptying out cupboards and smashing objects at random, the handheld camera's shaky movements mean that the ridiculous scene is treated as if it possessed the seriousness and high drama conventionally associated by other genres with the 'immediacy' of this style.

While not all occurring within parody movies, it might still be possible to describe all the aforementioned uses of visual style as constituting parodic moments in the films in which they appear. It is therefore also worth considering a use of the camera that still seems to represent an ironic pretence but that cannot be quite so easily explained as parody *per se*. Adrian Martin suggests that *Scarlet Street* (Fritz Lang, 1945) 'offers a veritable primer on the ways, means, forms and resonances of cinematic irony' (2011: 39). In the course of this argument, he refers to one arcing crane shot that descends from a high view of an outdoor café, past the leafy branches of a tree, towards a seated couple, Chris (Edward G. Robinson) and Kitty (Joan Bennett) (Fig. 3.7). Following a chance

Fig. 3.7 *Scarlet Street*: The camera cranes down towards the couple

encounter, Chris, a middle-aged cashier and middling amateur painter, is becoming increasingly infatuated with the younger Kitty. Kitty, by contrast, unbeknownst to Chris, is continuing to see him only in order to extort money from him on the advice of the man she really loves, her boyfriend and petty criminal Johnny (Dan Duryea). We have faded in on this shot after having faded out from a scene that saw Kitty and Johnny hatching the plan to pump Chris for money, which ended with Kitty writing Chris a letter to arrange their next meeting. The crane shot is, as Martin notes, 'atypically flamboyant' for the film, and—especially due to its accompanying score, which features 'a particularly florid arrangement of "My Melancholy Baby"'—it also seems self-conscious in its evocation of the conventional visual rhetoric of romance scenes (ibid.: 39). In its long, floating path down towards the outwardly content couple (and particularly as accompanied by this music), it already suggests a camera movement more usually used to introduce a lovers' meeting than a cynically clandestine shakedown. The shot is also careful to take in the tree, which (we soon learn) contains the birds whose twittering we can hear competing with the score on the soundtrack—thereby demonstrating the camera's concern to present us with clichéd romantic signifiers of nature. Also important is the complicity between the shot's movement and the dialogue that is to begin the scene, which itself relies on the very clichés that the style is invoking: as we draw close to the pair, who are now looking up at the tree, Chris comments, 'That robin sings just like I feel', continuing, 'Hey look, there's a pair of them up there—they're building their nest!' This camera movement can thus be described as pretending to adopt sincerely a visual style that brings to mind a number of conventionally romantic associations, when the film is in fact using those associations precisely to indicate its ironic distance from them.

What this crane shot also clearly does, however, is something that we have by now encountered repeatedly in relation to many aspects of film style: it combines ironic pretence with dramatic irony. The film adopts its ironic pretence, in part, to create a bitter 'register of mockery concerning Chris' romantic idealisation of Kitty' (Martin 2011: 39): he does not know, whereas we do, that romance clichés are entirely inappropriate to the real transactions at work in this scene. Before considering the relationship between dramatic irony and the camera more generally, though, it is necessary to make a few observations about some intrinsic properties of both.

As noted in the previous chapter, many critical discussions about films adopting ironic distance towards characters can be fundamentally understood as being about dramatic irony. John Gibbs, for instance, refers to this concept explicitly when he notes that a film's style may 'be used to establish forms of dramatic irony' if it 'provides a perception which is available only to the audience, who are privileged over the characters' (2002: 51). Similarly, though without using the term specifically, Thomas Elsaesser asserts that 'irony privileges the spectator, vis-à-vis the protagonists', by granting the audience 'a superior position' (1987: 66). Such characterisations clearly capture the key perspectival logic of dramatic irony; yet I suggest that they also demand an addendum in the case of film.

A novel, for example, can theoretically be told entirely through one character's words and, thus, from his or her exclusive perspective. A film, by contrast, will, for the vast majority of its running time, unavoidably provide us with multiple perspectives that remain unavailable to its characters. This is due to nothing less fundamental than the camera itself. Unless we are speaking of the very few films in which everything that appears on screen represents a character's optical point of view,[25] as Celestino Deleyto points out, 'the almost permanent external presence of the camera ensures a vantage point...which continually tends to dissociate itself from and supersede that of the...characters' (1991: 165). This does not mean, of course, that the camera somehow permanently creates dramatic irony. It *does*, however, mean that when we watch fiction films, our perspectives are almost perpetually 'privileged over the characters'. Given this fact, in order to speak of dramatic irony in relation to the camera, we must be speaking not only of our visual, spatial, or cognitive superiority over characters, but of particularly pointed kinds of superiority that the camera not only creates but also stresses.

One way in which the camera can not only grant us a superior perspective but actually make a point of that superiority is by ostentatiously detaching itself from characters entirely. A particularly radical example of this is found in the film *Cabin in the Woods* (Drew Goddard, 2012). Leaving aside a prologue set in a corporate-looking scientific facility whose relationship to the story is thus far unclear, the film begins with the familiar conceit of a group of young characters setting off for a weekend getaway in nature. Given not only the movie's title but also its credit sequence— which features foreboding music and decontextualised images of blood and carvings depicting ancient rituals—we are likely to feel that we are in the generic terrain of the horror movie. These generic expectations already (as in *Halloween*) create the potential for dramatic irony in the early portions of the movie, during which we watch our five carefree leads preparing for their trip and hitting the road in a camper van. The degree of irony created at their expense is heightened considerably, however, in one startling shot about a quarter of an hour into the film. It begins as a high-angled helicopter shot looking down on our protagonists' van heading along a winding mountain road and towards a rocky tunnel. As the van disappears into the tunnel, an eagle glides into frame, flying rightwards towards the mountain tunnel's exit, the camera now following its swooping trajectory. Soon, however, the bird collides spectacularly with what seems to be some previously undetectable force field that stretches across the screen. Apparently an electrical fence-like mesh of interlinking hexagonal shapes, this barrier becomes visible only upon the eagle's making contact with it, electrocuting the shrieking animal with a small explosion of buzzes and sparks. Visible but briefly, the force field fades from view almost precisely in time with the van emerging from the other side of the tunnel—stressing further our protagonists' blindness to the extraordinary sight to which we have been privileged. We may not yet know what exactly this strange phenomenon portends, but we certainly now know a great deal more about these characters' circumstances than do they (and might also begin to connect this mysterious technological marvel with the mysterious corporate building seen in the opening). This is an extreme example of a camera detaching itself from characters to give us a privileged viewpoint over them—its extremity lying not merely in its great height, nor in the protagonists' perspectives being extremely restricted (by the tunnel), but also in how these extreme gestures find their equivalent in how wildly remote this revelation feels even from our already superior, genre-driven, expectations.

As well as resulting from the camera's wholesale detachment from characters, pronounced instances of dramatic irony can also arise within any single shot if the image is composed so as to stress stark contrasts in degrees of knowledge between the audience and characters. We encountered examples of this in Chapter 2 when looking at moments of *Rope* that create dramatic irony through the camera's reframing. Yet camera movement is clearly not the only way films might create dramatically ironic compositions.

One common strategy, for instance, involves a character facing us in the foreground of a composition, unaware of something significant that we can see in the background. Such an image can be comic, as in *Modern Times* (Charlie Chaplin, 1936). At one point in this film our nameless protagonist (Chaplin) tries to help a truck driver by returning to him a flag that has fallen off the rear of the vehicle. As he picks up the flag and strides purposefully down the middle of the road towards the retreating camera, waving his arms to catch the driver's attention, a swarm of Communist protesters wielding placards suddenly flood the street in the background, marching behind Chaplin so that he appears to be leading their demonstration. Charlie, needless to say, remains unaware of their presence until it is too late, when mounted police officers charge in and round him up as the protest's apparent leader. Equally, though, such a dramatically ironic composition can just as easily be made to assume tragic overtones, as in *Drums Along the Mohawk* (John Ford, 1939). Here, Gil (Henry Fonda), an eighteenth-century American pioneer and farmer, tends to his fields in the foreground of a wide shot, which allows us to see in the deep background what he cannot: plumes of smoke rising from the nearby house where he lives with his wife and children, their homestead having been set on fire (we also know) by Seneca Indians acting under the orders of British Loyalists (Fig. 3.8). Since both rely on granting the viewer degrees of knowledge strikingly superior to that of the protagonist, albeit to very

Fig. 3.8 *Drums Along the Mohawk*: Gil in the foreground while his homestead burns behind him

different effects, these single images might remind us (as does *Rope*) how closely related dramatic irony can be to suspense.[26] Yet the gesture of baldly presenting in one shot these characters *and* the facts of which they are unaware has an effect that is both suspenseful and ironic—encouraging us to wish the characters would turn round, while also visually parading the filmmakers' (and our) superior knowledge over them.

Although it might seem paradoxical, dramatic irony can even be created by the camera's including in the frame not more, but pointedly *less*, than certain characters can see. In *Gilda* (Charles Vidor, 1946), Johnny (Glenn Ford), a small-time gambler, is introduced by his boss, casino owner Mundson (George Macready), to Mundson's new wife. By this point in the film we have been told little of Johnny's past, one of the only things we know being that he may once have been hurt badly by a woman (when Mundson questions him on the subject, Johnny momentarily becomes rather defensive). Mundson's new wife is Gilda (Rita Hayworth), a barroom singer to whom Mundson impulsively got married while away on a trip. The camera's framing when Gilda and Johnny are introduced to each other is such that, by the end of this two-minute scene—lacking any confirmation from the dialogue—we are nonetheless left in little doubt that, unbeknownst to Mundson, his wife is the mysterious woman from Johnny's past. During what Mundson presumes to be their first meeting, the conversation between the three characters consists primarily of conveying to Johnny the news of Mundson and Gilda's recent nuptials. There certainly seems to be slightly more tension in the room than we might expect given the circumstances: Johnny appears curt in the congratulations he offers, while Gilda seems to pivot between haughty offhandedness and moments of (unnoticed) private umbrage. Yet it is the camera's framing that confirms for us that, to say the least, this cannot possibly be the first time this man and woman have met. Throughout what remains a three-way conversation, the compositions almost exclusively include Johnny and Gilda alone, with the film cutting back and forth repeatedly between shots and reverse shots of them looking intently at one another, while Mundson is kept forever out of the frame. Our sense that Mundson is not merely not being included in these compositions but is more emphatically being *excluded* from them builds each time we are prevented from seeing him, even when he is delivering any of his several lines ('I wanted to keep it a surprise'; 'You don't congratulate the bride, Johnny, you congratulate the husband'; and so on). The culmination of the framing pattern comes, though, with the shot in which Mundson is kissing Gilda goodbye. Here, filmed from over Gilda's shoulder, his body is first bisected by the frame's edge, before the camera remains static as he leans in for his kiss, and Johnny's unwavering gaze at his wife is revealed from behind his back; even here, the camera's field of vision remains as intensely focused on this couple as they are on one another. The framing in this scene thus creates dramatic irony not by letting us see aspects of the world that certain characters cannot, but rather by giving us a pointedly *partial* perspective, which nonetheless serves to reveal a great deal.

I noted at the beginning of this section that the camera will, of course, more than likely make crucial contributions to almost any moment of irony in film. In particular, 'the almost permanent external presence of the camera' (Deleyto 1991: 165) will usually play an important role in a film's ironising of its characters. To acknowledge this is thus also to begin a conversation about the final topic considered in this chapter: film performance.

Irony and Performance

One outcome of the camera's almost perpetual visual superiority is simply that we are frequently permitted to observe characters while they undertake actions that they cannot see themselves performing. This in turn allows us to notice ironically revealing facts about their behaviour, of which they may remain unaware. As such, the performances of actors will frequently be cardinally important to any irony created at their characters' expense.

McCabe and Mrs. Miller (Robert Altman, 1971) tacitly exploits the basic perceptual privilege afforded the cinematic audience by allowing us to witness an actor ironically modulating his performance from one scene to the next. John McCabe (Warren Beatty), the proprietor of a small brothel in the early-nineteenth-century Pacific Northwest, is faced with the unfortunate choice of either selling his business to, or being murdered by bounty hunters sent by, a powerful mining company. Seeking legal protection, he visits a lawyer, Samuels (William Devane), who uses this opportunity to give McCabe what seems an oft-rehearsed patriotic pitch. Samuels proudly opines that 'the law is here to protect the little guy', pontificating that 'busting up these trusts and monopolies is at the very root...of creating a just society' and convincing McCabe that standing up to this mining company will make him a national hero. Throughout this scene, the lawyer is in lecturing mode, pacing pompously around his office, thumbs hooked in his waistcoat pockets; Beatty as McCabe, by contrast, projects an overwhelmingly nervous, cowed, and submissive figure: he answers with vague, unsure agreements ('Er, uh-huh...') and asks questions that reveal him struggling to keep up ('I guess what you're sayin' is...'/'...is that right?'). Physically too, he is utterly unprepossessing. Frequently clearing his throat and stuttering, he sits hunched on a chair, hat clutched in his lap; he follows Samuels with his neck as the lawyer struts about the space; Beatty also persistently avoids and breaks eye contact, his gaze constantly flitting away from, back to, and away from this more imposing man. In the scene that immediately follows Samuels' lecture, however, we see an ostensibly very different McCabe. Back at the brothel, McCabe is now in the midst of explaining his plan of action to his business partner, Constance Miller (Julie Christie). Beatty's performance here reveals McCabe trying to ape both Samuels' lofty ideals and his pretentious, posturing manner. Speaking in close-up, gesturing with firm nods towards Mrs Miller, McCabe asserts confidently that 'There comes a time in every man's life, Constance, when he's just got to stick his hand in the fire and, er...'—McCabe's flow crumbling, Beatty nods, looks off to the left, and furrows his brow as if searching for inspiration—'... and, er'—now reassuming his original assured expression—'and see what he's made out of'. Seemingly ignoring the dismissive tone of Constance's response, 'What are you *talking* about?', and now framed in a medium shot, McCabe goes on to parrot various aspects of Samuels' speech and comportment: 'I'm talkin' about bustin' up these trusts and monopolies', he declaims roughly, his hands pocketed, performing a diminutive version of Samuels' circular pacing, thrusting out his chin for extra emphasis on certain words. 'Somebody's gotta protect the small businessman...', he goes on, leaning into Constance in an attempt at towering, 'and I'm gon' be the man.'

While certainly creating an ironic distance towards his character, Beatty's embodiment of McCabe's pretentions also makes his pathetic stabs at loftiness somewhat endearing—more so, at least, than Samuels, whose equivalent pompous speechifying projects mere self-satisfied self-assurance. Nonetheless, Beatty's remains a consummately ironic performance, offering what James Naremore dubs a 'performance-within-performance', wherein an actor ensures that his character's self-presentation 'is revealed as a "mere act"' (1988: 70). It also demonstrates the ironic potential in simply allowing us to observe a character unconsciously betraying themselves to us—here in large part through a performance's development between scenes and in relation to other actors.

I have frequently noted that films may use our assumed familiarity with genre conventions—particularly the likely trajectory of a film's plot—to create dramatic irony. This is a strategy in which performance can also assist. In this case, though, the approach seems more obviously apt to create both dramatic irony *and* ironic pretence. To acknowledge the ways in which these effects can often be interlinked, I will consider both possibilities in relation to one moment from a single film: *The Scarlet Empress* (Joseph von Sternberg, 1934).

About forty-five minutes into this film, Catherine (Marlene Dietrich), who has recently married into eighteenth-century Russia's royal family, is being dressed in her bedroom by her maid, Marie (Marie Wells). Marie notes how inordinately happy Catherine seems: she has been smiling brightly and bouncing energetically around the room with the ebullience of an excitable child (because, we soon learn, she will be receiving her mother later today). 'If Your Highness were not so new to our court', Marie comments with a glint in her eye, 'I'd suspect you were going to see your lover…'. Popping up her head suddenly from beneath the bulbous crinoline of her sumptuous dress, Catherine inquires with eager curiosity, '*Lover*? And what may a "lover" be?' However, upon learning the answer (a lover is 'a man, not a husband, who loves you with all his heart and whom you love in return'), Catherine responds in scandalised fashion: 'But *Marie*', she offers in shocked reproach, 'that's *wicked*!' (Fig. 3.9).

There is, first, dramatic irony at play in this moment thanks to our knowledge of the film's likely narrative trajectory as a historical biopic. By this point, *The Scarlet Empress* has already made several references to the historical reputation of Catherine the Great, including intertitles to the effect that she is 'soon to become Russia's most powerful and most sinister Empress'; indeed, the film's title itself has effectively promised a violent and quite possibly salacious future for her. The film, having thus presumed its audience to have some familiarity with Catherine's imminent reputation (or at least having evidenced no desire to withhold it), has also already exploited expectations about the sort of monarch she will become for ironic foreshadowing: the keen interest Catherine has shown in tales of war and torture as a child, for example, or early intertitles that described her as being 'full of innocent dreams for the future'. Catherine's puritanical response to the concept of a lover is another example of this approach, since the audience is presumed to know full well that she will herself come to be famous (in part) for her historic number of extramarital affairs. Moreover, though, it is Dietrich's performance specifically that

Fig. 3.9 *The Scarlet Empress*: Catherine/Dietrich scandalised by the concept of a 'lover'

heightens the possibility of this dramatic irony and creates its particular effects. There is, for instance, the childlike enactment of excitement she has offered before the exchange, and the comical manner with which she bobs her head over her dress as if playing peek-a-boo—on not one, but *both* of her lines. There is also the way she inquisitively opens her eyes saucer-wide upon hearing that mysterious word, as well as the means she finds for projecting utter, indignant disbelief at the concept. The latter is achieved partly via her intonation (the pitch and stress of her voice rising on the second half of 'Mar-eee!'), and partly by an accompanying slight nod of the head that suggests her trying to make her reprimand stern, regardless of her own naïveté. In the context of our knowledge of where—given generic convention and historical precedent—this narrative is almost certainly leading, Dietrich's performance seems to hint by omission at her character's fate: the greater her claims to innocence, the greater Catherine is ironised.

This moment from *The Scarlet Empress* thus offers a demonstration of one possibility available to film performance, wherein, as Alex Clayton puts it, 'the same gesture reveals both the sincerity of the character and the irony of the actor' (2012: 54). In this particular case, though, I suggest that the irony itself must also be understood as being of two kinds. If Dietrich's performance helps create dramatic irony, then we might say it also implies an acknowledgement of the shape of the unfolding plot. It is a small step from here to acknowledging the fact that she is also an actress playing a role. In this sense, another key dimension of this performance relates to ironic pretence.

Writing of the ironic possibilities of film performance, Tom Brown notes that 'characters may be performed in a knowing way, with "tongue in cheek", ...or may even appear cognisant of the trajectory of the film narrative in which they participate' (2012: 172). As Brown notes, at its most extreme, this strategy might involve a performer/character 'breaking the fourth wall' to comment directly on the unfolding story; yet there are also subtler ways of creating similar effects. George Wilson describes Dietrich's acting style in *The Scarlet Empress* during this earlier, 'innocent' portion of Catherine's life as 'fun and utterly preposterous,' suggesting that she 'seems to be playing with her role more than playing it' (Wilson 2005: 55). The very excessiveness of her portrayal of innocence here does seem to encourage us to take it as teetering on the edge of parody—offered, indeed, as a pretended, 'tongue-in-cheek' embodiment of inexperience. In addition, though, this exaggerated performance also demands relating to another inter-/extratextual consideration beyond genre or history alone: Dietrich's star image. A persona of sultriness, worldliness, and—perhaps above all—*knowingness* about sexuality had by this point in her career been firmly established,[27] and *The Scarlet Empress'* makers (including Dietrich herself) could absolutely assume that a sizeable proportion of the film's contemporary audience would be familiar with this. Thus, when Dietrich accompanies her second line with a slight raised eyebrow and a disapproving pout that seems to teeter for a millisecond on the precipice of a smile, we can feel a performer ironising her role by suggesting her teasing awareness not only of this character's fate, but also of the absurdity of an actress like her delivering lines like these. Offering such a 'knowing', overstated enactment of a character is a key way in which performers in general may create ironic pretence, and an actor's playing upon his or her established star persona may make crucial contributions to this effect.

As well as via exaggeration, another way in which an actor might project something like ironic pretence is by doing the opposite; as Elsaesser puts it: 'highly emotional situations [may be] *under*played to present an ironic discontinuity of feeling' (1987: 66; emphasis mine). The set-up for a famous sight-gag from *Steamboat Bill, Jr.* (Charles Reisner, 1928), for example, involves Willie (Buster Keaton) being caught up in the middle of a tremendous storm that is ripping a town literally to pieces. He has been blown, in a bed, to the foot of a house whose structural integrity is failing. Having been rudely ejected from the bed, Willie has taken refuge from the winds by cowering beneath it. By this point we have already seen (while Willie has not) that the front of this house is gradually being torn apart from the rest of the building's frame, a seam apparently opening up from the top down. Once Willie's scant protective covering has been blown away, we cut out to a wide shot of him standing looking down at the ground, rubbing the back of his neck in discomfort—the looming building imposing itself behind him with dramatically ironic heft. The camera still holding this shot, the front of the house now begins to give way, toppling directly forward, all set to squash Willie flat. However, when this portion of the building reaches him, Willie is miraculously spared by the fact that he happens to be standing in precisely the right spot for his body to slip through the one solitary gap in the house's front: a glassless top-storey window. The façade thus now crashes to the ground around Willie but leaves him standing bolt upright. As it does, Keaton initially plays his character as oblivious, almost nonchalant. His left arm gives the tiniest jolt of recoil, but he is otherwise entirely impassive. He continues rubbing his neck all the while the building is careening past him—still looking downwards, entirely absorbed with easing his annoying minor twinge. Equally, when he looks around him to see what has landed, then up at what remains of the building, his first reactions seem to be intrigued perplexity and curiosity—rather than profound fear mixed with awe-inspired gratitude at his unbelievable good fortune. Only after a few moments of inspection does he eventually evince something like a conventional emotional response to the situation, and he bolts away, out of frame, in alarm. It is thus the incongruity between a character's extremely emotionally intense conditions and a performer's extremely downplayed manner of expression that creates the humour, and irony, here. Keaton's underplaying undermines expectations in a manner characteristic of comedy in general; but it also creates a distance between emotional registers—and between actor and character—that is more suggestive of irony in particular. This is one way of describing a common effect of what we often call deadpan: an actor draining away emotionality from an emotionally heightened moment, creating a sense of ironic distance from the affective demands such a moment seems logically to make.[28]

Finally, one of the least commented upon—perhaps because most common—ways that irony finds its way into fiction films is via characters themselves communicating ironically. So familiar is this phenomenon that it is easy to forget all the—often surely subconscious, but nonetheless essential—interpretive activities required to comprehend it. Some aspects of that activity are in fact likely to be similar in fundamental ways to grasping irony in everyday conversation: we must take account of the speaker's context, certainly, but also the tone and manner with which his or her words are spoken. Apprehending such ironies therefore requires, among other things, attention to performance. I touched briefly in Chapter 2 on how a skilful actor can imbue even the most apparently innocuous of lines with ironic intent (James Stewart as Rupert in *Rope* asking, 'Is he...good?'). Of course, however, sometimes dialogue itself encourages an ironic delivery; even in such cases, though, performance will still play a decisive role in making that irony meaningful.

In *Citizen Kane* (Orson Welles, 1941), millionaire newspaper magnate Charles Foster Kane (Orson Welles) is throwing a party for the staff of his paper, *The Daily Inquirer*. In high spirits, he announces that he will be leaving imminently on an overseas vacation, having long promised his doctor he would do so. 'Say, Mister Kane—as long as you're *promising*', pipes up his business manager Mr Bernstein (Everett Sloane), 'there's a lot of pictures and statues in Europe you haven't bought yet...'. Laughter erupts from all present at this reference to what is becoming Charles' increasingly costly art-collecting habit. As the laughter dies down, Charles responds, 'You can't blame *me*, Mister Bernstein: they've been making statues for two thousand years—and I've only been buying for five'; the staff again guffaw at this riposte. Both these lines represent small but deceptively complex acts of ironic pretence. Bernstein pretends to be complaining not that Charles is purchasing too many expensive artefacts, but rather that he has not yet accrued *enough*; Charles, meanwhile, pretends to ignore Bernstein's irony, defending himself not against the accusation of being a spendthrift, but against the (pretended) charge that he is not acquiring artworks with sufficient alacrity. Beyond these unspoken meanings that the lines themselves imply, the two actors' performances suggest several further inflections at work in their characters' exchange. The playful nature of the comments helps, first, to veil an indirect criticism and its rebuttal. Sloane's jumping up with a raised hand and using the table to lean forward suggests some pointedness beneath Bernstein's (slightly tipsy?) jocularity; while Welles' careful, steady, lower tone not only heightens the poker-faced nature of Charles' pretended misunderstanding, but also quietly asserts his character's superior status and capacity to deflect minor impudence coolly. Both characters' ironic admonishments also, though, dramatise their shared tastes in wit. Sloane's smile, which collapses into a laugh at the line's end, tells us Bernstein anticipates his real meaning will be understood; and Welles' mock-teacherly nod on 'years' suggests Charles' play-acting along with a friend. The exchange also, of course, represents a show for the benefit of the room. Sloane sells 'as long as you're *promising*' through a flourish of a head movement, while Welles finishes his response with an arched left eyebrow and a turn to those assembled, both these beats expressing these characters' acknowledgement of a diegetic audience, who must follow along their ironic play too.

Understanding film narratives at very fundamental levels often involves understanding when and how characters are speaking ironically, and interpreting such irony clearly requires attending not only to words, but also the particular manner of their delivery. However, so multifarious are the expressive possibilities of performance—and so attentive can the camera be to the most minute intricacies of the actor's craft—that performers can also sometimes communicate ironically without uttering a single word.

Such is often the case for Bill Murray's character, Bob, in *Lost in Translation* (Sofia Coppola, 2003). In one scene, a series of looks and small gestures given across a crowded room initiates what will become a friendship between Bob and one of the few other Americans in the Tokyo hotel at which Bob is staying, the newly married Charlotte (Scarlett Johansson). Bob and Charlotte are sitting twenty-or-so metres apart in the hotel's bar, separately watching a female lounge singer and her pianist give a musically competent but breathy, ponderously slow, and rather overripe rendition of Simon and Garfunkel's song 'Scarborough Fair'. From across the room, Charlotte is amused to notice Bob seeming not to be especially enjoying the music, and Bob notices her noticing. As the singer finishes and invites applause with her closing remarks, Charlotte claps politely while smiling somewhat wryly. She then looks back over at Bob, who we now discover—rather than applauding—snapping his fingers in a burlesque of jazz club etiquette. As he does so he also nods with a furrowed brow in faux-earnest appreciation, before breaking into a slight smile upon glancing back at Charlotte. While she laughs quietly, he continues his little routine; still snapping and nodding, his face becomes pretend-serious again, his raised eyebrows and the movement of his gaze now indicating that Charlotte should direct her attention back to the band. Rather than being a gesture of overt scepticism, the particular way Murray raises his eyebrows here—in combination with his snapping, expression, and head movements—seems instead a parody of sober appreciation, as if to communicate, 'Yeah, check these guys *out*'. In this sense, Bob's is a play of ironic pretence at enjoyment, and it has entertained Charlotte enough that she will soon buy this stranger a drink. The fact that the relationship between this man and woman gets its start in this manner suggests it will be based at least partly on the sort of kinship of which Edith Wharton once spoke: 'the real marriage of two minds is for any two people to possess a sense of humour or irony pitched in exactly the same key' (in Booth 1974: 13). And Murray's wordless embodiment of these characters' ironic taste in humour—his routine managing to be understated and subtle in all the ways the lounge performer's is not—allows this silent moment of shared irony to sing.

*

It is fitting that our critical survey should conclude with two dramatisations of what amount to successful instances of ironic communication: a two-sided process in which both ironist and interlocutor or audience participate. We have thus far explored our medium's capacities for ironic expression and investigated how some of its properties and characteristic devices can be used to ironic effect. Yet, of course, in order even to call any of these films or moments ironic, I first had to interpret them *as* ironic. It is the question of what precisely this means, and what might be involved in or required of the interpretation of irony in film, that we shall take up in Chapter 4.

NOTES

1. See, for instance, Kalinak (1992: 26) and Stam (2005: 64).
2. See, for example, Gorbman (1987) and Kalinak (1992).
3. In *Film Music, A Very Short Introduction*, for instance, Kathryn Kalinak proceeds from a discussion of the ways in which Tarantino's films frequently 'pair brutal images with frothy music for ironic effect' to the claim that 'Stanley Kubrick pioneered the practice in *A Clockwork Orange* (Stanley Kubrick, 1971)' (2010: 2).

4. These lyrics may be absent from the instrumental arrangement of the piece used in the film, but *The Public Enemy*'s filmmakers could safely assume that a good percentage of the film's audience would both be familiar with them and could perhaps also be relied upon to call them to mind along with the tune's waltzing melody.

5. The final shot of the montage features US soldiers sitting by a radio, following which we return to Cronauer in the studio as the recording finishes.

6. Of course, Cronauer's radio programme is broadcast across Vietnam, and the final shot of the montage does show soldiers sitting by a radio; yet we do not seem invited to imagine that the song could conceivably be playing during all of the various events depicted.

7. This will be even more ostentatiously the case when the music is given not even a *semblance* of diegetic motivation. For an example of this, we might consider the final montage of atomic explosions in *Dr. Strangelove*, which is accompanied by the song 'We'll Meet Again', as performed by Vera Lynn (Gorbman 2006: 3–18).

8. The immanent potential for irony in this process holds true for the aesthetic appropriation of any cultural object. As Jaimie Baron notes, 'all appropriations of found documents are potentially ironic…because there is always a certain double awareness inherent in [the practice]' (2013: 37).

9. Greg M. Smith, for instance, writes illuminatingly about the incorporation of 'Happy Birthday' into the score of *Stella Dallas* (King Vidor, 1937) in a manner that creates a 'nondiegetic ironic commentary on the action' (2003: 105).

10. As Colebrook notes, 'tragic irony is exemplified in ancient drama, …[wherein] the audience watched a drama unfold, already knowing its destined outcome' (2004: 14).

11. Roche identifies this possible means of ironising voice-over narrators when he writes of 'irony at the expense of an intradiegetic narrator…"originating" from the [voice-over] narration' itself (2015: 9).

12. Following this shot we cut to Jim (Matthew Broderick) asking Dave in disbelief, 'You did it in your *house*? In your own house?'

13. As Kozloff notes, 'compromised, unreliable [voice-over] narrators' (1989: 110) are not always characters in the fiction; she mentions,

for instance, the possibility that voice-over narrators might be used to parody the style of documentaries (which would constitute one way in which the device could also help create ironic pretence). Nonetheless, ironised character voice-overs are probably considerably more common; examples that have received extended critical commentary include *Badlands* (Terrence Malick, 1973) (Bignell 2005) and *The Sweet Hereafter* (Atom Egoyan, 1997) (Roche 2015).

14. Again, Roche notes this approach, describing it as 'irony at the expense of…intradiegetic narrators, "originating" from other elements of the narration' (2015: 9).
15. Örjan Roth-Lindberg goes so far as to define contradictions established by cutting as the only 'pure' form of filmic irony (1995: 158–165). Clearly, I do not agree on this point, but it does highlight the importance of editing for any full account of irony in this medium.
16. Of course, Conner's title itself might be similarly described as an act of ironic pretence: far from being an example of the kind of popular cinema usually associated with the term *movie*, *A Movie* is in fact plainly and avowedly an 'art *film*'.
17. Pye (2007: 42–44) offers a useful demonstration of this in relation to *Strangers on a Train* (Alfred Hitchcock, 1951).
18. See King (2005: 197–198) for a discussion of this moment's relationship to Hollywood stylistic conventions and the 'transgressive' use to which *Happiness* puts them.
19. We might think, too, of course, of the camera revealing the chest at particular moments in *Rope*, or indeed of the paired shots in *Letter from an Unknown Woman* (Chapter 2), and so on.
20. See Gibbs (2013) for a historical overview and Martin (2014) for contemporary debates.
21. Indeed, we might say that I am interested here primarily in the ironic potential of certain elements of filmmaking indebted most ostentatiously to the 'dramatic' aspects of the medium (Chapter 2). While, as noted earlier, the 'dramatic' and 'narrative' dimensions of filmmaking are always in practice inseparable, this does not mean that we cannot profitably distinguish between them for the purposes of analysis.
22. For one argument that *Blue Velvet* is far less ironic (and less 'postmodern') than is frequently assumed, see Rombes (2004).

23. For more on this film's particular ironic tone, which he defines in terms of 'mass-camp', see Cohan (2005: 200–245).

24. It is tempting to account for their differences by invoking the distinction between *parody* and *satire*—wherein 'the ironic echo of artistic material (styles, genres, ..., etc.) is parody, and the ironising of social habitus (persons, ... groups, etc.) is satire' (Vandaele 2002: 237). As I have suggested, not all 'ironic echoes' of aesthetic conventions are so neatly defined as straightforwardly parodic, and perhaps not all exaggerated ironising of 'social habitus' need necessarily be called satirical. Nonetheless, such terms do at least catch the difference between a film employing exaggeration in order to ironise the whole of its address and doing so in order to ironise only specific elements of its fictional world.

25. And even films pursuing this exceedingly uncommon strategy—a famous example would be *Lady in the Lake* (Robert Montgomery, 1947)—seldom restrict themselves throughout to showing us only their protagonists' optical perspectives.

26. See Smith (2000: 49–75) and Allen (2007: 38–71), both of whom touch upon this notion in relation to Hitchcock's films.

27. Especially via her roles in other collaborations with von Sternberg: *Dishonored* (1931), *Blonde Venus* (1932), and *Shanghai Express* (1932).

28. On deadpan as a performance strategy that can 'call attention to performance *as* performance' see Peberdy (2012: 46).

BIBLIOGRAPHY

Allen, Richard. (2007). *Hitchcock's Romantic Irony*. New York: Columbia University Press.

Baron, Jaimie. (2013). *The Archive Effect: Found Footage and the Audiovisual Experience of History*. New York: Routledge.

Berry, Betsy. (1988). 'Forever, In My Dreams: Generic Conventions and the Subversive Imagination in *Blue Velvet*', *Literature/Film Quarterly* 16: 2, 82–90.

Bignell, Jonathan. (2005). 'From Detail to Meaning: *Badlands* and Cinematic Articulation', in Gibbs, John & Douglas Pye (eds), *Style and Meaning: Studies in the Detailed Analysis of Film*. Manchester: Manchester University Press, 42–52.

Booth, Wayne C. (1974). *A Rhetoric of Irony*. Chicago: University of Chicago Press.

Brown, Tom. (2012). *Breaking the Fourth Wall: Direct Address in the Cinema.* Edinburgh: Edinburgh University Press.

Chatman, Seymour. (1990). *Coming to Terms: The Rhetoric of Narrative in Fiction and Film.* Ithaca: Cornell University Press.

Chion, Michel. (1994). *Audio-Vision: Sound on Screen* (Translated and edited by Claudia Gorbman). New York: University of Columbia Press.

Clayton, Alex. (2012). 'Play-Acting: A Theory of Comedic Performance', in Taylor, Aaron (ed), *Theorizing Film Acting.* New York: Routledge, 47–61.

Cohan, Steven. (2005). *Incongruous Entertainment: Camp, Cultural Value, and the MGM Musical.* London: Duke University Press.

Colebrook, Claire. (2004). *Irony.* New York: Routledge.

Deleyto, Celestino. (1991). 'Focalization in Narrative Film', *Atlantis* 8: 1/2, 159–177.

Elsaesser, Thomas. (1987). 'Tales of Sound and Fury: Observations on the Family Melodrama', in Gledhill, Christine (ed), *Home is Where the Heart is: Studies in Melodrama and the Woman's Film.* London: BFI, 43–69.

Evans, Bertrand. (1960). *Shakespeare's Comedies.* Oxford: Clarendon Press.

Garwood, Ian. (2000). 'Must You Remember This? Orchestrating the "Standard" Pop Song in *Sleepless in Seattle*', *Screen* 41: 3, 282–298.

Gehring, Wes D. (1999). *Parody as Film Genre: Never Give a Saga an Even Break.* Westport: Greenwood.

Gibbs, John. (2002). *Mise-en-Scène: Film Style and Interpretation.* London: Wallflower Press.

Gibbs, John. (2013). *The Life of Mise-en-Scène: Visual Style and British Film Criticism, 1946–78.* Oxford: Oxford University Press.

Gorbman, Claudia. (1987). *Unheard Melodies: Narrative Film Music.* London: BFI.

Gorbman, Claudia. (2006). 'Ears Wide Open: Kubrick's Music', in Powrie, Phil & Robynn J. Stilwell (eds), *Changing Tunes: The Use of Pre-existing Music in Film.* Burlington: Ashgate, 3–18.

Graham, T. Austin. (2013). *The Great American Songbooks: Musical Texts, Modernism, and the Value of Popular Culture.* Oxford: Oxford University Press.

Gunning, Tom. (1991). *D. W. Griffith and the Origins of American Narrative Film: The Early Years at Biograph.* Chicago: University of Illinois Press.

Hatch, Kevin. (2012). *Looking for Bruce Conner.* Cambridge: MIT Press.

Hodsdon, Barrett. (1992). 'The Mystique of *Mise en scène* Revisited', *Continuum*, 5: 2, 68–86.

Kalinak, Kathryn. (1992). *Settling the Score: Music and the Classical Hollywood Film.* Madison: University of Wisconsin Press.

Kalinak, Kathryn. (2010). *Film Music: A Very Short Introduction.* Oxford: Oxford University Press.

King, Geoff. (2005). *American Independent cinema.* New York: I. B. Tauris.

Kozloff, Sarah. (1989). *Invisible Storytellers: Voice-over Narration in American Fiction Film*. Los Angeles: University of California Press.
Lastra, James. (2000). *Sound Technology and the American Cinema: Perception, Representation, Modernity*. New York: Columbia University Press.
Martin, Adrian. (2011). 'Guess-Work: *Scarlet Street*', *Movie: A Journal of Film Criticism*, Issue 3, 35–42. Available at: http://www2.warwick.ac.uk/fac/arts/film/movie/contents/scarlet_st._final.2.pdf (Accessed 20 January 2016).
Martin, Adrian. (2014). *Mise en scène and Film Style: From Classical Hollywood to New Media Art*. London: Palgrave Macmillan.
Muecke, Douglas Colin. (1970). *Irony and the Ironic*. London: Methuen.
Mulvey, Laura. (1996). *Fetishism and Curiosity*. London: BFI.
Naremore, James. (1988). *Acting in the Cinema*. Berkley: University of California Press.
Orpen, Valerie. (2003). *Film Editing: The Art of the Expressive*. London: Wallflower Press.
Peberdy, Donna. (2012). '"I'm Just a Character in Your Film": Acting and Performance from Autism to Zissou', *New Review of Film and Television Studies*, 10: 1, 46–67.
Perez, Gilberto. (1998). *The Material Ghost: Films and Their Medium*. Baltimore: Johns Hopkins University Press.
Perkins, V. F. (1972). *Film as Film: Understanding and Judging Movies*. London: Penguin Books.
Pye, Douglas. (1989). 'Bordwell and Hollywood', *Movie* 33, 46–52.
Pye, Douglas. (2007). 'Movies and Tone', in Gibbs, John & Douglas Pye (eds), *Close-Up 02: Movies and Tone/Reading Rohmer/Voices in Film*. London: Wallflower Press, 1–80.
Robertson, Pamela. (1990). 'Structural Irony in *Mildred Pierce*, or How Mildred Lost Her Tongue', *Cinema Journal* 30: 1, 42–54.
Roche, David. (2015). 'Irony in *The Sweet Hereafter* by Russell Banks (1991) and Atom Egoyan (1997)', *Adaptation* 8: 2, 237–253.
Rombes, Nicholas. (2004). '*Blue Velvet* Underground: David Lynch's Post-Punk Poetics', in Sheen, Erica & Annette Davison (eds) *The Cinema of David Lynch: American Dreams, Nightmare Visions*. London: Wallflower Press, 61–76.
Roth-Lindberg, Örjan. (1995). 'Skuggan av ett Leende: Omfilmisk Ironi och den Ironiska Berättelsen', PhD Thesis, University of Stockholm: Bokförlaget T. Fischer & Co.
Sconce, Jeffrey. (2002). 'Irony, Nihilism and the New American "Smart" Film', *Screen* 43: 4, 349–369.
Sitney, P. Adams. (2002). *Visionary Film: The American Avant-Garde, 1943–2000*. Oxford: Oxford University Press.
Smith, Greg M. (2003). *Film Structure and the Emotion System*. Cambridge: Cambridge University Press.

Smith, Susan (2000). *Hitchcock: Suspense, Humour and Tone*. London: BFI.

Stam, Robert (ed). (2005). *New Vocabularies in Film Semiotics*. New York: Routledge.

Vandaele, Jeroen. (2002). 'Humor Mechanisms in Film Comedy: Incongruity and Superiority', *Poetics Today*, 23: 2, 221–249.

Wilson, George M. (2005). 'Narrative and Visual Pleasures in *The Scarlet Empress*', in Gibbs, John and Douglas Pye (eds) *Style and Meaning: Studies in the Detailed Analysis of Film*. Manchester: Manchester University Press, 53–67.

Wood, Robin. (1960/1961). 'New Criticism?', *Definition*, Winter (1960/61), 8–12.

Zemach, Eddy & Tamara Balter. (2007). 'The Structure of Irony and How it Functions in Music', in Stock, Kathleen (ed), *Philosophers on Music: Experience, Meaning, and Work*. New York: Oxford University Press, 178–206.

CHAPTER 4

Interpreting Irony in Film: Intention, Rhetoric, and Irony's Edge

So far, this book has largely been concerned with the possibility of creating filmic irony and with how different aspects of the medium can and have been used ironically. This chapter turns its attention from the matter of creating irony in film towards the matter of interpreting it.

Irony is, as Wayne Booth puts it, 'an extraordinarily good road into the whole art of interpretation' (1974: 44). This is to say that, taken seriously, it fundamentally demands that we risk staking out positions on a number of questions central to interpretation in general. Analysing various kinds of irony in film has, of course, already required me to undertake numerous interpretations. Even to dub any given moment of a film ironic is, among other things, to interpret that moment as ironic in the first place. But how can we know such interpretations are justified? How do we determine a film is addressing us ironically? Moreover, I have repeatedly referred to irony as an *effect* films create. If this description is accurate, then irony could seem to be less something that can be present in a film and more something that simply may—and equally well may not—be experienced by audiences. This could in turn suggest that we should not in fact speak of the irony *in* films at all.

Might it be the case that, as Mary Ann Doane puts it, 'without the effect of irony, there is no irony' (1979: 137)? Answering this question with a yes has become commonplace in much critical literature on irony, and film scholarship is no exception. David Roche, for instance, writes that irony in

© The Author(s) 2016

J. MacDowell, *Irony in Film*, DOI 10.1057/978-1-137-32993-6_4

film 'depends on individual viewers...to make it happen' (2015: 13); simi-larly, Jamie Baron argues that 'if the interpreter does not perceive irony, the irony does not "happen"' (2013: 37). Going further still, Kimberly Davis suggests that filmic irony 'is not...in the text, but must be produced by the audience' (1999: 27–28); while Lars Elleström similarly argues that ironies are not 'actual qualities of...filmic texts' (2002: 150), but rather the product of 'an interpretive strategy employed by the spectator' (2002: 149). Davis and Elleström in particular here echo theorists of the subject such as Stanley Fish, who claims that 'irony...is not the property of works' but instead 'a way of reading, an interpretive strategy...that produces the ironic meanings' (1989: 194). Of course, propositions to the effect that an artwork's meanings depend more on its reception than its properties have been commonplace within the humanities for many decades. Yet there might seem to be something about irony specifically that especially encourages a focus on readers before works.

'Irony', writes Fish, 'is a risky business because one cannot be at all certain that readers will be directed to the ironic meanings one intends' (1989: 181). And indeed, the potential for misinterpretation appears to be not merely one possible outcome of ironic expression, but almost its necessary corollary. Jonathan Culler, for example, proposes that 'irony *always* offers the possibility of misunderstanding' (1975: 154; emphasis mine), while Doane argues that 'the possibility of misreading [irony] is always present and, in fact, *necessary*' (1979: 137; emphasis mine). This is because 'the double vision of ironic art' (Babington/Evans 1990: 48) seems innately to depend upon creating the possibility for a division between 'those who "get" it and those who don't' (Hutcheon 1994: 2). David Kaufer (1977) refers to this property of irony as 'audience bifurca-tion', and H.W. Fowler calls linguistic irony 'a form of utterance that pos-tulates a double audience', being 'intended to convey one meaning to the uninitiated...and another to the initiated' (1926: 305–306). Irony is thus, as Doane puts it, 'in some sense a wager. It entails a necessary uncertainty that the meaning will ever reach its destination' (1979: 129). Moreover, whether or not irony *will* reach its destination clearly depends in large part on the interpreter. Doane notes of her reading of *Once Upon a Time in the West*, for instance, that to grasp this film's irony, 'the spectator must have a certain knowledge': 'a spectator who has never seen a Western can-not "get" the irony' of Leone's film (ibid.: 137). Whether or not one will even regard an aspect of a work as ironic at all, then, assuredly depends on which side of its 'double audience' one finds oneself on. To recognise this is to recognise that irony plainly requires interpretation in order for its effects to manifest.

Having acknowledged 'the dependency of irony upon mutuality' (Storm 2011: 10), however, does it follow from this that 'irony isn't irony until it is interpreted as such' (Hutcheon 1994: 6) and that it is also therefore 'not the property of works' (Fish 1989: 194)? This is a crucial question, partly because the answer amounts to a referendum on whether attempting to identify and analyse irony *in* film is an essentially fruitless endeavour. This chapter will propose some reasons for answering no. It will do so by approaching from various angles a single famous moment of (what I claim is) filmic irony. This moment is one in which the risks of the ironic 'wager' seem particularly high: the 'Ride of the Valkyries' helicopter sequence from *Apocalypse Now* (Francis Ford Coppola, 1979).[1] By any reasonable standards an iconic moment of American cinema, this sequence has also been interpreted as both ironic and unironic by scholars and viewers. Because of its subject matter—a US military attack on a Viet Cong–affiliated village during the Vietnam War—it is a scene that is intensely ethically and politically charged; as such, the matter of whether one attributes irony to the sequence appears to be of particular consequence. We might express this by saying that this scene demonstrates strikingly and acutely what Hutcheon has evocatively called irony's 'edge' (1994).

As Hutcheon notes, irony's edge lies in the fact that—due partly to its 'evaluative' nature, and partly to its potential to divide audiences into 'those who "get" it and those who don't'—irony 'unavoidably involves touchy issues such as exclusion and inclusion' (ibid.: 2). Grappling with irony thus fundamentally requires grappling with these touchy issues. One particularly touchy subject irony raises is whether, as Wayne Booth puts it, 'we do in fact read *and misread* ironies' (1974: 2; emphasis mine). This matter is touchy because, if we are indeed capable of both reading and misreading irony, then it could seem also to follow that 'some readings are better than others' (ibid.: xi). To propose that we can reasonably speak of the irony *in* films seems to be to commit oneself to this simultaneously seductive and thorny premise. It is this possibility, and the difficult theoretical issues it raises for film interpretation, that I intend to explore through what I believe can justifiably be called the irony in this sequence from *Apocalypse Now*.

Apocalypse Now's 'Ride of the Valkyries'

The 'Ride of the Valkyries' sequence in *Apocalypse Now* comes about thirty-five minutes into the film. US Army Captain Benjamin Willard (Martin Sheen) has been dispatched to assassinate Army Special Forces Colonel Walter Kurtz (Marlon Brando), who has apparently lost his mind, foregone US military strategy, and established a settlement in Cambodia over which he seems to preside by force. Long before encountering Kurtz, though, Willard begins his mission by patrol boat, accompanied by a small crew. His first order is to enter the Nung River by sea with the help of an Airborne Cavalry Regiment, who have been instructed to ensure his boat's safe passage. Accessing this river will be dangerous because the beach at the mouth of the Nung is home to a Viet Cong village, meaning that any US vehicle attempting entry is sure to be met with violent resistance. The regiment's commanding officer, Lieutenant Colonel Bill Kilgore (Robert Duvall), is initially reluctant to help Willard and his men. He does agree to assist them, however, upon learning that the beach around the Nung is famed for its tall waves, which will allow him and his boys to indulge his favourite pastime, surfing. Willard and his team thus set off in one of a fleet of Bell UH-1 Iroquois—or 'Huey'—helicopters, whose job is to make the beach safe by decimating the Viet Cong encampment. Once in the sky, Kilgore announces, 'We'll come in low, out of the rising sun, and about a mile out we'll put on the music.' Upon being asked what he means, Kilgore explains, 'I use Wagner. It scares the hell out of the slopes [racist term for Vietnamese]. My boys love it.' Sure enough, as the Hueys approach the beach, Kilgore gives the order, and a reel-to-reel player is promptly turned on, causing Richard Wagner's 'Ride of the Valkyries' to begin blasting from loudspeakers mounted on the sides of the helicopter. This rousing music then accompanies most of the following military manoeuvre—as the helicopters' machine guns and missiles are used to mow down Vietnamese men and women, and the village's inhabitants launch a defensive attack; eventually a napalm airstrike is called in, levelling the surrounding forest.

One of the most immediately striking aspects of how this sequence addresses us is the high degree of congruence it creates between the bombast of the music and the violent intensity of the attack. We might begin to account for this congruence by considering the nature of 'Ride of the Valkyries' itself. In her own analysis of the sequence, Hutcheon suggests that this piece of operatic music carries 'vague suggestions of war' (1994: 18), and its propulsive rhythm and repeating, heavy, pounding melody do unquestionably possess a very assertive—perhaps aggressive—quality in and of themselves. Furthermore, while not featuring explicitly martial percussion, its distinctive rhythm has been characterised as 'military' in tenor (Tarasti 2012: 261), and its instrumentation and dynamic range make it almost brutally overpowering.[2] However, not only is there a general, abstract equivalence between 'Ride of the Valkyries' and the violent contents of this scene, but the sequence is notable for creating an overwhelming complementarity between its action, musical accompaniment, and visual style.

A reciprocal relationship between musical and filmic style starts to emerge from the very moment the Wagner piece strikes up. When the music is turned on, beginning to play from the reel-to-reel deck aboard Kilgore's chopper, the camera pointedly tilts steadily upwards, rising along with the first similarly rising flourishes of the piece. In one sense, this small but pointed camera movement simply makes a visual connection between the tape player and some higher-mounted speakers; what it also does, though, is immediately establish a logic of collaboration between the film's perspective and the dynamics of the music: as the music rises, so too does our view. This sense of the film's visual style complementing and contributing to the dynamic power of the piece is reinforced moments later by a sequence of aerial shots that zoom into the choppers to focus on numerous protruding machine guns and speakers—each of these cuts and zooms being timed perfectly to coincide with one of a series of fast, stabbing crescendos in the piece's opening. Furthermore—and more troublingly—the portion of the scene depicting the actual assault on the beach contains many similar accords. Upon the first rockets being launched, this image is accompanied by the return of the central exultant melody (Fig. 4.1); soon after, four

Fig. 4.1   *Apocalypse Now*: The helicopters launch their missiles

explosions that injure a group of fleeing Vietnamese figures are also timed to echo the rhythm of the refrain; later, after the music has momentarily dropped out, it comes roaring back in with the reprise of the central melody when we cut to the first helicopters touching down on the beach.[3] In addition to this, throughout the entirety of the attack, the pace of the editing echoes the heavy insistence of the music, giving us 110 cuts within five and a half minutes, resulting in an average shot length of three seconds.[4]

An emphatic sense of confluence is thus established between the Wagner, the dramatic content, and the visual style, with the ostensible purpose of each element being to reinforce the affective power of the others. Since the action of the scene is exceedingly violent, that affective power is certainly definable in one sense as fundamentally violent in character. This makes it unsurprising that we should find critical accounts referring to the sequence's 'kinesthetic excitement' (Tomasulo 1990: 149), its 'primitive power' (Norris 1998: 762), or its 'euphoria and grandeur' (Warshaw 2009: 195)—even suggestions that it offers a feeling of 'murderous elation…for the viewer' (Kolker 2011: 152–153). In one careful, extended analysis of the use of sound in the attack scene, Matthew Michael Sumera condenses a few strands of the characteristic critical response to the sequence when he admits that 'no matter how much I attempt to avoid it, every time I watch and listen to the scene I find myself amped up and filled with palpable aggression' (2013: 79).

We are surely obliged to admit that this scene gives the appearance of encouraging feelings of aggression in its audience. Given this far from insignificant fact, then, why do I nonetheless strongly suspect that the film itself desires that we at least 'attempt to avoid' interpreting this scene as an enthusiastic endorsement of the militaristic aggression it seems to be celebrating? The answer I propose, of course, is that the 'Ride of the Valkyries' sequence is—among other things—addressing us ironically. More specifically (and using terminology introduced in Chapters 2 and 3), I argue that the sequence is communicatively ironic since it can be described as undertaking an ironic pretence: the film *pretends* excessively to affirm Kilgore's use of the Wagner piece for what he calls 'psy-war' (psychological warfare), when in fact it is implicitly asking us to be revolted by this music's apparent emotional appeals in this context, as well as by the very congruence between music and action that the style ostensibly heightens.

It is important to make clear that these represent the horizons of this chapter's critical claims about *Apocalypse Now* specifically. In what follows I will not, for instance, be advancing an original interpretation of the film as a whole, nor offering an aesthetic, ethical, or political evaluation of it. Perhaps unsurprisingly, some critics of Coppola's film are willing to acknowledge that aspects of it may attest to ironic intentions yet nevertheless believe that *Apocalypse Now*, taken in its entirety, offers 'no real distance, no critical sense' (Baudrillard 1994: 60) in its depiction of the US military's involvement in Vietnam.[5] Questions such as this will not be my concern in what follows. Instead, I will be restricting myself to one seemingly straightforward issue in particular: whether or not we might be justified in describing the 'Ride of the Valkyries' sequence itself as ironic. It will soon become evident that if we are dedicated to confronting it thoroughly, this apparently simple question proves more than complex enough to demand our attention for the whole length of this chapter.

The reason this question is so difficult, of course, is that it requires us to engage in a sustained fashion not only with the film itself but also with the kinds of theoretical questions raised earlier concerning whether or not irony can reasonably be said to be 'the property of works' (Fish 1989: 194). I argue that the irony of the helicopter attack scene can indeed be demonstrated, and primarily (though by no means exclusively) via evidence drawn from the film itself—specifically: (1) numerous aspects of this sequence's address, (2) the ways in which music and violent action are combined *elsewhere* in the movie, and (3) this film's strategies of dramatic irony. However, whether this evidence is of any interpretive value at all clearly depends on whether ironies can even be 'actual qualities of... filmic texts' (Elleström 2002: 150) in the first place. Before examining and weighing such evidence, then, we must confront this vitally important question.

IRONY AND INTERPRETATION

The 'Ride of the Valkyries' sequence is one of the first artistic examples invoked by Linda Hutcheon in her invaluable monograph *Irony's Edge*. In a chapter called 'Risky Business', she first makes clear that she interprets this scene ironically and offers various reasons for this judgement. However, in a theoretical move in keeping with her book as a whole, Hutcheon then goes on to use the moment to demonstrate irony's tendency to complicate critical claims to interpretive validity. 'This is how *I* attribute and interpret irony here', she writes, arguing that she interprets the scene as ironic only because of her membership within particular 'discursive communities': as someone familiar with the work of Wagner, for instance (ibid.: 19; emphasis mine). I will return later to the specifics of Hutcheon's interpretation, but for now I wish to remain with the theoretical assumptions underlying her argument.

Despite seeing irony in the sequence, Hutcheon argues that we cannot simply call the scene ironic—indeed, according to her theoretical framework, no work or any aspect of it can be said simply to *be* ironic. Instead, it is her membership within certain discursive communities that 'makes the irony [in *Apocalypse Now*] possible in the first place....An American male soldier may well interpret that scene very differently', she notes; furthermore, 'so may a Vietnamese....And irony may not figure in their interpretations at all' (ibid.: 19). This fact, for Hutcheon, helps demonstrate that, as she puts it elsewhere, 'to call something ironic...is less a *description* of the entity itself than an *attribution* of a quality of response....Irony "happens" for you (or, better, you make it "happen")' (Hutcheon 1998: 1; original emphasis).

Would it be reasonable to say that the 'Ride of the Valkyries' sequence is not ironic in itself? Or, put another way: if an American male soldier who watched it, for instance, did not 'make it[s irony] "happen"', would this also mean that no irony was 'happening' in the film either? Such questions are essential to consider. They also need not be entirely hypothetical, since at least one male American soldier has in fact described reactions to *Apocalypse Now* very similar to those imagined by Hutcheon. In his memoir *Jarhead* (2003), ex-marine Anthony Swofford relates an anecdote about himself and his company watching Vietnam War films and cheering along with their depictions of warfare—'get[ting] off on the various visions of carnage and violence' (2003: 5–6). 'There is talk', writes Swofford, 'that many Vietnam War films are antiwar. But actually'

> Vietnam War films are all pro-war, no matter...what Kubrick or Coppola or Stone intended. Mr. and Mrs. Johnson in Omaha or San Francisco or Manhattan will watch the films and weep and decide once and for all that war is inhumane and terrible, and they will tell their friends at church and their family this, but Corporal Johnson at Camp Pendleton and Sergeant Johnson at Travis Air Force Base...and Lance Corporal Swofford at Twentynine Palms Marine Corps Base watch the same films and are excited by them, because the magic brutality of the films celebrates the terrible and despicable beauty of their fighting skills. Filmic images of death and carnage are pornography for the military man. (2003: 6–7)

This passage raises critical questions regarding Vietnam War movies that are ceaselessly asked of war films more generally—concerning, for instance, 'the very possibility of an anti-war film...that foregrounds the visceral reconstruction of violence' (Carruthers 2011: 259); the danger that 'any depiction of war [in film] necessarily lends itself to military-pornographic exploitation' (Weschler 2005: 69), and so on. And while his memoir does not mention *Apocalypse Now* by name, in an interview on the subject, Swofford has been more specific about the particular Coppola film he has in mind, as well as which particular sequence: 'It's Kilgore who you remember, at least if you're young and impressionable, with all his manly bravado. Him and those racing helicopters. Those are the images that have kids enlisting' (Weschler 2005: 73–74). Swofford's descriptions demonstrate he is aware that he and his compatriots' reactions to this film may not be the most commonplace, and probably even run contrary to the intentions of the film's makers. Indeed, we might suspect that such reactions in fact depend on ignoring willfully, rather than simply missing, an irony that may be suspected to be present. Nonetheless, his descriptions certainly seem designed to suggest that irony, at least, was far from the most significant thing 'happening' for himself and his comrades while watching and interpreting Kilgore's 'racing helicopters'.

The film *Jarhead* (Sam Mendes 2005), meanwhile, goes further still, dramatising Swofford (Jake Gyllenhaal) and his fellow marines not only 'get[ting] off on' *Apocalypse Now*'s air cavalry attack but singing along to it, too. It shows us dozens of US marines in a screening room at their base at Camp Pendleton, watching this sequence from Coppola's movie, raising their voices raucously to ape the stately, booming melody of the Wagner: 'Duh duh-duh daah daah, duh duh-duh daah daah...'. Throughout the scene we receive numerous shots highlighting different marines' responses. Some yell instructions or encouragements to the onscreen soldiers; others jump out of their seats and throw triumphant fists rhythmically in the air (Fig. 4.2). All, however, are made to seem nothing other than utterly enthralled and enthused by the spectacle of violence unfolding in front of them, none leaving any ambiguity as to with whom their sympathies lie. When Kilgore's soldiers begin to unload their firepower upon their human targets, the marines erupt in cheers, shouts, and fist-pumps. The energy in the room is almost hysterical, many of the soldiers rising from their seats, shouting aggressively, approvingly, jubilantly, at the sights of rockets being launched into the village and at machine-gun bullets ripping around and through groups of Vietnamese men and women. Like

Fig. 4.2 *Jarhead*: The marines cheer at *Apocalypse Now*'s helicopters

Swofford's personal testimonies, then, *Jarhead*'s fictionalised depiction of the marines' reaction to *Apocalypse Now* takes pains to represent irony as being far from the most significant thing 'happening' for them during this sequence. Indeed, the fact that these characters are responding to the scene *un*ironically seems rather important to an irony that *Jarhead* itself is directing towards them at this moment (more on this shortly).

As described by Swofford and more hyperbolically dramatised by the film of *Jarhead*, then, these scenarios seem to be presented almost as enactments of the very situation imagined by Hutcheon: American male soldiers watching *Apocalypse Now*'s helicopter sequence, and irony apparently 'not figur[ing] in their interpretations'. Moreover, the memoir explicitly frames these reactions as stemming precisely from the fact that Swofford, and those to whom he attributes similar responses, do indeed belong to a particular discursive community: 'the military man', for whom 'filmic images of death and carnage are pornography' (2003: 7). And, in a final echo of Hutcheon, Swofford also appears effectively to endorse the premise that it is reception strategies—rather than the intentions of films or their makers—that determine a movie's meanings: for such an audience, he claims, 'Vietnam War films are all pro-war, no matter...what [their directors] intended' (ibid.: 6).

Particularly given the high stakes of irony's 'edge' here (some of which Swofford himself articulates), the pressing question becomes: 'What do you do, then, with the obvious fact that...there are ironies you might intend, as ironist, but which remain unperceived by others' (Hutcheon

1994: 10)? The importance of this question is undeniable, and Hutcheon recognises that any answer must acknowledge in some fashion a concept that lies so ostentatiously at its heart: intention.

Hutcheon reports that 'it is not without nervousness and self-consciousness that I raise issues of intentionality in a post-Derridean, post-Barthesian, and post-Foucaultian age'; however, as she acknowledges, 'in the study of irony's edge, it seems...to be unavoidable' (ibid.: 11). The particular way Hutcheon chooses to pursue the issue of intention, though, is not in the manner of all scholars of irony. 'The party line', she suggests, 'says that there is an intending "ironist" and her/his intended audiences—the one that "gets" and the one that doesn't "get" the irony' (ibid.: 10). This 'party line'—which is frequently critiqued by theorists such as Hutcheon, Fish, and Elleström[6]—is essentially the one adhered to by those who understand communicative irony first and foremost as *rhetorical*. To treat communicative irony as a rhetorical device was for many centuries the most common approach to interpreting irony (e.g. Quintilian 1977), and broadly rhetorical approaches to the subject have continued to hold sway in many quarters—from Burke (1969), to Muecke (1970), to Booth (1974), to Currie (2006). To approach communicative irony rhetorically is to treat it in something like the fashion that this book has thus far: fundamentally as (1) an indirect form of expression in which (2) one pretends to express a viewpoint or attitude that one does not hold; this indirect expression is (3) intended to be recognised as such by (at least some of) one's audience and thus (4) requires interpretation in order for its intended, implied meaning to be grasped (or, in Booth's terminology, 'reconstructed' [1974]). The intention of the ironist is thus indispensable to rhetorical understandings of irony and, therefore, also serves as the key to what might count as a 'successful interpretation' (Booth 1974: 36). As her arguments have already suggested, however, this is not the theoretical approach to intention taken by Hutcheon.

While agreeing that 'many cogent reasons for abandoning intentionality as the guarantee of meaning have been advanced over the years' (1994: 112), Hutcheon nonetheless argues that fully understanding irony requires 'extending further rather than tossing out the notion of intention' (ibid.: 113). Yet the concept of intentionality should be expanded, she suggests, by incorporating the intentions of the *interpreter*. Hutcheon argues that 'to call something ironic is to frame...it in such a way that, in fact, an intentionalist statement has already been made—either by the ironist or by the interpreter (or both)' (ibid.: 112). Hutcheon thus grants intention a central place in her theory of irony, but does so by proposing that the intentions of interpreters should be treated as equally fundamental to the creation of irony as the intentions of ironists.

This proposition seems to me absolutely valid—depending, that is, on what one hopes to discover about irony and what kinds of irony one is concerned with. Hutcheon, for instance, mentions the case of 'ironies… that are not intended, but are most certainly interpreted as such' (ibid.: 10). A filmic example of this might be fans of a cult film deemed 'so bad it's good' taking ironic enjoyment from its unintentional failings.[7] In such cases, it is certainly true to say that it will not be the intentions of artists or works but rather those of interpreters which make irony 'happen'. What, though, of situations like those hypothesised about by Hutcheon and described by Swofford—in which it seems likely that irony *has* been intended but certain interpreters (perhaps because of the discursive communities to which they belong) do not treat it as such?

For the sake of argument, let us momentarily assume that *Apocalypse Now*'s 'Ride of the Valkyries' scene is indeed intended ironically—that it pretends to endorse violent actions and a stylistic register that it is in fact determined to ironise. If this were so, then how should we describe what is going on in a screening room if this sequence is being watched by a group of young men who sing joyfully along with the Wagner, shouting encouragements to the fictional American soldiers depicted slaughtering Vietnamese villagers? Should we say, with Hutcheon, that, because 'irony isn't irony until it is interpreted as such' (Hutcheon 1994: 6) and is not a quality 'intrinsic to a text' (ibid.: 117), there is no irony 'happening' in this screening room at all? Or should we rather say that a film is playing that is addressing its audience ironically—and can also therefore be said to contain irony—but that this irony has seemingly failed to 'reach its destination' (Doane 1979: 129)? I suggest that the latter characterisation offers the better explanation and that irony can be described as 'happening' in a work even when it is not 'happening' for audiences.

I propose, then, that there are many legitimate debates to be had about the reach, purpose, and value of irony in the 'Ride of the Valkyries' scene; but I submit that one thing that should not be up for debate is whether the scene is ironic at all. Arguing this case convincingly, however, is in fact a challenging task. I have already suggested that it will require, in part, an in-depth analysis of this sequence of *Apocalypse Now* and its relationship to the surrounding film. I would now add that I believe such an analysis must seek in the film—and articulate in language appropriate to this medium—precisely the kind of evidence about intention that is demanded by the 'party line' approach to irony-as-*rhetoric*. In making this claim, though, I am also in need of theoretical grounding for the argument that some form of intentionalist approach to irony is even legitimate. I believe that such grounding can be found in the nature of irony itself and in the fact that, while fraught, the concept of intention does indeed seem inseparable from the concept of ironic expression.

IRONY, INTENTION, AND RHETORIC

Hutcheon suggests that 'to call something ironic is to frame…it in such a way that, in fact, an intentionalist statement has already been made— either by the ironist or by the interpreter (or both)' (1994: 112). One question to consider, however, is whether the intentionalist statements that interpreters might make when 'call[ing] something ironic' (or indeed *not* ironic) could ever be anything other than statements about the intentions of an artist or work.

Take, for instance, the scene from *Jarhead* mentioned earlier. I have suggested in passing that (leaving aside for now questions concerning the irony of the *Apocalypse Now* sequence itself) the marines who are watching Coppola's film in this manner are themselves being made the victims of *Jarhead*'s own irony. By advancing this interpretation, it would seem that I am necessarily claiming to have discerned from the film an *intention* to ironise the marines' responses. Specifically (and again using terms introduced in Chapters 2 and 3), I am claiming that the film has been intentionally constructed to evoke at this moment a sense of ironic distance from these characters' attitudes and actions—an effect we can describe as dramatic irony being created at their expense.[8] In attempting to demonstrate the validity of this interpretation, meanwhile, I suggest I would need to seek evidence for these intentions. I might, for example, cite the stated intentions of the film's director, Sam Mendes, who describes the scene this way on *Jarhead*'s DVD director's commentary: 'They're watching what is, by common consent, one of the greatest anti-war movies of all time, *Apocalypse Now*, and they're treating it entirely as a pro-war movie. I thought it was very ironic that it should be this great movie.' Or, if I am more wary of basing my interpretations on the public proclamations of artists (more on this below), I might instead attempt to identify *textual* evidence of ironic intentions in this scene or the surrounding film. I could, for instance, draw attention to the fact that the marines continue singing the famous Wagner melody at a moment when, in Coppola's film, the music is pointedly made to drop out: when we cut away to the village towards which the helicopters are hurtling, where we see a group of children being evacuated from a school; in Mendes' film, we are shown a rapt Swofford responding to this image by mouthing intensely, 'Shoot them, shoot those motherfuckers...'. Equally, I could note a parallel between this sequence and a moment towards the end of the film, when these soldiers celebrate the end of their Gulf operations with an impromptu party, during which they cathartically unload their weapons into the sky to the strains of a hip-hop track bursting from a nearby boombox; that track, I could point out, is Public Enemy's 'Fight the Power', thus making this another instance where the marines appear to be ironised for indulging in the stylistic aggression of an artwork without first reflecting on its political implications.

What I am suggesting is that when an interpreter calls something ironic, he or she is indeed making an 'intentionalist statement'; yet at least one of this interpreter's intentions must necessarily be to attribute intentions to a work or its makers. This fact becomes clearer still when we are speaking of what is commonly called verbal irony but which in this book I have been referring to as communicative irony or ironic pretence (Chapters 2 and 3). In the case of this kind of irony, it seems especially clear that intention is the only thing that makes irony definable as irony in the first place. If I express myself ironically by turning to my friend in the pouring rain and announcing, 'Lovely weather!', what exactly is it that makes this an instance of communicative irony? It is the fact that I am momentarily pretending to possess (what I would consider) poor powers of perception and that I intend to communicate indirectly a contrary assessment of the weather. If I did *not* intend to communicate this alternative meaning, instead of speaking ironically, I would either be mistaken, revealing myself to have unusual taste in weather, or lying. *With* my intention to communicate the alternative meaning, however, my statement becomes not incorrect, eccentric, or deceptive, but ironic. It thus seems to be only my intention that makes this an instance of irony rather than an instance of something else. Hutcheon in fact acknowledges this, noting that 'intention is one of the few ways we have of distinguishing lying from irony' (1994: 113). It therefore appears logical to conclude that intention is in fact a non-negotiable component of what defines communicative irony as a distinct phenomenon in the first place (Carroll 2002). As Douglas Muecke puts it: 'being ironical means deliberately being ironical' (1969: 57).

Since intention appears indispensable to the very definition of communicative irony, it seems to follow that it must also be indispensable to the interpretation of such irony. For this reason, as Daniel Nathan puts it, 'irony can seem especially problematic for anti-intentionalism' (1992: 184). In his article 'Why Intentionalism Won't Go Away', Denis Dutton goes so far as to argue that 'ironic works are *decisive* in supporting the need for appeals to authorial intentions' (1987: 203; emphasis mine); he offers the following example as support:

> Consider Strauss's only work for piano and orchestra, his *Burleske*, written in 1885. The...listener who supposes the piece to be a straight attempt to compose a one-movement piano concerto will no doubt find it in many ways attractive and rewarding. But the meaning, for example, of Strauss's mad double-octave passages, which evaporate at the top of the keyboard (rather than leading into big cadences), or the long runs that go nowhere, will elude such a listener. In this instance the composer has helpfully provided a title that gives a hint that the work is intended as a sendup of the romantic virtuoso piano concerto. But authors are not always so helpful; and in any event, whether they are is immaterial so far as the purely conceptual question is concerned. (ibid.: 200–201)

In such cases, Dutton argues, 'intentions appear to constitute a bedrock without which valid interpretation is impossible' (ibid.: 200). This is largely because, as we have seen, communicative irony involves pretending to behave in precisely the manner that one wishes to ironise. Nathan notes that, in speech, the meaning of an ironic sentence 'cannot just be "read off" the meanings of the words that make it up. Instead, some "extra" interpretive move appears necessary to capture the special twist of language at work' (1992: 184). That 'extra' move is precisely to attribute ironic intention: it is only by assuming my *intention* to say 'Lovely weather!' ironically that my friend can distinguish an ironic use of such words from a lying (or perhaps peculiar, or mistaken) use of them. Something very similar seems bound to be true for non-linguistic media. In the case of *Burleske*, we do not need to invoke intention to argue that Strauss's piece uses Romantic musical conventions in unusual ways. We do need to invoke intention, however, to argue that the work employs these conventions not only unusually, but also ironically. I suggest that we must extend the same assumption to film. When we interpret a film or a portion of it as being ironic in this way, we appear necessarily to be inferring an intention—specifically, an intention to imply an 'attitude [or an] evaluative judgment' towards materials that the film is employing or perspectives it is adopting (Dynel 2014: 540).

The relevance of this for the 'Ride of the Valkyries' scene should already be clear. I referred earlier to a widespread concern regarding cinematic depictions of warfare: that the very representation of combat in this medium might unavoidably render it spectacular, which might in turn compromise a film's ability to critique that which it depicts. Yet this sequence from *Apocalypse Now* does not merely '[foreground] the visceral reconstruction of violence' (Carruthers 2011: 259); it seems positively to *revel* in it. This is partly due, again, to the Wagner music itself. I have noted that the stylistic register of this piece is aggressive and assertive and, thus, seems in some sense conducive to the depiction of a battle. Yet what is perhaps even more striking about it is its utterly *triumphant* nature. Thanks to the sheer, joyous ebullience of its resoundingly major-key melody, the mood created through Wagner's composition and orchestration in fact seems appropriate not so much to a battle as a victory march—evoking less the struggle of war than something closer to the jubilation of a celebration. In this sense, as used in this context, this music not only carries 'vague suggestions of war' (Hutcheon 1994: 18) but also suggests very much a particular perspective on and attitude *towards* this act of war. Meanwhile, as we have already noted, the film's visual style frequently aligns itself with the style of the music—cutting to its rhythms, the camera moving in time with its propulsive melodic dynamics, and so on. Rhetorically speaking, then, the filmmaking creates a sense that it might be attempting to persuade us that this spectacle of slaughter should indeed be regarded as triumphant. This in turn means that, as Frank Tomasulo puts it,

> The sheer kinesthetic excitement of this sequence—especially its sweeping and majestic helicopter shots—might even provoke a 'gung-ho' response from those who revel in deeds of derring-do....The editing is quick and fast-paced, simulating the highly charged emotional state of...Kilgore and his men. The scene is synchronized to a triumphant musical score.... The audience is thus cinematically implicated in the exhilarating superiority of the American attack. (1990: 149)

If, however, I as an audience member do not support and endorse the music's apparent collusion in this slaughter, and resent my implication in the attack—and if I furthermore suspect that this may be exactly the response the sequence seeks to provoke—then it would seem, as Booth puts it, that 'I must somehow determine whether what I reject is also rejected by the author' (1974: 11). As such, because of the nature of irony itself, it appears that I am unavoidably required to explain the sequence not only in terms of its stylistic qualities, but also in terms of the intentions informing those qualities.

If we wish to continue interpreting irony at all, it does thus appear that we are also bound to continue speaking in some fashion about intention. This clearly brings us back, though, to the problems with intentionalist approaches to interpretation. These have, of course, been well-rehearsed in literary theory, film theory, and the humanities more broadly for many decades. As Peter Kivy puts it, 'The mere mention of the word "intention" in regard to any art-critical or art-theoretical question is liable to elicit, these days, the most violent reaction, as if one had just dropped a snake in a crowded room' (1993: 9). There do indeed exist numerous familiar, tangible problems with supporting our interpretations by referring to (what we take to be) the real intentions of real artists. There is, for instance, the problem of the 'accessibility' of the artist's intention (Elleström 2002: 45). If we listen to a film's director's commentary—or even converse with an artist ourselves—this can still provide us only with what an artist (wishes publicly to claim) s/he *remembers* intending, and intending *consciously* (Wimsatt/Beardsley 1946). This latter point highlights the extraordinarily complex nature of intentions themselves. As a mental activity, intention invariably consists of a tangled mass of conscious and instinctive impulses, which will be affected by any number of factors—both psychological and environmental—and whose precise character we may never be able to comprehend, let alone verbalise (Dickie 2006). This offers another reason for doubting the usefulness of basing one's interpretations on 'psychological states or events in [the artist's] mind' (Beardsley 1958: 17). Equally, granting interpretive authority to a real artist's statements about their intentions would seem also to grant them the ability to change the meaning of a work simply via what they happen to claim about it—regardless of the nature of that work (Wilson/Dickie 1995). Finally, there is the obvious fact that certain artworks—and, in particular, films—are the product not of a single artist but many artists working in concert; clearly, we cannot reasonably attribute a single mental intention to a collection of individuals (Elleström 2002: 46).

These are only a handful of the reasons why interpretive critics might justifiably be wary of invoking the real intentions of real artists.[9] Yet, as we have also by now acknowledged, if we are speaking of ironic expression at all, we are also necessarily speaking of an intention to be ironic. George Wilson conveys the general quandary well when he notes that, upon sensing certain personal qualities or intentions manifested in an artwork,

> no doubt, we frequently suspect that the flesh-and-blood author...had, in reality, the personal qualities that we find thus manifested, but we are cognizant of the various ways in which these suspicions may be historically false, and thus require a terminology that permits us to articulate the character of the relevant impressions...without incurring any direct commitment about the artist's psychic biography. I take it that the concept of 'implied author'... was designed to contribute to such a terminology, and I believe that a parallel concept of 'implied (version of the) film maker' can play a similar role. (1986: 134–5)

Wilson thus proposes that one solution to the problem of intentionality may be to adapt the notion of 'the implied author' to film. This famous term was proposed by Wayne Booth to address exactly the kinds of problems with invoking real artists' intentions touched on earlier. For Booth, the implied author is not a work's flesh-and-blood creator, but an *inferred* 'ideal, literary, created version of the real man [*sic*]; he is the sum of his own choices' (1961: 74–5).[10] Wilson is just one of several scholars who have argued that the term may be equally applicable to film as literature (e.g. Currie 1995; Robertson 1990). Jerrold Levinson, for example, argues that 'the need for this concept is clear,' defining it as 'the picture we construct of the film's maker—beliefs, aims, attitudes, values, and personality—on the basis of the film' (1996: 253). And indeed, it is difficult not to agree that the concept of the implied author in some sense appears *especially* appropriate for film—a medium in which artistic labour is carried out by myriad agents making myriad choices but that still frequently creates the sense of 'a creative voice uniting all of the choices' (Booth 2002: 125). Applied to questions of irony, the concept of the implied author could thus usefully serve as a figure to whom we attribute the intentions necessary for a film, or any aspect of it, to be considered ironic. If discussing *Apocalypse Now*, for instance, we might plausibly refer to the ironic intentions of 'Coppola', the implied filmmaker.

There are, however, additional concepts that could allow us to put aside hypotheses about the workings of filmmakers' minds while still incorporating the crucial matter of intention. Discussing what is involved in discerning

a film's tone, Douglas Pye suggests that 'these interpretative manoeuvres...
depend on what we intuit, as the film develops, about the film's intentions'
(2007: 13). Attributing intentions to a film itself does seem another possible approach, and it is one that has much in common with what Umberto
Eco calls the 'intention of the text'. 'Between the unattainable intention
of the author and the arguable intention of the reader', claims Eco, 'there
is the...intention of the text, which disproves an untenable interpretation'
(1992a: 78). This concept is closely related to that of the implied author, as
Eco makes clear when he refers to 'a model author that is not the empirical
one and that, in the end, coincides with the intention of the text' (1992b:
64). It has the added benefit, though, of retaining a focus on intention
while also avoiding any reference to an *individual* figure (however hypothetical) who possesses those intentions, which could seem inappropriate
to a medium such as film. In what follows, then, when discussing intention,
I will for the most part restrict myself to references to the *film's* intentions. I suggest that, while inevitably imperfect, this may be the best available response to the troublesome but necessary requirement of attributing
intentionality to filmmaking.[11] The only remaining question, then, is the
small matter of how we might best discern a film's intentions.

The concept of the intention of the text (like the implied author) relies
fundamentally upon inference; as Eco notes, 'the text's intention is not
displayed by the textual surface....One has to decide to "see" it. [It is] the
result of a conjecture' (ibid.: 64). Yet that conjecture must nonetheless
be built in large part upon what is indeed displayed on a text's 'surface':
the strategies employed by its story, narration, point of view, tone, style,
and so on. If attempting to infer a film's intentions, we must examine
such aspects of its address for guidance as to the interpretations a film
is inviting us to make. As Terry Eagleton puts it in relation to literature,
'when we understand the intentions of a piece of language, we interpret
it as being in some sense *oriented*, structured to achieve certain effects'
(1983: 114; original emphasis). Another way of putting this would be to
say that determining a film's intentions can only be, after all, a matter of
identifying the nature of its *rhetoric*. Nick Browne notes that discerning
the nature of a film's rhetoric consists, in part, of discerning the 'ensem-
ble of attitude, judgement, and intention' implied by its narration (1975:
30). Furthermore, to study a film's rhetoric is also crucially to study what
appear to be its 'means of persuasion' (Perez 2000: 1)—the innumerable
ways in which it seems designed with the purpose of urging us to watch,
understand, and experience it in the manner the film intends.

If we are attempting to determine the presence of *ironic* intentions specifically, then we are clearly concerned with an aspect of rhetoric that Kenneth Burke calls 'persuasion "to attitude"' (1969: 50). And, if we try to establish whether a film's intention is to persuade us to experience it with an ironic attitude, then we will likely need to seek evidence for the kinds of rhetorical strategies that are often called 'irony markers': conventional clues as to the presence of irony (Muecke 1978). Although we have not been referring to them as such, we have in fact been encountering numerous conventional rhetorical markers throughout this book and have examined some forms they may take in film: clashes of perspective, shifts in style, excess, various kinds of juxtaposition, incongruity, distance, and so forth. As even adherents to the intentionalist view of irony are usually quick to acknowledge, these rhetorical markers will 'not *constitute* the irony; rather, they are evidence of the presence of irony' (Hermerén 1975: 73; emphasis mine). That is to say: they can serve only as signals as to the possibility or likelihood that irony has, precisely, been intended.[12]

As this characterisation suggests, it will always be true that, as Dan Sperber and Deirdre Wilson put it, 'there is no such thing as a fail-safe diagnostic of irony' (2007: 47); this is because, as they rightly observe, 'intentions…must be inferred by a fallible process of hypothesis formation'; thus, 'even the best hypothesis may turn out to be wrong' (ibid.: 47). However, although accurate, this very formulation admits that there is such a thing as a 'wrong' (and by implication 'right'?) hypothesis. I submit that, if we admit the existence of such a thing as ironic expression,[13] and if we are interested in interpreting it, then the ever-present possibility of our hypotheses about texts' intentions being wrong cannot prevent us from striving for the hypotheses that seem 'best'. It is in such a spirit that we must hypothesise about the ironic intentions of *Apocalypse Now*.

THE IRONY IN *APOCALYPSE NOW*: RHETORIC AND ITS CONTEXTS

Where, then, should we seek rhetorical evidence that irony is intended in the 'Ride of the Valkyries' sequence? As we have established, one of the most pressing interpretive questions raised by the scene is what to make of the rhetorical consonance it creates between the Wagner piece and the narration's presentation of the violence. There is, of course, an obvious reason why this close alignment between sound, dramatic material, and narration might initially suggest intentions *other* than irony: a widely acknowledged 'irony marker'—especially as regards film music—is not rhetorical consonance, but rather rhetorical *incongruity*. When discussing ironic uses of music in Chapter 3, for instance, we encountered *Good Morning, Vietnam*, in which Louis Armstrong's 'What a Wonderful World' soundtracked a montage depicting various distressing scenes of violence associated with the Vietnam conflict—including, indeed, US helicopters bombing a Vietnamese village. In a case like this, the film's rhetorical strategies seem to ensure that our decision to interpret ironic intentions in the use of music is made (almost?) inevitable. By contrast, *Apocalypse Now* unmistakably creates more stylistic consonance than incongruity between the tenor of its music and the images of hammering artillery and death on screen. Given this, how exactly are we to determine that its ultimate intention is not to elicit responses like, for instance, those of *Jarhead*'s 'gung-ho' marines?

The answer, I suggest, is that the rhetoric of this sequence in fact *does* create incongruities, but that to discern them we must look beyond the individual sequence alone. That is to say that the scene's rhetoric demands somehow to be *contextualised*. As Eco puts it: interpreting the intentions of a text is always 'a kind of interpretive bet'; yet, as he goes on to note, 'the contexts allow us to make this bet less uncertain than a bet on the red or the black of a roulette wheel' (1992b: 63). 'Contexts' of various kinds will indeed always be key to discerning ironic intention. They can fruitfully be understood as consisting of two broad types, both of which must have a bearing on our interpretation of *Apocalypse Now*.

First, there are the contexts provided for an individual moment by the surrounding text. These encompass all the various rhetorical strategies adopted throughout a film, any of which could inform our judgements about the intended purpose of the film's address at any given moment: where and how a particular device or strategy is placed relative to other established tendencies of the work, whether the rhetoric of this moment seems to chime or clash with rhetorical strategies adopted elsewhere, and so on. Second, though, contexts beyond the rhetoric of the work itself will also be important. These might include conventions established by comparable types of texts, some awareness of the historical and cultural moment in which a text was produced, normative moral frameworks we associate with that time and culture, and so on and so forth. Again, it will usually be impossible to reach a judgement about whether a work is addressing us ironically without some reference to inter- and extra-textual contexts of these far more general kinds.[14] Indeed, while often tacit, every interpretation of irony offered by this book will rely somewhere and to some degree upon such contexts.[15]

Demonstrating ironic intentions in *Apocalypse Now* will thus certainly be a matter of attending to the film's rhetorical strategies; but to explain the significance of those strategies, we may also need to refer to a potentially limitless array of broader contexts. Given, though, that no interpretation can ever account for all the external contexts to which a text's rhetoric could *conceivably* be related, the question necessarily becomes: which contexts should be treated as most relevant? Booth approaches the matter this way:

> What determines the *relevant* context out of the infinite number of surrounding details are the [implied] author's choices and the reader's inference about those choices..., with every detail referring reciprocally to every other in the work. But at the same time, it is impossible to say that only what is 'in the work' is relevant context, because at every point the [implied] author depends on inferences about what his [*sic*] reader will likely assume or know—about both his [*sic*] factual knowledge and his experience of literature. And the reader depends on inferences about what the [implied] author could assume. (1974: 99–100; original emphasis)

Booth's point here can help us articulate why external contexts will always be relevant to our sense of a film's intentions and, thus, to the interpretation of irony. Inferring the intentions of a work's rhetoric involves, in part, inferences about what contexts the work seems to assume its audience to be conversant with: facts about the world, knowledge of particular aesthetic conventions, and so on.[16] Take, as an especially clear-cut example, Doane's aforementioned observation that someone who has never seen a Western will surely find it difficult to 'get' the irony of *Once Upon a Time in the West* (1979: 137). This is because Leone's film invites us to interpret it in relation to this cultural context and assumes our familiarity with it.[17] Films thus *intend* us to understand them in relation to broader contexts, meaning that one task of interpretation must be to determine the most relevant of those contexts. This, then, is one of our responsibilities when interpreting *Apocalypse Now*: discerning the intentions of the film's rhetoric, yes, but also discerning the contexts to which that rhetoric seems intended to relate.

What contexts might be most relevant to the intentions of the 'Ride of the Valkyries' sequence? In her own interpretation of how irony 'happens' for her during this scene, Hutcheon begins by acknowledging the rhetorical strategies of the surrounding film; yet she quickly abandons her consideration of this internal context in favour of external contexts of a quite particular kind. It is worth quoting her interpretation at some length:

> Hearing [the] rhythmic power and strong dynamics [of 'Ride of the Valkyries'] while viewing a military maneuver might suggest to you a certain appropriateness, either because of vague suggestions of war or because the characters' response on screen reveals it as functioning [as a kind of violent aphrodisiac]....Yet, in the context of the film, this 'high-art' music is highly incongruous and clashes with the rock music that has dominated the sound-track to this point. What if, in addition to this, among your many discursive communities there was one framed by some knowledge of Wagner's work, and therefore you knew that this was called the 'Ride of the Valkyries' and perhaps even that, in Wagner's mythic universe, the Valkyries were supernatural women? Then, suddenly out-of-place suggestions of the feminine and the otherworldly might well intrude on your viewing of what has so far in the film been a very male and material, not to say earthy, world. If you know even more about this, the second opera of the cycle known as *Der Ring des Nibelungen*, you might add to these now multiple incongruities, the fact that this music is used in the opera to accompany the warrior maidens as they search the battlefield for the dead bodies of those fallen heroes worthy of being taken to Valhalla, the home of the gods. However, the male-piloted helicopter[s], you may then notice, [are] just going into battle in the film: this is a killing mission, a conscious attempt to create—and not reap and redeem—dead bodies.
>
> I have been writing 'you' here but, of course, I mean 'me,' for this is how I attribute and interpret irony here. (1994: 18–19)

It strikes me as telling, first, that Hutcheon in fact does not write 'you' and mean 'me' when referring to a context that has been established by the surrounding film itself. That the Wagner clashes with the kinds of music used elsewhere is not suggested to be an interpretation that we might or might not hazard but is rather treated, on the contrary, as an indisputable fact about *Apocalypse Now*: 'in the context of the film, this...music is highly incongruous'. This rhetorical context will indeed be indispensable for discerning the intentions of the sequence and will be returned to shortly.

Second, though, it also seems significant that Hutcheon goes on to ground her interpretation in quite such specialised intertextual contexts: the gender of the beings referred to in the title 'Ride of the Valkyries', the piece's narrative functions within the original opera, and so on. Of course, basing her reading upon these comparatively arcane contexts helps serve her argument that it will not be texts but one's discursive communities that make irony 'happen'. Yet, although I have no reason to doubt that this interpretation captures how irony personally 'happens' for Hutcheon during the helicopter attack scene, I also suggest that it fails to account for several other more pressingly relevant contexts that encourage us to infer ironic intentions in this sequence. And, as I have suggested, if we wish to call something ironic, then we are necessarily hypothesising about its intentions. Given this, we need to seek the most relevant contexts to which this sequence in *Apocalypse Now* intends us to relate it—both the rhetorical contexts established by the surrounding film and broader cultural contexts.

In terms of cultural contexts for the scene, Wagner's music does loom large. Yet I propose that the most relevant aspects of that context are not the narrative specifics of the *Ring* cycle but rather far more widely available cultural associations of Wagner's music more generally. Perhaps the most important of these is, of course, a longstanding association with racism and Nazism.[18] Even leaving aside commonly cited and debated evidence of Wagner's own anti-Semitism, it has long been public knowledge that Adolf Hitler was an admirer of Wagner's and that the composer's music was frequently used at high-profile Nazi events, with certain (unsubstantiated) rumours persisting that it may also have been routinely played at Nazi concentration camps.[19] The reason I consider this a relevant context—and more relevant than the particulars of the opera for which 'Ride of the Valkyries' was written—rests partly on my sense of what, as Booth would put it, 'the [implied] author [could] infer...about what his reader [*sic*] will likely assume or know' (1974: 99–100). Wagner's association with Nazism has been treated as relatively common currency within US popular culture since at least *The Great Dictator* (Charlie Chaplin, 1940), when the Hitler-like dictator Adenoid Hynkel (Chaplin) performed his dance routine with a floating globe to the strains of Wagner's *Lohengrin* prelude. I do not claim, of course, that every member of *Apocalypse Now*'s audience will be familiar with this association, any more than they will all be familiar with the specifics of Wagner's opera. I do claim, though, that it represents a cultural context that this film is more likely to assume its audience could possess.[20] For instance, in support of the premise that American films of *Apocalypse Now*'s period were prepared to assume widespread awareness of this association, we might note an oblique joke about Wagner and anti-

Semitism made in 1977's *Annie Hall*, which depends absolutely upon knowledge of this context in order to be understood.[21]

Especially given that the helicopter sequence has Kilgore mention Wagner by name—announcing 'I use Wagner. It scares the hell out of the slopes'—I thus suggest that the film strongly invites us to draw upon such general associations pertaining to Wagner's cultural reputation. Furthermore, this line of Kilgore's also makes plain the second reason for inferring the relevance of this context: the fact that the 'Ride of the Valkyries' scene depicts both explicit racism (such as this racial slur) and a more general dramatisation of assumptions of racial superiority—Kilgore's later exclamation, 'Fuckin' savages', for instance, as well as the very fact of the attack being launched on an exclusively Vietnamese population. This relates in turn to another cultural context for the Wagner that would seem to demand our attention.

Prior to *Apocalypse Now*, the most notorious popular-cultural association of the 'Ride of Valkyries' in American cinema was surely its use in the infamous *The Birth of a Nation* (D.W. Griffith, 1915), and particularly its role in that film's heroic depiction of the Ku Klux Klan (KKK). While *The Birth of a Nation* was made before the advent of synchronised sound, scores by composer Joseph Carl Breil accompanied prints of the film on its initial release, and variations on that score have soundtracked almost every subsequent reissue (Hickman 2006: 68–78). Breil's score melds original compositions with stretches of existing classical pieces. Notable among these is 'Ride of the Valkyries', which is used in the film to accompany an action set-piece in which members of the KKK charge into a small South Carolina town on horseback to prevent the forced wedding of a white woman to a villainous 'mulatto', killing numerous members of a black militia in the process. As employed here, the piece is thus aligned with the spectacle of a military triumph by the KKK, its assertive and celebratory tone made to assist in the film's laudatory representation of the violent deeds of this racist paramilitary organisation.

While I would argue that this might still be assumed to be a considerably more widely available context than the comparatively recondite facts about the *Ring* cycle cited by Hutcheon,[22] my argument for its relevance rests less upon what I presume the film could assume about its audience's knowledge. Rather, it is the many suggestive links between *Apocalypse Now*'s dramatic and thematic materials and Griffith's film that makes this context seem particularly relevant to the text's intentions—more relevant than, for instance, suggestions of feminine otherworldliness or the aims of

Wagner's Valkyries. Although feminine and otherworldly overtones could be said to clash in a very general fashion with the sequence's contents, I suggest that the connections with *The Birth of a Nation* are specific and numerous enough to appear pointed: the depiction of a military triumph; the fact that, like the Klan, Kilgore's airborne division is equipped with superior weaponry; the 'charge' of the fleet of helicopters suggesting a contemporary iteration of an armed offensive by horseback[23]; and, of course, the fact that Coppola's scene too depicts a predominantly white (North American) force launching a sneak attack upon members of another race. These echoes cause me to suspect strongly that Griffith's film is not simply one context among innumerable others to which we *could* conceivably refer but rather a deliberate allusion that has been intended.[24]

I thus suggest that *Apocalypse Now* intends us to draw upon these contexts when interpreting this sequence. We might debate the precise resonances we should feel encouraged to take from these associations, but I argue that they must be considered relevant to our hypotheses about the film's rhetoric and its intentions.[25] We could hypothesise about what those intentions might be by invoking a final, broader context. *Apocalypse Now* is about the Vietnam War. America's involvement in this war came to be opposed by a vast majority of the US population and was, moreover, widely and publicly accused at home of being based in imperialist and racist ideologies (Hall 2005: 60). Despite this, the film chooses to accompany a violent US military victory with music that carries strong cultural associations of both Nazi genocide and US racism. Yet it also adopts stylistic strategies during this sequence that appear to amount to a rhetorical endorsement of combining this triumphant piece of music with this murderous spectacle. By doing so, this scene, which seems so defined by its rhetorical congruence, in fact implicitly creates significant *in*congruence: the film's rhetoric gives the impression of affirming something that various relevant cultural contexts strongly suggest may not be being affirmed. If 'discovering an ironic intention in a work depends upon... the decision that the [text] cannot have intended such-and-such a meaning' (Booth 1974: 19), then these contexts go a certain distance towards convincing me to decide, at least, that it appears unlikely *Apocalypse Now* can be using this music entirely *un*ironically. Specifically, the incongruities they create play a key role in encouraging me to suspect that the helicopter scene is adopting an ironic pretence: intending to create the *appearance* of expressing one thing, when in fact it intends to express something else.

This, though, is far from the only evidence we can cite in support of an interpretation of the sequence's ironic intentions. Taking account of the additional evidence requires engaging in some depth both with the musical incongruity raised passingly by Hutcheon and with other contexts established for the sequence by the surrounding film. It is worth acknowledging that interpreting these internal rhetorical contexts will, in fact, still on occasion require me to invoke various broader contexts—from fairly specific historical or cultural associations to much more general assumptions about normative moral frameworks. Nonetheless, the difference between the film's internal contexts and those cultural contexts considered thus far is, as Hutcheon acknowledges, that the former constitute undeniable, observable facts of the film itself, regardless of how we might interpret them. As such, to make decisions about what interpretive judgements they intend us to make, we must support the sorts of inferences about intention we have hitherto practised with sustained close analysis.

IRONIC PRETENCE: MUSIC AND INCONGRUITY

I have so far hypothesised that one way of defining the nature of *Apocalypse Now*'s rhetoric during the helicopter sequence would be to say that it may be engaging in ironic pretence, and that one reason for inferring this is the incongruity created by Wagner's cultural associations. Yet, as Hutcheon argues, something else that might encourage this interpretation is the aural incongruity the film creates between this piece of music and the kind of music featured elsewhere. Before pursuing and extending this observation, though, we must first note an important incongruity that is actually created within the sequence itself.

In my earlier interpretation of the screening room scene from *Jarhead*, I suggested that one thing that heavily implied the marines were being ironised was the fact that they continued singing the melody of 'Ride of the Valkyries' during a moment when in Coppola's film that music drops out. This moment in *Apocalypse Now* comes when we transition suddenly from aerial shots of the advancing helicopters—accompanied by the blasting Wagner—to the village towards which the fleet is headed. The thirty seconds that follow this abrupt cut introduce us to a seemingly serene, meagerly appointed encampment. A low, slowly tracking wide shot positions us in a yard where a few women are tending to plants and arranging baskets; next to one of them crouches a young child. After a brief moment in which only the sounds of a dog barking and a duck quacking break the silence, we hear the distant voices of children singing from inside one of the small nearby buildings, suggesting that it is a school. Soon, the Wagner is heard edging its way onto the soundtrack, growing gradually louder, alerting both us and the villagers to the helicopters' proximity. The alarm is raised: a woman runs out of the building to begin an evacuation, and a warning bell starts ringing. As a group of kids are hurried out (Fig. 4.3), one boy pauses, standing and staring off curiously in the direction of the music, almost getting left behind, before a classmate runs back to fetch him. Following this, we cut to a distant shot of the advancing helicopters as seen from the beach, the music now a little louder, then find ourselves suddenly thrown back into the fleet's midst, the Wagner reinstated to its initial booming volume.

As situated within the sequence, this brief passage appears highly incongruous in several respects. Most obviously, the decision to give us a glimpse of the village momentarily wrenches our point of view away from a focus on the characters we have hitherto been following. More specifically, we are introduced to the location they are about to assault, before being thrust back again to the helicopters. Visually, too, the contrasts between the images of the aircraft and the village could hardly be made starker. From a crowded sky we cut to an initially sparsely populated yard. The helicopters appear high-tech and robust, whereas the village looks comparatively archaic—its buildings' structures all too penetrable and the children more vulnerable still. We move from shots of male-piloted machines of war plunging through the sky to women and kids in a calm, still, presently peaceful location. This last fact especially reinforces

Fig. 4.3 *Apocalypse Now*: Our glimpse of the serene village prior to the attack

the sense that the shift in perspective intends to create as many clashes as possible. We will soon learn that this village contains many armed combatants, as well as anti-aircraft gun posts; however, since the primary purpose of the shift in point of view seems to be to create juxtapositions, we are not initially shown any sights that could establish any significant parallels between the advancing helicopters and their target. The overall sense of juxtaposition is, furthermore, at least as indebted to sounds as imagery. The Wagner is made to move higher and lower in the sound mix at different points across the sequence; at the particular instant we cut away from the helicopters its volume is rendered especially thunderous, ensuring that its sudden cutting-out feels even more markedly abrupt. Contributing further to that sense of abruptness is the fact that the piece is broken off *just* before the main melodic line is about to resolve, leaving it hanging, its trajectory interrupted. Finally, in its place we hear not simply silence but bucolic sounds of nature (the duck and dog), before the reedy noise of the children's singing causes a further musical clash with the overpowering sounds in which we were previously immersed.

Taken together, these decisions concerning perspective, imagery, and soundtrack thus create a multitude of incongruities with those elements of the sequence preceding and following the transition to the village. The fact that the film's point of view jumps so rudely away from and then back to the helicopters in this manner should, I think, be understood as a rhetorical gesture, whose purpose is to guide our interpretation of Kilgore's fleet once we return to it. The intentions implied by that gesture can, I suggest, be defined as ironic—encouraging our point of view and evaluation of the imminent attack to become distanced from the points of view and values apparently possessed by its perpetrators, including our protagonists. This is partly simply a matter of normative moral frameworks: particularly given the decision to highlight the presence of children, the brief introduction to the village seems intended to distance our moral sympathies from those who are set on obliterating its inhabitants, and also from the belief that the Wagner might represent an appropriate musical score for this impending slaughter. Equally, though, to pursue this matter of distance a little further: the point of view we are retrospectively urged to adopt towards the Hueys' occupants depends precisely on the film having momentarily allowed us to get far closer than these soldiers to the potential victims of their assault. The wide shots we see of the villagers may in fact remain relatively distant (we are not suddenly provided with emotive close-ups of frightened children's faces, say), but they nonetheless guarantee we are momentarily granted views of this village that are infinitely less detached than those of the men currently perched on high in Kilgore's advancing helicopters, who can see this encampment less as a community featuring domestic tasks and schools than as an inconvenient military target on a map. While I would not go quite so far as Jeffrey Chown in describing this shift from the helicopters to the village as '*the* key cut in facilitating the ironic point of view' (1988: 137; emphasis mine), this aspect of the scene's rhetoric does make a pivotal contribution to my decision to interpret the sequence as I do.

This rhetorical incongruity therefore forms a part of the attack sequence itself. Coming as it does after the film's style has already begun to collude with the music—moving in time with its cadences, cutting to its rhythms—the tranquil interjection constitutes a disruption of the precise collaboration between image, music, and action that the film had begun to develop. In doing so, it also allows for a brief moment of distance within a sequence that is otherwise defined by an overwhelming consonance and closeness between the film's narration, the mood of the Wagner, and the dramatic events depicted. Following this momentary interruption, though, the rest of the sequence reverts largely to precisely the patterns of rhetoric that had already begun to be established.

Indeed, the remainder of the time during which 'Ride of the Valkyries' plays is for the most part characterised by an *intensified* sense of closeness and stylistic appropriateness between the ferocity of the music, the action, and the manner of its presentation. For instance, when Wagner's main melody strikes up with renewed force upon our return to the fleet, we cut to a close-up of a pilot's thumb launching the inaugural missile, then to a shot of that missile speeding off towards the beach, and soon to several hurtling aerial shots that apparently represent the perspectives of the advancing helicopters themselves. Equally, after one of the choppers sustains minor damage from the Viet Cong, the resumption of this rousing melody accompanies images of the US pilots retaliating by blowing up the responsible anti-aircraft weapon and its operators. Another way the film creates an increased sense of rhetorical closeness is by gradually excising any viewpoints that appear to any extent disengaged from the manner in which this military action is being conducted. When the music first begins playing (prior to the cut to the village), we are provided with a couple of shots of Willard and *his* team, who are strangers to Colonel Kilgore's methods. They initially respond to the sounds of the music either with some confusion or with (perhaps somewhat gleeful) incredulity: Willard and Lance (Sam Bottoms) are shown sharing a sideways glance, while Chef

(Frederic Forrest) laughs and shakes his head. However, such acknowledgements of any comparatively sceptical perspectives on the scene soon recede into the background. This is partly because we begin to be more frequently shown the faces of nameless members of Kilgore's troops, who are far more enthusiastic—shouting encouragements, shooting, whooping, giving one another thumbs-up signs, and so on. It is also due to the fact that Willard and his team themselves appear quite quickly to get into the spirit of the operation: early on we see Clean (Laurence Fishburne), for instance, high-spiritedly shouting, 'Run, Charlie!' (before we cut, indeed, to a shot of one man fleeing for his life); later, Willard himself is shown letting off several rounds from his perch in the chopper.

Overt incongruity of the kind created by the cut to the village is thus in short supply during the rest of the attack. If we wish to seek more evidence for the sequence's ironic intentions, then, we must look beyond this scene itself. What we must try to establish by doing so is whether the context supplied by the rest of the film appears to support, complicate, or even invert our sense that the film's rhetoric might be endorsing the violent triumphalism that 'Ride of the Valkyries' appears to represent for, and helps instil in, Kilgore and his men.

The first place to which we might profitably turn is the incongruity identified by Hutcheon between the Wagner and the music used elsewhere: the fact that, 'in the context of the film, this "high-art" music is highly incongruous and clashes with the rock music that has dominated the sound-track to this point' (1994: 18). It is absolutely true that one way in which the rhetoric of the attack sequence differs from that of the surrounding film is through its foregrounding of classical music at all. Almost all other pieces of prerecorded music featured prominently in *Apocalypse Now* are indeed popular songs contemporaneous to the film's 1969 setting, and even Carmine Coppola's originally composed score largely eschews classical instrumentation, consisting primarily of electronic and synthesised sounds. However, while this in itself ensures the Wagner's atypicality, more can be said about how the film's rhetoric elsewhere contributes to this scene's incongruity in context.

One strong hint that 'Ride of the Valkyries' may be being deployed ironically is the incongruity between the rhetorical register evoked by this scene's combination of image-track and soundtrack, and the ways this film combines music and imagery elsewhere—particularly at other moments of violence. The film's opening dream-like sequence is especially instructive in this regard. In *Apocalypse Now*'s first moments we fade in to a static wide shot of the edge of a jungle, our view of a row of palm trees immediately somewhat compromised by a smoke that hangs between the camera and its subject. This is the first of many choices establishing this sequence's distanced, indistinct, almost impressionistic nature. After a few seconds, initially mysterious distorted and sporadic whirring sounds begin to fade in. As soon as the appearance of a Huey helicopter seems to confirm the sound's apparent source, the dark yellow mist that has blurred our view of the trees begins to thicken further. With these variously disorienting features already in place, The Doors' 'The End' starts to play. It opens with three sparse cymbal hits that are oddly separated from the rhythm of the ensuing song, before a melody belatedly edges in slowly, and in a near-improvisatory fashion, a single high-register electric guitar string occasionally spiralling up and down a minor scale. Before long, the pulse of a cymbal begins, which starts to lend the music some shape; yet the comparative sense of structure this affords is also offset by the occasional return of the distorted whirring sounds, which fade in and out arhythmically. Suddenly, as Jim Morrison's voice begins softly singing the opening lines ('This is the end, / Beautiful friend; the end'), multiple explosions rip silently through the trees, completely engulfing them—and virtually the entire screen—in flames and thick smoke. We do not hear the noise of the blast or fire, but the song gradually increases in intensity, becoming more frantically formless and meandering: the guitar part improvises on minor and sometimes atonal notes; inscrutable lyrics intone, 'Can you / Picture what will be? / So limitless and free, / Desperately in need of some / Stranger's hand'. At the same time, the images descend further into indecipherability: superimposed atop the obscured shot of the burning jungle is, first, an upside-down close-up of Willard's impassive face; this is next overlaid on the right of the frame by a shot of a ceiling fan; finally, for just a moment, an image of what looks like the face of a stone statue of Eastern origin dissolves in and then out of the frame (Fig. 4.4).

Given that this opening depicts an act of US (aerial) military violence—and is indeed the *only* representation of such violence in the film prior to the 'Ride of the Valkyries' scene—it creates an important rhetorical context for the second helicopter assault that will follow some thirty minutes later. Numerous stark differences between these two moments are immediately apparent. Considering even the music in isolation, we might note several key contrasts: not only is the Wagner of the relative historical past whereas this song is comparatively contemporary, but the latter is sombre and elegiac while the former is celebratory and bombastic; 'The

Fig. 4.4 *Apocalypse Now*: The burning jungle, Willard's face, and statue superimposed

End' often shifts into a minor key, where the Wagner is resolutely major; it is periodically melodically discordant, while Wagner's piece is unremittingly tuneful; and so on. In terms of the interaction between music and images, meanwhile, so much of the rhetoric of this opening montage can be described as disorienting and distancing in various ways. The first words heard in the film's first sequence announce that, on the contrary, 'This is the end'. A soothing combination of musical timbre and hushed voice disconcertingly accompany an image of total devastation. The source of sounds we are initially encouraged to attribute to helicopter blades is made ambiguous by the image of the ceiling fan. We cannot hear the noise of the huge explosions and furthermore are initially given no narrative context to help us understand their significance. And when we *are* provided with something that might serve this purpose, via the shot of Willard, his face is upside down—another pointedly disorienting gesture.

As soon becomes clear, the stylistic register of this sequence must be understood partly as an attempt to render affectively memories of combat as passed through the mind's eye of our war-weary protagonist and voice-over narrator; in a few moments, Willard will say in voice-over that 'every day I expect to wake up back in the jungle'. Chatman describes him as 'drunk, half-remembering, half-dreaming' (1997: 209) the helicopter sequence, which would seem to capture something of his ambiguous relationship to these images. The distance at which the trees are held, the hazy visual field, the associative editing, and the abstract song that replaces diegetic sound—all these aspects of the film's style thus suggest his, and encourage our, detachment from military violence that could theoretically have been made to feel far more immediate, present, proximate. Instead, it seems reasonable to say that dissonance, opacity, and estrangement of various kinds are this sequence's defining rhetorical characteristics.

The contrasts between the film's opening montage and the later helicopter sequence are thus manifold. Whereas the 'Ride of the Valkyries' scene is characterised by utter consonance between exultant music, visual style, and the violence wrought by its US helicopters, the film's only preceding combination of music and combat has placed us emphatically and in several respects at a remove from its depiction of a comparable military action. And while less contextually relevant to the Wagner sequence on first viewing, similar contrasts are observable in the music accompanying later combat scenes, too. For instance, the battle at the Do Lung Bridge shows us only disoriented US soldiers unloading copious firepower indiscriminately and blindly into the surrounding night-time jungle—never their elusive targets—and is accompanied for the most part by Carmine Coppola's original score, whose minor-key synthesised drones could hardly be further removed from the major-chord triumphalism and rhythmic clarity of the Wagner. At another extreme, perhaps the most explicitly presented act of violence in the film—Willard's men mistakenly gunning down all the unarmed Vietnamese passengers of a sampan boat—is accompanied by no music at all and, thus, attempts nothing like the kind of kinaesthetic complementarity of sound and image that characterises the helicopter sequence's depiction of military slaughter.

Any war film will implicitly establish what it deems an appropriate rhetorical register with which to render violent acts of war: as horrifying, tense, exciting, heroic, comic, and so forth. Identifying a film's overarching rhetorical tendencies in this regard will help us make well-informed hypotheses about the film's likely reasons for departing noticeably from those general tendencies. The register in which militarised violence tends to be depicted in *Apocalypse Now* varies to some degree: sometimes it is suggested to be being remembered, almost hallucinated; sometimes it is characterised as hellish and futile; sometimes it is shown to be tragically misdirected; and in each instance the film's soundtrack contributes to our experience of such actions. What appears common to every one of the film's scenes of warfare *other* than the 'Ride of Valkyries' sequence, though, is some kind of rhetorical and stylistic distance. In each case, choices concerning subject matter, point of view, and sound combine to invite a sense of perspectival—and, I would suggest, moral—detachment from the US perpetrators of violence, which is wholly alien to the strategies of the helicopter attack scene.

We should note, in this respect, that the prelude to Kilgore's helicopter assault—the sequence depicting the Hueys beginning their journey towards the beach—is actually presented in something like the distanced register introduced by the film's opening montage. While Coppola's murky, dissonant synth score plays, the fleet is shown flying off on their mission via a series of dissolves; the sun begins to rise over a nearby mountain, causing some lens flare, obscuring our view; and overlapping shots of the helicopters dotting a burnt orange sky are superimposed atop a close-up of Willard's face in profile as he stares off blankly to the right. However, having to some extent evoked the eerie, foreboding, detached mood of the opening, once the Wagner begins playing and the fleet start their attack, the rhetoric of the sequence shifts completely—coming to adopt the almost *too* close, *too* fitting, relationship between jubilant music, violent action, and narration that we have previously identified.

The context in which the 'Ride of the Valkyries' sequence is situated thus makes the scene incongruous, not merely—as Hutcheon notes—in terms of the kind of music it employs, but also in terms of its wholesale departure from the film's established rhetorical strategies concerning the representation of warfare. And again, the scene's rhetorical incongruity in relation to the rest of the film should, I argue, be taken to imply certain things about its intentions. The very fact that *Apocalypse Now* renders scenes of US military violence in such wildly divergent registers implies, at the very least, that this film adopts at different moments distinct perspectives towards such material. When one of those perspectives appears to depart so completely from those surrounding it, we are confronted with the question of the film's likely intentions for doing so. I propose that the hypothesis of ironic pretence offers the best explanation for that incongruity: we are intended to infer the film's implicit distance from this aberrant perspective, which is made aberrant precisely because of its contrasting rhetorical *congruence* between triumphant music and violent action.

There is, however, one final vital context established by the film that Hutcheon's interpretation neglects to mention but that would seem to add considerable further support to my hypothesis. This concerns the highly significant fact of the music's diegetic source and which character has elected for the slaughter to be soundtracked this way: Lieutenant Colonel Kilgore.

Dramatic Irony (and Ironic Pretence): Kilgore

We encountered earlier Swofford's claim about his (and reportedly other marines') reactions to *Apocalypse Now*: 'It's Kilgore who you remember, at least if you're young and impressionable, with all his manly bravado. Him and those racing helicopters. Those are the images that have kids enlisting' (Weschler 2005: 73–74). The film itself, however, seems to provide us with little evidence that we should feel encouraged to respond to the character of Kilgore with anything approaching admiration. In fact, I suggest that *Apocalypse Now*'s rhetorical treatment of Kilgore can be characterised as systematically critical and distanced—indeed, as being dedicated to mounting a sustained campaign of dramatic irony at his expense. So many aspects of John Milius' script, Robert Duvall's performance, and Coppola's direction contribute to the rhetorical condemnation and mockery of Kilgore that to itemise them all in detail could take up an entire chapter; in fact, considered together, these measures combine to create the sense that he is to some extent less a fully fledged character than a pointedly exaggerated figure of satire.[26] Let us look, though, at some of the most obvious strategies by which the film positions him as a man from whose attitudes and perspectives the film, at a minimum, seems to invite us to recoil.

The way characters are introduced will always be important for establishing what we intuit will come to be a film's attitudes towards them. Willard's crew first meet Kilgore and his soldiers at a beach where the latter have recently concluded some combat operations. As Willard's riverboat approaches, we see flames and smoke rising into the air and choppers circling; crucially, we will never learn the strategic purpose of these operations. Before we even see Kilgore, the film is thus rhetorically positioning him through what is revealed of the beach over which we know he and his regiment currently have dominion. We witness the arrival of our protagonists' boat from the shore; as the camera pans and tracks left to follow their path into the beach, in the foreground of the shot emerges what is to serve as our first clear view of the battleground: a crying, very young child, with what looks to be a sizeable chemical burn on her cheek. Not allowed to stay in frame longer than an instant, this image is nonetheless key for how the film is orienting us towards the action.[27] Further sights we are presented with quickly reinforce a sense that what is intended to strike us most forcefully about these military operations is their chaotic and callous nature: an armoured amphibious vehicle, whose nose is painted to resemble the mouth and eyes of a cartoon shark, flattens a rickety, uninhabited bamboo hut for no discernible reason. As fires rage in the background and Vietnamese locals huddle in the fore, a soldier declaims through a loudspeaker, 'We will not hurt or harm you; we are here to extend a welcome hand...'. And, framed against a backdrop of a tank spewing fire and smoke, a makeshift Christian service is under way, a reverend leading a group of troops in the Lord's Prayer. Perhaps especially these last two images, which themselves pointedly stage ironic contrasts, such details play significant roles in establishing the film's implied attitudes towards this regiment and, thus, its commanding officer.

Kilgore himself is introduced in the midst of this scene when Willard approaches him to explain how the colonel is expected to assist his team in its mission. Upon meeting him, Kilgore deals gruffly and curtly with Willard, quickly dismissing him in favour of marching off to ritualistically flip playing cards onto the nearby dead bodies of murdered Vietnamese men, women and (it seems important to acknowledge) children. 'Six of clubs, eight of spades', he intones roughly, 'There isn't one worth a Jack in the whole bunch!' ('Death cards', explains Willard to Lance, 'Lets Charlie [slang for Viet Cong] know who did this...'.) This task completed, Kilgore next passes by a young soldier sitting on a wall, staring straight ahead, looking near-catatonic. 'Cheer up, son!' he off-handedly offers the boy by way of comfort, tapping him lightly on the shoulder as he walks by.

These initial decisions about how to frame and introduce Kilgore would, by themselves, have great importance for how we should feel we are being encouraged to respond to the imminent Wagner sequence. First, I believe we are entitled to assume that, despite its eccentricities and fascination with extremes of human depravity, *Apocalypse Now* is—again—not a film that is unconcerned with encouraging normative moral judgements in its audience. For example, surely a crying baby with a chemical burn cannot deserve this fate; platitudes about extending a 'welcoming hand' must appear empty in the face of such apparently pointless carnage; a colonel should crow less over the bodies of dead children and care more for a traumatised kid in his charge. Importantly, however, Kilgore is not only implicitly critiqued by the film prior to the Wagner attack; he is also *mocked*. This is a slightly different proposition, and one that, I suggest, should prepare us further for the strategies adopted during the 'Ride of the Valkyries' sequence.

A significant moment comes a few minutes after Kilgore's introduction, during an incident between himself and a wounded Viet Cong soldier who is sprawled on the ground begging for water. Informed that the only thing keeping this man's insides from spilling out is the pot lid he clutches to his stomach, Kilgore initially seems to take pride in performing a humanitarian act of kindness. Furiously dismissing with a violent shove a Vietnamese translator who suggests they only let the man drink paddy water, Kilgore yells, 'I'll kick your fuckin' ass! Any man brave enough to fight with hits guts strapped into him can drink from my canteen any day!', grabbing a vessel from one of his men and kneeling down to dispense water into the frantic invalid's mouth. This uncharacteristically compassionate act towards the enemy proves short-lived, however, when a member of Kilgore's regiment approaches to share some news. 'Colonel', says the soldier, gesturing towards Willard and his crew, 'I think one of those sailors is Lance Johnson—the surfer!' Immediately Kilgore's priorities change. 'What?' he demands, getting up from his kneeling position, 'Are you sure?' Now framed in a wide shot that pointedly keeps in view the wounded man desperately grasping around Kilgore's legs for the canteen he still holds in his hand (Fig. 4.5), the colonel immediately strides away with the purpose of meeting this quasi-famous member of Willard's crew. As the camera then tracks and pans rightwards with Kilgore's movements, several things happen in sequence: the injured man and his pained cries recede from our view and hearing; a soldier relaying the battle's body-count into a field phone is momentarily passed by in the foreground; and flames and helicopters become visible, rising into the air in the background. All of this is ignored by Kilgore, whose sole purpose has become to introduce himself to the recreational sporting celebrity who is revealed

Fig. 4.5 *Apocalypse Now*: Kilgore with the invalid

as the target of this sweeping camera movement. 'It's an honour to meet you, Lance', enthuses Kilgore as he pumps the young man's hand upon reaching him: 'I've admired your nose-riding for years!' (Fig. 4.6) 'Thank you, sir!' smiles a flattered Lance before Kilgore leads him away to introduce two other surfing enthusiasts in his regiment.

Several elements of dramatisation and style thus conspire here to pass specifically ironic judgement upon Kilgore. Simultaneously echoing and exposing the character's limited perspective, the aforementioned tracking shot ensures that our own focus is shifted from suffering to surfing, just as is Kilgore's, while at the same time making prominent within our view everything that is all too easily excluded from his. Whereas the news of Lance's identity seems immediately to render the colonel blind to everything else around him, as the camera moves deliberately with Kilgore to the right, we might reasonably feel our concern being encouraged to drift back to the left—to everything else in the scene that he has now forgotten. Moments like this, in which the film's concerns and attitudes appear so markedly separated from those of Kilgore, need to be made central to any appropriately contextualised interpretation of the impending Wagner scene. Perhaps most important of all, though, is the reason the film establishes for why the helicopter assault even comes to be waged in the first place.

The night before the attack, Kilgore, his troops, and Willard's men relax with food and drinks around a campfire. Willard approaches Kilgore with a map, pointing out the beach at the mouth of the Nung into which Kilgore is supposed to ensure his boat's safe passage. Initially, Kilgore tries

Fig. 4.6 *Apocalypse Now*: Kilgore abandons the invalid to welcome Lance

to dismiss Willard's plan as too dangerous. As before, however, his tune is soon to change when his favourite subject is introduced. He asks one of his men, Mike (Kerry Rossall), if he knows anything about this beach. 'That's a fantastic peak', comes the reply. 'Peak...?' Kilgore enquires, intrigued. 'About six foot', Mike continues, 'Yeah, it's an outstanding peak....It's just tube city' ('tube' being surfing slang for the barrel of a large wave). We now watch Kilgore as his whole conception of the mission begins to shift in light of this new information: in a moment of deep consideration he looks up at Willard, down at the map, off towards Mike, back at the map, and up at Willard again. 'Well why didn't you tell me that before?' he eventually fires back at Mike. 'A good peak? There aren't any good peaks in this whole shitty country: it's all goddamn beach break!' Seeing his chance, Willard capitalises on what he now recognises may be the only way to get Kilgore to do the job required of him: 'Sir', he begins, deliberately flatteringly, 'we can go in there tomorrow at dawn', before adding, after a pause and with emphasis: 'There's *always* a good off-shore breeze in the morning...'. Kilgore takes this bait whole, and the scene closes with him wasting no time in barking orders for the imminent action, but giving far more emphasis to his recreational—rather than military—aims: 'Okay, take a gunship back to the division', he all but mumbles to one soldier before issuing other instructions with much greater clarity: 'Lance', he says, addressing his surfing hero, 'go with Mike, let him pick out a board for you. And bring me my Yater Spoon, the 8'6.' 'Well...', responds Mike as he rises, clearly uneasy with the plan, 'it's pretty hairy in there, isn't it? It's *Charlie's* point...', this last complaint prompting an irritable Kilgore to cap the scene by yelling one of the film's most famous lines: 'Charlie *don't surf!*'

We are thus invited to view the helicopter attack sequence in the light of this preceding scene, in which it is made clear that—while its ostensible aim for Willard is to allow him access to the Nung—for Kilgore, the military action is worthwhile only insofar as it may allow him to experience the heady peaks of 'tube city'. Before we can fully account for the significance of this fact, though, it is necessary to place it in the context of one final way in which dramatic irony is created at Kilgore's expense.

Before we have even met him, but while we are witnessing the carnage his regiment is wreaking, Kilgore is becoming associated by the film with a particular cluster of historical imagery. As we take in sights like the crying baby and the shark-painted amphibious vehicle, Willard's voice-over tells us that '1st of the 9th was an old Cavalry division that had cashed in its horses for choppers and gone tear-assing around 'Nam, looking for the shit.' Then, when we meet Kilgore soon afterwards, we are permitted to notice his attire. The generic green fatigues he wears are the same as those of the troops around him, but this similarity only invites us to register more precisely where his outfit differs. Most ostentatiously, there is his hat. Rather than the standard-issue helmets and canvas camouflaged caps worn by his surrounding soldiers, Kilgore sports a distinctive 'Hardee'-style hat, familiar from depictions of the older, traditional uniform of the US Cavalry: black with a wide brim, a feather protruding from its side, prominently displaying on its front the distinctive cross-sabre emblem and dangling cord tassels. As well as this, emerging from under his standard-issue shirt is what would seem to be a yellow kerchief, also recalling those worn by previous generations of Cavalry officers. These details are only the first of several that suggest Kilgore's preoccupation with the iconography of the Civil War-era US Cavalry. For instance, he continues wearing his Hardee hat in the campfire scene, where it is made to clash with his T-shirt, which features a logo of a surfboard and the name of a Santa Barbara surf camp. We also see the crossed-sabres emblem again on the nose of the helicopter that takes Kilgore into battle, here made to frame the words 'DEATH FROM ABOVE'. Finally, when the helicopters take off on their mission, they are accompanied by a bugler playing the 'Cavalry Charge', who also wears the same hat as the colonel (Fig. 4.7).

Just prior to and during the helicopter attack, then, *Apocalypse Now* places significant emphasis on the visual and aural iconography of the US Cavalry of an earlier century. This thus represents another specific cultural

Fig. 4.7 *Apocalypse Now*: The Cavalry bugler accompanies the helicopters' departure

context that the film seems to intend us to draw upon in our interpretations. We might begin to hypothesise about the purpose behind invoking that context by noting that the US Cavalry is, historically, an institution that is conventionally made to represent nobility and heroism within American national mythology and popular culture (if not always within the American historical record)—having been frequently associated by numerous Hollywood Westerns in particular with what are represented as courageous acts of rescue.[28] We might further note that it is plainly Kilgore specifically who is made to seem so invested in this nostalgic imagery, decking out both himself and some of his troops (or at least his bugler) in its patriotic regalia.[29] Finally, we must place this in the context of what we have already established about Kilgore: that he is a Colonel who elects to send his troops on a dangerous military mission with the main strategic purpose (for him) of exterminating the inhabitants of a beach so that he and his men might enjoy the quality of its surf; as Walter Benn Michaels put it in a contemporaneous review, Kilgore regards the attack as 'an attempt to make the world safe for surfing' (1979: 1173). Short of establishing wholly malicious goals for the character, I can imagine a war film imputing few motives to a colonel's military decision-making that would more forcefully frame that character's actions as *less* noble and courageous.

We might propose different interpretations of what precisely the film intends by juxtaposing Kilgore's clichéd pretentions to patriotic nobility against his character's ignoble actions. We might, for instance, argue that mapping the former onto the latter invites us to measure Kilgore unflatteringly against his ideals. We might equally suggest that some continuity is in fact being satirically implied between the US Cavalry of yore and Kilgore's present military actions. This interpretation might seem particularly persuasive, for a few reasons: because of Willard's description of this regiment as having 'cashed in its horses for choppers'; because of the emphasis placed on the 'Cavalry Charge' as the helicopters depart; and because the later cut to the peaceful village prior to the attack allows us to hear the sounds of the Wagner growing louder as the fleet encroaches, thereby grotesquely inverting the Western generic convention of distant bugle calls heralding an imminent rescue.[30] Both possible interpretations, though, would require us to claim that Kilgore is being positioned by the film as possessing a trait common to much ironic characterisation: self-delusion. While he seems to want to create an image for himself that implies he is continuing a military tradition enshrined in patriotic national myth, almost everything we are shown of his aims and methods helps to undermine that self-image, the truth of that myth, or both. To argue this is to argue that he is made a victim of the film's dramatic irony, which we might, indeed, further extend to his employment of 'Ride of the Valkyries'. Are we intended to imagine that Kilgore is unaware of the kinds of racist cultural associations carried by this piece, addressed earlier? Or might we assume that he *is* aware of them, but that he either does not care or in fact considers them apropos to his purposes? Such questions are patently unanswerable as matters of fact, but making any of these arguments means arguing that this constitutes another way in which the film encourages a distance between our perception and moral assessment of Kilgore and his own perception and moral assessment of himself.

This brings us back, finally, to the helicopter sequence itself. I have hypothesised that the rhetorical endorsement implied by the scene's emphatic consonance between music, action, and visual style might best be interpreted as an ironic pretence. I have also suggested the film offers us several reasons for inferring that it is undertaking such a pretence: the cultural associations of the Wagner, the early shift of our point of view to the village, the difference between this scene's rhetoric and the way scenes of military violence are presented elsewhere, the fact that the attack only takes place to facilitate surfing. All these gestures create incongruities within a scene that could initially appear so characterised by its utter rhetorical congruity. This means, of course, that they also provide the kind of signals that conventionally indicate ironic intent. However, the final piece of evidence I would cite in support of this interpretation is also, I suggest, the most decisive: 'Ride of the Valkyries' represents *Kilgore's* choice of music.

The playing of 'Ride of the Valkyries' during the assault occurs not merely at Kilgore's behest but is actually represented as being something of a sacred ritual for this character. The first time we hear anything of the Wagner is as a snatch of melody being sung off screen by one of Kilgore's troops during the campfire scene. Once Kilgore has been persuaded to assist Willard's men, he announces this decision by declaiming, 'This is Air Cav, son—Air Mobile!'; the very mention of these terms prompts an unidentified off-screen member of his cavalry regiment to launch high-spiritedly into a couple of bars of the tune—'Bah bah-bah baah baah, bah bah-bah baah baah...'. Clearly, then, 'Ride of the Valkyries' has become so routine a part of the colonel's airborne deployments that it is something to which his men can look forward eagerly; as Kilgore claims: 'my boys love it'. Indeed, by seemingly serving a quasi-ritualistic function for Kilgore, the grandness of the Wagner is suggested to play a role in his military routines comparable to the self-aggrandising functions apparently performed by the cavalry regalia or the 'Death Cards'. Furthermore, during the attack sequence itself Kilgore is depicted taking special pleasure in the music. Having ordered the commencement of this 'psy-war op' with the accompanying instruction to 'make it *loud*', we are shown Kilgore responding to the piece by turning to share a haughty laugh and a raised fist of solidarity with a member of his company; a few moments later, he is revealed smilingly bobbing his head and keeping time to the music's rhythm, again with a clenched fist.

Given all this, when we are made to listen to the Wagner during the assault sequence, we are, first of all, being made to experience this scene with a musical accompaniment conducted to the terrifying logic of a madman—albeit a madman making a calculated, apparently routine, choice about how best to fire-up his boys. Moreover, though, when the film's rhetoric appears to imply its wholesale endorsement of playing this music throughout this combat operation, it appears to adopt an attitude towards the slaughter that Kilgore himself would most certainly endorse. In fact, by effectively subjecting us to the same sort of inducement to violent aggression that the music performs for Kilgore's men, the film is enacting upon us similar methods of coercion as he himself subjects his troops to. In this way, then, the sequence appears to echo the point of view of a character whose perspectives have hitherto seemed to remain perpetually, pointedly at odds with those of the film—in other words, a character who has himself already been the victim of a great deal of the film's irony. This being the case, I suggest that we are required to seek an explanation for the rhetoric of the attack sequence in which ironic intentions play at least some role.

We saw in Chapters 2 and 3 that dramatic irony and ironic pretence need not by any means be mutually exclusive and that each can in fact be synthesised with and heighten the other. I claim that this is the best way of describing *Apocalypse Now*'s intentions during this sequence. Having laid the rhetorical groundwork by ironising Kilgore and what he represents by distancing us from his actions and perspectives,[31] the film's rhetoric then proceeds to ironise him and his worldview by instead pretending to endorse excessively precisely the kinds of perspectives towards the war which he holds. Of course, we are required to ask, as Claire Colebrook does: 'what distinguishes an ironic use of excessive…rhetoric from a text that simply is excessive?' (2004: 11); and it seems that the only possible answer is: the *intention* to use such rhetoric ironically. My interpretation has attempted to present as much persuasive evidence as possible—drawn both from the text and its relevant contexts—for attributing to the film precisely such intentions. It remains true that none of this evidence, no matter how voluminous or suggestive, can guarantee 'a fail-safe diagnostic of irony' since intention must always 'be inferred by a fallible process of hypothesis formation' (Sperber/Wilson 2007: 47). Nonetheless, I argue that the nature of this evidence, whose significance I have tried to elucidate, makes this the best hypothesis available. I think we can, ultimately, hope for no firmer grounds when interpreting irony in film.

IRONY'S EDGE, INTERPRETATION, AND EVALUATION

I began this chapter by acknowledging that it is eminently possible for irony to fail to 'reach its destination' (Doane 1979: 129) and, thus, for its effects to fail to 'happen' for audiences. I have gone on to argue, however, that this fact should not lead us to conclude that irony is therefore 'not the property of works' (Fish 1989: 194) or that it 'isn't irony until it is interpreted as such' (Hutcheon 1994: 6). I have suggested that, because intention is what defines irony as a distinct means of expression, we should conclude that, if irony has been intended by an artwork, irony can be said to be a property of that artwork. This is by no means to claim that a work's irony will always reach its destination; it is merely to say that there does indeed exist something that is attempting to reach a destination in the first place. As such, I argue that—because irony resides in intention, and because ironic intentions can be discerned in *Apocalypse Now*—the 'Ride of the Valkyries' sequence would remain ironic even in a hypothetical world in which it had only ever been viewed by audiences like those dramatised in *Jarhead*. Where, though, does this leave us regarding the thorny issues raised by irony's 'edge'?

To speak of irony's edge is, fundamentally, to speak of its evaluative nature: the innate tendency of irony to imply value judgements, the fact that it 'generally has victims' (Clark/Gerrig 2007: 27), and its potential to create hierarchies of understanding among interpreters. It is this last outcome of irony especially that ensures 'irony involves relations of power' and 'unavoidably involves touchy issues such as exclusion and inclusion' (Hutcheon 1994: 2). To argue that we can justifiably speak of the irony *in* films, as this chapter has, is to argue that 'we do in fact read and misread ironies' (Booth 1974: 2); it therefore seems also to suggest that 'some readings are better than others' (ibid.: xi). It is worth finally nuancing this last proposition, though, by acknowledging that which readings are deemed 'better' will crucially depend on the particular *purposes* of those readings.

As I have acknowledged, it may be that the interpretations of *Apocalypse Now* offered and reported by Swofford in his memoir result not necessarily from *missing* the irony in Coppola's film so much as *resisting* it. This is an ever-present possibility of ironic expression and interpretation; as Hutcheon notes, a particular audience 'may reject the ironic meaning, or find it inappropriate or objectionable in some way...; it may simply choose not to see irony' (1994: 118). If ironic rhetoric involves the 'persuasion "to attitude"' (Burke 1969: 50), then these young men have either failed or refused to be persuaded to adopt such an attitude. As such, rather than having their interpretations guided by the intentions of the text, Swofford and his fellow marines could instead be described as *using* the text or appropriating it in an alternative manner—one that seems perfectly appropriate to their purposes.[32] To help understand this, we might say that, by responding to the scene as they do, they are simply not aligning themselves with this text's 'preferred reading'. Drawing upon Stuart Hall's (1980) canonical 'encoding/decoding' theory of communication,[33] Charlotte Brunsdon and David Morley define a text's 'preferred reading' as the interpretation of a text 'towards which the audience is actively directed' (1999: 36). Brunsdon and Morley employ this concept to help account for the fact that, while 'most texts do indeed propose a preferred reading', every text also 'retains the potential, if decoded in a manner different from the way in which it has been encoded, of communicating a different meaning' (ibid.: 15). The meanings Swofford and his fellow marines apparently take from *Apocalypse Now* may diverge from those the film prefers, but they clearly constitute the more valuable, indeed 'better', reading for these particular interpreters.

We could extend this point to theoretical and critical approaches to irony in film. Meanings that diverge from a film's 'preferred reading' will become more or less valuable depending on what we seek to know about irony and film. Readings other than those 'preferred' by a film are likely to be of only limited value if what we are seeking to discern and demonstrate is whether a film is addressing us ironically. However, readings of the kind described by Swofford will be of much greater value than a film's 'preferred' reading if we are instead seeking to answer different kinds of questions, for instance: How might audience members' discursive communities affect their interpretations of this film, and to what relations of power might those interpretations be instructively related? Or what interpretations is this film capable of prompting under certain circumstances, how might those circumstances affect audiences, and what might be the implications of this? These are not the kinds of questions this chapter has sought to address, but of course that is not to say that their answers would not provide valuable insights into how filmic irony can 'happen', or indeed *not* 'happen'.

Finally, we might also apply a similar logic to a critical project that this book in general has largely eschewed: *evaluating* a text's irony. My primary interpretive question in this chapter has been whether we are justified in calling the 'Ride of the Valkyries' sequence in *Apocalypse Now* ironic—which is to say, whether we can discern from the scene an intention to be ironic. There are, however, many additional interpretive questions we could ask of this sequence. In particular, having discerned the film's intentions, we could then seek to evaluate them aesthetically, ethically, or indeed politically. As Booth acknowledges, having established the intentions of a work, 'often we do not want to stop there: having understood what the [work] really says and does, we may quite legitimately say that we wish it said or did something else' (1974: 126). Thus, we might ask: what is the value of the irony in this scene, and how might it affect our evaluation of *Apocalypse Now* as a whole? Partly because of the film's subject matter, such questions are likely to move 'beyond the issue of whether, in this particular case, irony was used *well* to question its very appropriateness as a discursive strategy' (Hutcheon 1994: 188). For instance, some critics and scholars have attacked Coppola's film with variations on the charge that, via its 'elaborate and expensive spectacle...the film seeks to excite the very appetites that, at the same time, [it] ostensibly denounces' (Britton 2009: 87). Questioning the aesthetic, ethical, and ideological aims and achievements of the helicopter attack sequence's ironic address is likely to be cardinally important for any such criticism. After all, it is precisely because this scene elects to address its audience ironically that it becomes capable of being responded to as an exultant and thrilling action sequence by viewers like Swofford. Clearly, to evaluate this scene's irony negatively would—again—be to read it in ways that the film does not intend or prefer, and yet we might quite reasonably regard this as another valid task of interpretation. This, then, represents one more way in which readings other than those a film intends can come to be regarded as 'better than others'.

None of this, however, detracts from the need to discern a film's intentions in the first instance—if, that is, we are interested in making interpretive claims about irony in film. It is a fact about interpretation in general that, as Noël Carroll puts it, even 'in order to interpret against the grain, one needs to find the grain in the first place' (1998: 12).[34] Similarly, it is only by first identifying irony that we can then elect to evaluate, criticise, or even potentially repudiate it; and, as I have argued, the very nature of irony ensures that we can only ever hope to identify it by discerning a text's intentions. As such, it is certainly true that interpretive and theoretical moves of the kind practised by this chapter barely scratch the surface of the ways in which we might fruitfully read the irony of this or any other scene or film. However, I believe that together they represent something like the groundwork from which any interpretation of irony in film is compelled to begin.

*

I would propose something similar about the arguments offered by this book as a whole. Partly because it is the first of its kind, this study has focused on posing, and offering some answers to, a number of fundamental and rather general questions about irony in film. What capacities does film have for creating irony? What kinds of irony is it capable of creating? How have particular features common to the medium assisted in ironic expression? What is involved in interpreting irony in film, and how should we undertake this task? I hope I have succeeded in presenting some convincing, or at least productive, answers to these questions.

Chapter 2 argued that, despite claims to the contrary, there is nothing intrinsic about film that should necessarily make irony difficult for this medium to achieve. Indeed, I have suggested that—partly because of its 'mongrel' nature (Durgnat 1976)—the live-action fiction film is in fact capable of creating several different kinds of irony by a host of different means: its pictorial qualities help it depict *situational* ironies, its dramatic and storytelling properties assist in creating *dramatic* irony, and its narrative dimensions aid its potential to be *communicatively* ironic. Chapter 3, meanwhile, proposed that many individual features of the medium can serve to make their own particular contributions to irony in film. Even though no aspect of a film ever operates in isolation, properties and devices like film sound, editing, mise-en-scène, the camera, and performance nonetheless all offer distinctive possibilities for different forms of ironic expression. Finally, Chapter 4 has made the case that when we speak of the irony in a film, we are necessarily making claims about the ironic intentions of that film; given this, interpreting such irony seems to demand that we seek in the film evidence for such intentions.

The questions this book has sought to address do strike me as being among the most pressing for any serious consideration of this topic. Of course, one of my hopes is that the answers I have offered strike the reader as persuasive. Another, though, is that this study might conceivably represent only a starting point for a renewed, more sustained consideration of its subject. This would mean, in part, that other potential responses to such questions must be offered and weighed. This will also doubtless involve posing other questions altogether—perhaps of the kind I have gestured towards, but also of a wholly different sort, perhaps relating to wholly different aspects of and definitions of irony. No inaugural book on a topic can hope to address all the issues it raises, and so vast and confounding a topic as irony in film will assuredly be capable of prompting pivotal critical and theoretical questions far beyond any that this study has even attempted to tackle. Indeed, were I to believe that I could have arrived at anything close to the final word on any aspect of this subject, I would effectively be making myself hostage to precisely the kinds of self-delusion and limited perspectives that irony characteristically serves to puncture.

Nevertheless, as in the case of the arguments set forth in this particular chapter, I do have hopes that this book might offer not a destination, nor even perhaps a map, but a potential base from which future critical and theoretical journeys could begin. The reason this hope seems to me not entirely misplaced is that, wherever we many find or seek to discuss irony in film—and whatever the arguments we wish to advance—it appears certain that we will be forced to confront many of the same questions with which this book has been grappling. I thus look forward to others continuing to contend with the innumerable imposing but invigorating critical challenges we invite when we undertake to interpret irony in film.

NOTES

1. I will be basing my discussions around the original version of this film rather than the expanded *Apocalypse Now Redux* (2001).
2. In his musicological analysis of 'Ride of the Valkyries', Eero Tarasti notes its use of the 'old musical topic of "galloping horses"', one of the musical figures linked to the military...ever since the Baroque' (2012: 261).

3. Matthew Michael Sumera also argues that 'the sounds of gunfire…
are edited through explicitly musical approaches…, creating poly-
rhythms against one another as well as against Wagner's soaring
strings' (2013: 80).

4. This covers the portion running from the first rocket being
launched to Kilgore's helicopter touching down.

5. In addition to those already mentioned, see also Britton (2009: 87).

6. See: Hutcheon (1994: 85–134), Fish (1989), and Elleström
(2002); see also, for instance, de Man (1996: 164–181).

7. See Sconce (1995), McCulloch (2011), MacDowell/Zborowski
(2013), and Bartlett (2015).

8. As we have been defining it, dramatic irony creates 'dissonance
between what the audience…see and the limitations of the character's own self-awareness' (Storm 2011: 5–6); see Chapter 2 for a
more thorough discussion.

9. For a far more exhaustive recent overview and discussion, see
Maynard (2009).

10. The usefulness of the concept of the implied author is suggested by
the fact that, even if they ostensibly reject the term, both those
theorists concerned with the *flesh-and-blood* author's intentions
and those concerned to account for the *reader's* intentions frequently come close to positing very similar concepts. For instance,
Noël Carroll notes that 'the primary evidence for…inferences
[about the flesh-and-blood author's intentions] is generally the
artwork itself' (2002: 327). Equally, in her 'reader-focused and
contextual definition of intentionality', Hutcheon suggests that
'the producer of the text (at least from the reader's point of view)
is…one inferred by the reader' (1989: 81). It also should be noted,
though, that several theorists also remain convinced by the need
for 'actual author intentionalism'; for a recent overview of such
arguments, see Irvin (2006).

11. Clearly, there are ways of objecting to the concept. George Wilson,
for instance, argues that 'it is unclear that films can imply anything
at all unless some responsible agent has had the relevant communicative intention' (1997: 224). Yet we have also seen that Wilson
himself accepts the usefulness of the concept of the 'implied film-
maker', which is closely related to that of the intention of the text.

12. We might note that Hutcheon in fact reaches a similar conclusion.
Having cast significant doubt on the possibility that irony is a

property of texts, and thus the possibility that its presence is designated by 'irony markers', Hutcheon nonetheless concedes that 'we might be able to speak of…signals that function meta-ironically', the presence of which 'sets up a series of expectations that frame the utterance as potentially ironic' (1994: 148). She defines such 'meta-ironic' markers as consisting of 'a complex of things clustered around the notions of contradiction, incongruity, contrast, and juxtaposition' (ibid.: 151), arguing that such features 'do not so much constitute irony in themselves as signal the possibility of ironic attribution' (ibid.: 148). I suggest that this formulation ultimately positions Hutcheon's theory as being not so very different from those of more traditionally author-focused rhetorical theorists: Muecke, for instance, who argues that irony markers represent clues to ironic intentions but that they also 'cannot be defined as infallible pointers to irony' (1978: 365).

13. In refusing to acknowledge a distinction between ironic expression and unwilled, situational irony, a devout anti-intentionalist such as Elleström, for instance, does effectively seem willing to deny the existence of the former (2002: 47).

14. See Colebrook (2004: 94–109) for a useful discussion of this.

15. See, for instance, the many moments in Chapters 2 and 3 when I had reason to invoke particular conventions or clichés that films seem to be engaging with.

16. Interpreting a literary irony, suggests Booth, will tend to rely upon a reader's familiarity with at least three interlinking kinds of context—all of which an (implied) author is, in turn, likely to assume or hope that their reader possesses: a familiarity with the language employed, some degree of shared cultural experience and assumed moral norms, and some awareness of literary genres relevant to the work (1974: 100).

17. In literary theory, the concept of the *implied reader* or *implied auditor* would be relevant here: the kind of reader that a work apparently assumes itself to be addressing, an image of which is 'revealed only by what the narrator implicitly takes for granted as needing or not needing explanation or justification' (Abrams 1999: 218). I have no objection on principle to applying a comparable concept (perhaps *implied audience* [Barker/Austin 2000: 42–48]) to film, though doing so seems inessential to my argument here.

18. One reason it is surprising that Hutcheon makes no reference to this context here is the fact that later in her book she engages with Wagner's cultural associations with Nazism at some length (1994: 126–135).
19. See Gutman (1968).
20. It is also worth acknowledging that, as Marc Weiner notes, while there are those 'who bemoan the association of Wagner's works with Nazism as a regrettable and unfair distortion and aberration..., in terms of our understanding of his place in the modern film, such concerns are besides the point' (2010: 206).
21. Alvy's (Woody Allen) paranoia regarding anti-Semitism is demonstrated by his telling the following anecdote: 'I was in this record store....There's this big, tall, blond crew-cutted guy, and he's looking at me in a funny way, and smiling, and he's saying, "Yes, we have a sale this week on Wagner." *Wagner*, Max, *Wagner*—so *I* know what he's really trying to tell me, very significantly: *Wagner*.'
22. Melanie Lowe, for one, claims that knowledge of this context has long been commonplace among at least a relatively sizeable proportion of the American population when she suggests that, following *The Birth of a Nation*, '"Ride of the Valkyries" became suddenly repugnant for many liberal-minded Americans, as it was difficult to erase the image of the Ku Klux Klan rushing in, summoned forth by Wagner's call' (2007: 166).
23. Prior to the attack sequence we are told that Kilgore's regiment has effectively 'cashed in its horses for choppers'; I will return later to further implications of this description.
24. This reference to allusion is intended to evoke Carroll's (1982) discussion of allusion in Hollywood cinema from the 1970s onwards. Carroll's article assumes that such allusions to other texts are intentional, and his description of allusionism as a strategy in fact recalls characteristic strategies of irony itself: films are claimed to develop 'a two-tiered system of communication which sends [one]...message to one segment of the audience and an additional hermetic, camouflaged, and recondite one to another' (ibid.: 56).
25. Lawrence Kramer, for instance, refers generally to the film asking us to ponder 'the implications of associating Wagner with a racially charged triumphalism' (2002: 152–153); Marsha Kinder argues that 'the music...can't help but remind us of our German enemies in previous wars' (1979: 19); while Maria Pramaggiore and Tom

Wallis assert that its 'intertextual reference to *The Birth of a Nation*...emphasises Kilgore's racism and bigotry' (2005: 233).

26. Kinder (1980: 20) makes a suggestive link between Kilgore's exaggerated characterisation and the satirical mode of anti-war novels such as *Catch-22* (1961). It is also worth briefly acknowledging another potentially relevant literary context, suggested by Kilgore's name: as well as suggesting bloody brutality, it could also very easily be interpreted as an allusion to Kilgore Trout, a character in (among other books) Kurt Vonnegut's *Slaughterhouse Five* (1970), another satire about the madness and futility of war.

27. Not least for its invocation of famous Vietnam War photography showing injured children as 'collateral damage'; see, for instance, Nick Ut's 1972 Pulitzer Prize-winning picture that is sometimes called 'Accidental Napalm' and sometimes 'The Terror of War', with its depiction of crying, injured children fleeing from a bombing at the village of Trång Bàng.

28. Perhaps most famously in *Stagecoach* (John Ford, 1939), though the convention stretches back much further—at least to early Westerns such as, say, D.W. Griffith's *The Battle at Elderbush Gulch* (1913). Through its particularly extreme demonising of Native Americans, the latter reminds us bluntly of the blatantly racist potential of this particular trope, which, as in the case of *Apocalypse Now*'s invocation of Griffith's *The Birth of a Nation*, also seems significant to a full interpretation of the 'Ride of the Valkyries' scene. Relatedly, see Dee Brown's *Bury My Heart at Wounded Knee: An Indian History of the American West* (1971) for a popular, Vietnam War-era historical account concerning, in part, the United States Cavalry's violence against Native American communities.

29. This remains significant even if we accept that, as Sharrett notes, it is a matter of historical fact that 'the Air Cavalry in Vietnam *did* wear the antiquated hats and neckerchiefs, and blow the same bugle calls of Bull Run and The Little Big Horn' (1986: 27; original emphasis). Even so, the film was clearly under no obligation to include—let alone stress, and so associate with Kilgore—these anachronistic sights and sounds, making their presence and treatment entirely relevant to a consideration of the film's rhetorical strategies. We might recall here the emphasis *Dr. Strangelove* places

on the historical fact that Strategic Air Command's motto really *was* 'Peace is our profession' (Chapter 2).

30. As with the film's allusions to Nazism and the Ku Klux Klan via Wagner, our interpretation of *Apocalypse Now*'s use of cavalry imagery might be bolstered by reference to historical discourses concerning American involvement in the Vietnam War. As Carpenter (1990) notes, the language, images, and ideology of frontier mythology were frequently mobilised by both supporters and opponents of the war during the 1960s and 1970s.

31. It should be noted that similar strategies suggesting the film's ironic distance from Kilgore also continue once the attack sequence is under way. For instance, he is shown taking a swig from a coffee mug precisely as we hear another soldier utter the compliment 'nice shot, Bill!'—the carefree ease of the gesture and the relaxed domesticity conjured by the prop clashing horribly with the words' meaning in this context. More damning still is when Kilgore pauses during the attack to draw Lance and Willard's attention to the surfing potential of the sea below them: gesticulating animatedly, he exclaims, 'The waves, the waves! Look: they break both ways—watch, watch!'

32. Eco (1992a, b) in fact suggests that we should make a distinction between the practices of interpreting and 'using' a text.

33. Hall (1980) famously argued that the different ways readers 'decode' texts may stand in varying relationships to the meanings 'encoded' in a text: readings may be characterised as 'dominant', but they may also be 'negotiated' or even 'oppositional' to a text's preferred readings.

34. See, for instance, Burke (1998: 116–169) on this point, and in particular its relevance for poststructuralist theories of literature.

Bibliography

Abrams, M. H. (1999). *A Glossary of Literary Terms*. New York: Holt.

Babington, Bruce & Peter Evans. (1990). 'Another Look at Sirkian Irony', *Movie* 34/35, 47–58.

Barker, Martin & Thomas Austin. (2000). *From Antz to Titanic: Reinventing Film Analysis*. London: Pluto Press.

Bartlett, Rebecca. (2015). 'How Failure Works: Understanding and Analysing the Characteristics of Badfilm, 1950–1970'. PhD Thesis, University of Glasgow.

Baron, Jaimie. (2013). *The Archive Effect: Found Footage and the Audiovisual Experience of History*. New York: Routledge.

Baudrillard, Jean. (1994). *Simulacra and Simulation*. Ann Arbor: University of Michigan Press.

Beardsley, Monroe C. (1958). *Aesthetics: Problems in the Philosophy of Criticism*. NewYork: Harcourt, Brace, and World, Inc.

Booth, Wayne C. (1961). *The Rhetoric of Fiction*. Chicago: University of Chicago Press.

Booth, Wayne C. (1974). *A Rhetoric of Irony*. Chicago: University of Chicago Press.

Booth, Wayne C. (2002). 'Is there an "Implied" Author in Every Film?', *College Literature* 29: 2, 124–131.

Britton, Andrew. (2009). *Britton on Film: The Complete Film Criticism of Andrew Britton*, Barry Keith Grant (ed). Detroit: Wayne State University Press.

Brown, Dee. (1971). *Bury My Heart at Wounded Knee: An Indian History of the American West*. New York: Bantam Books.

Browne, Nick. (1975). 'The Spectator-in-the-Text: The Rhetoric of *Stagecoach*', *Film Quarterly* 29: 2, 26–38.

Brunsdon, Charlotte & David Morley. (1999). *The Nationwide Television Studies*. New York: Routledge.

Burke, Kenneth. (1969). *A Rhetoric of Motives*. Los Angeles: University of California Press.

Burke, Sean. (1998). *The Death and Return of the Author: Criticism and Subjectivity in Barthes, Foucault and Derrida*. Edinburgh: Edinburgh University Press.

Carpenter, Ronald H. (1990). 'America's Tragic Metaphor: Our Twentieth-Century Combatants as Frontiersmen', *Quarterly Journal of Speech* 76: 1, 1–22.

Carroll, Noël. (1982). 'The Future of Allusion: Hollywood in the Seventies (and Beyond)', *October* 20, 51–81.

Carroll, Noël. (1998). *Interpreting the Moving Image*. Cambridge: Cambridge University Press.

Carroll, Noël. (2002). 'Andy Kaufman and the Philosophy of Interpretation', in Krausz, Michael (ed), *Is There a Single Right Interpretation?* University Park: Pennsylvania State University Press, 319–344.

Carruthers, Susan L. (2011). *The Media at War*. London: Palgrave Macmillan.

Chatman, Seymour. (1997). '2 1/2 Film Versions of *Heart of Darkness*', in Moore, Gene M. (ed), *Conrad on Film*. Cambridge: Cambridge University Press, 207–223.

Chown, Jeffrey. (1988). *Hollywood Auteur: Francis Coppola*. London: Praeger Publishers.

Clark, Herbert H. & Richard J. Gerrig. (2007). 'On the Pretense Theory of Irony', in Gibbs, Raymond W. & Herbert L. Colston (eds), *Irony in Language and Thought: A Cognitive Science Reader*. London: Lawrence Erlbaum, 25–34.

Colebrook, Claire. (2004). *Irony*. New York: Routledge.

Culler, Jonathan. (1975). *Structuralist Poetics: Structuralism, Linguistics and the Study of Literature*. New York: Routledge.

Currie, Gregory. (1995). *Image and Mind: Film, Philosophy and Cognitive Science*. Cambridge: Cambridge University Press.

Currie, Gregory. (2006). 'Why Irony is Pretence', in Nichols, Shaun (ed), *The Architecture of the Imagination: New Essays on Pretence, Possibility, and Fiction*. Oxford: Oxford University Press, 111–133.

Davis, Kimberly Chabot. (1999). 'White Filmmakers and Minority Subjects: Cinema Vérité and the Politics of Irony in *Hoop Dreams* and *Paris Is Burning*', *South Atlantic Review*, 64: 1, 26–47.

De Man, Paul. (1996). *Aesthetic Ideology*. Minneapolis: University of Minnesota Press.

Dickie, George. (2006). 'Intentions: Conversations and Art', *British Journal of Aesthetics*, 46: 1, 70–81.

Doane, Mary Ann. (1979). '*The Dialogic Text: Filmic Irony and the Spectator*'. PhD Thesis, University of Iowa.

Durgnat, Raymond. (1976). 'The Mongrel Muse', in *Durgnat on Film*. London: Faber & Faber, 17–28.

Dutton, Dennis. (1987). 'Why Intentionalism Won't Go Away', in Cascardi, A. J. (ed), *Literature and the Question of Philosophy*. Baltimore: Johns Hopkins University Press, 194–209.

Dynel, Marta. (2014). 'Linguistic Approaches to (Non)humorous Irony', *Humor*, 27: 4, 537–550.

Eagleton, Terry. (1983). *Literary Theory: An Introduction*. Oxford: Blackwell.

Eco, Umberto. (1992a). 'Between Author and Text', in Collini, Stefan (ed), *Interpretation and Overinterpretation*. Cambridge: Cambridge University Press, 67–88.

Eco, Umberto. (1992b). 'Overinterpreting Texts', in Collini, Stefan (ed), *Interpretation and Overinterpretation*. Cambridge: Cambridge University Press, 45–66.

Elleström, Lars. (2002). *Divine Madness: On Interpreting Literature, Music, and the Visual Arts Ironically*. London: Bucknell University Press.

Fish, Stanley. (1989). 'Short People Got No Reason to Live: Reading Irony', in *Doing What Comes Naturally: Change, Rhetoric, and the Practice of Theory in Literary and Legal Studies*. Durham: Duke University Press, 180–196.

Fowler, H. W. (1926). *A Dictionary of Modern English Usage*. Oxford: Oxford University Press.

Gutman Robert W. (1968). *Richard Wagner: The Man, His Mind and His Music.* New York: Harcourt.

Hall, Simon. (2005). *Peace and Freedom: The Civil Rights and Antiwar Movements in the 1960s.* Philadelphia: University of Pennsylvania Press.

Hall, Stuart. (1980). 'Encoding/Decoding', in Hall, Stuart, Dorothy Hobson, Andrew Lowe & Paul Willis (eds), *Culture, Media, Language.* London: Hutchinson, 128–138.

Hermerén, Göran. (1975). 'Intention and Interpretation in Literary Criticism', *New Literary History*, 7: 1, 57–82.

Hickman, Roger. (2006). *Reel Music: Exploring 100 Years of Film Music.* New York: W. W. Norton & Company.

Hutcheon, Linda. (1989). *A Poetics of Postmodernism: History, Theory, Fiction.* New York: Routledge.

Hutcheon, Linda. (1994). *Irony's Edge: The Theory and Politics of Irony.* New York: Routledge.

Hutcheon, Linda. (1998). 'Irony, Nostalgia, and the Postmodern', *University of Toronto English Library.* Available at: http://www.library.utoronto.ca/utel/criticism/hutchinp.html (Accessed 13 June 2015).

Irvin, Sherri. (2006). 'Authors, Intentions and Literary Meaning', *Philosophy Compass*, 1:2, 114–128.

Kaufer, David. (1977). 'Irony and Rhetorical Strategy', *Philosophy and Rhetoric*, 10, 2: 90–110.

Kinder, Marsha. (1979). 'The Power of Adaptation in *Apocalypse Now*', *Film Quarterly*, 33: 2, 12–20.

Kinder, Marsha. (1990). 'Ideological Parody in the New German Cinema', *Quarterly Review of Film & Video* 12: 1/2, 73–103.

Kivy, Peter. (1993). *The Fine Art of Repetition.* Cambridge: Cambridge University Press.

Kolker, Robert. (2011). *A Cinema of Loneliness.* Oxford: Oxford University Press.

Kramer, Lawrence. (2002). *Musical Meaning: Toward a Critical History.* Los Angeles: University of California Press.

Levinson, Jerrold. (1996). 'Film Music and Narrative Agency', in Bordwell, David & Noël Carroll (eds), *Post-Theory: Reconstructing Film Studies.* Madison: University of Wisconsin Press, 248–282.

Lowe, Melanie. (2007). *Pleasure and Meaning in the Classical Symphony.* Bloomington: Indiana University Press.

MacDowell, James & James Zborowski. (2013). 'The Aesthetics of "So Bad it's Good": Value, Intention, and *The Room*', *Intensities*, Autumn/Winter 2013, pp. 1–30.

Maynard, John. (2009). *Literary Intention, Literary Interpretations, and Readers.* Peterborough: Broadview Press.

McCulloch, Richard. (2011). '"Most People Bring Their Own Spoons": *The Room*'s Participatory Audiences as Comedy Mediators', *Participations: Journal of Audience & Reception Studies,* 8: 189–218.

Michaels, Walter Benn. (1979). 'The Road to Vietnam', *MLN* 94: 5, 1173–1175.

Muecke, Douglas Colin. (1969). *The Compass of Irony.* London: Methuen.

Muecke, Douglas Colin. (1970). *Irony and the Ironic.* London: Methuen.

Muecke, Douglas Colin. (1978). 'Irony Markers', *Poetics,* 7, 363–375.

Nathan, Daniel. (1992). 'Irony, Metaphor, and the Problem of Intention', in Iseminger, Gary (ed), *Intention & Interpretation.* Philadelphia: Temple University Press, 183–202.

Norris, Margaret. (1998). 'Modernism and Vietnam', *Modern Fiction Studies* 44: 3, 730–766.

Perez, Gilberto. (2000). 'Toward a Rhetoric of Film: Identification and the Spectator', *Senses of Cinema*, Issue 5 (April 2000). Available at: http://sensesofcinema.com/2000/society-for-cinema-studies-conference-2000/rhetoric2/ (Accessed 4 April 2015).

Pramaggiore, Maria & Tom Wallis. (2005). *Film: A Critical Introduction.* London: Laurence King Publishing.

Pye, Douglas. (2007). 'Movies and Tone', in Gibbs, John & Douglas Pye (eds), *Close-Up 02: Movies and Tone/Reading Rohmer/Voices in Film.* London: Wallflower Press, 1–80.

Quintilian. (1977). *The Institutio Oratoria* (Translated by H.E. Butler). Cambridge: Harvard University Press.

Robertson, Pamela. (1990). 'Structural Irony in *Mildred Pierce*, or How Mildred Lost Her Tongue', *Cinema Journal*, 30: 1, 42–54.

Roche, David. (2015). 'Irony in *The Sweet Hereafter* by Russell Banks (1991) and Atom Egoyan (1997)', *Adaptation*, 8: 2, 237–253.

Sconce, Jeffrey. (1995). 'Trashing the Academy: Taste, Excess, and an Emerging Politics of Cinematic Style', *Screen*, 36: 4, 371–393

Sharrett, Christopher. (1986). 'Intertextuality and the Breakup of Codes: Coppola's *Apocalypse Now*', *Sacred Heart University Review*, 6: 1/2, 1–20.

Sperber, Dan & Deirdre Wilson. (2007). 'On Verbal Irony', in Gibbs, Raymond W. & Herbert L. Colston (eds), *Irony in Language and Thought: A Cognitive Science Reader.* New York: Lawrence Erlbaum Associates, 35–55.

Storm, William. (2011). *Irony and the Modern Theatre.* Cambridge: Cambridge University Press.

Sumera, Matthew. (2013). 'War's Audiovisions: Music, Affect, and the Representation of Contemporary Conflict'. PhD Thesis, University of Wisconsin-Madison.

Swofford, Anthony. (2003). *Jarhead.* New York: Simon and Schuster.

Tarasti, Eero. (2012). *Semiotics of Classical Music: How Mozart, Brahms and Wagner Talk to us.* Berlin: De Gruyter.

Tomasulo, Frank P. (1990). 'The Politics of Ambivalence: *Apocalypse Now* as Prowar and Antiwar Film', in Dittmar, Linda & Gene Michaud (eds), *From Hanoi to Hollywood: The Vietnam War American Film*. New Brunswick: Rutgers University Press, 145–158.

Vonnegut, Kurt. (1970). *Slaughterhouse Five*. London: Cape.

Warshaw, Hilan. (2009). '"The Dream Organ": Wagner as Proto-Filmmaker', in DiGaetani, John Louis (ed), *Wagner Outside the Ring: Essays on the Operas, Their Performance and Their Connections with Other Arts*. London: Mcfarland & Company, 184–198.

Weiner, Marc A. (2010). 'Hollywood's German Fantasy: Ridley Scott's *Gladiator*', in Jeongwon, Joe & Sander L. Gilman (eds), *Wagner & Cinema*. Lanham: Rowman & Littlefield, 186–209.

Weschler, Lawrence. (2005). 'Valkyries Over Iraq: The Trouble with War Movies', *Harper's Magazine*, November 2005, 65–77.

Wilson, George M. (1986). *Narration in Light: Studies in Cinematic Point of View*. Baltimore: John Hopkins University Press.

Wilson, George M. (1997). 'On Film Narrative and Narrative Meaning', in Allen, Richard & Murray Smith (eds), *Film Theory and Philosophy*. Oxford: Oxford University Press, 221–238.

Wilson, Kent & George Dickie. (1995). 'The Intentional Fallacy: Defending Beardsley', *Journal of Aesthetics and Art Criticism*, 53, 233–250.

Wimsatt, William Kurtz & Monroe C. Beardsley. (1946). 'The Intentional Fallacy', *The Sewanee Review*, 54: 3, 468–488.

INDEX

Note: Page numbers with "n" denote notes.

© The Author(s) 2016

J. MacDowell, *Irony in Film*, DOI 10.1057/978-1-137-32993-6